WATERSTONES LF 7244
£14-99 281964

INSIGHT GUIDES

BAHAMAS

D0487324

DISCOVERY
CHANNEL

APA PUBLICATIONS
Part of the Langenscheidt Publishing Group

INSIGHT GUIDE
Bahamas

ABOUT THIS BOOK

Editorial

Editor
Lesley Gordon
Editorial Director
Brian Bell

Distribution

UK & Ireland
GeoCenter International Ltd
The Viables Centre, Harrow Way
Basingstoke, Hants RG22 4BJ
Fax: (44) 1256-817988

United States
Langenscheidt Publishers, Inc.
46–35 54th Road, Maspeth, NY 11378
Fax: (718) 784-0640

Canada
Prologue Inc.
1650 Lionel Bertrand Blvd., Boisbriand
Québec, Canada J7H 1N7
Tel: (450) 434-0306. Fax: (450) 434-2627

Worldwide
**Apa Publications GmbH & Co.
Verlag KG (Singapore branch)**
38 Joo Koon Road, Singapore 628990
Tel: (65) 865-1600. Fax: (65) 861-6438

Printing

Insight Print Services (Pte) Ltd
38 Joo Koon Road, Singapore 628990
Tel: (65) 865-1600. Fax: (65) 861-6438

©2002 Apa Publications GmbH & Co.
Verlag KG (Singapore branch)
All Rights Reserved

First Edition 1986
Fifth Edition 2002

CONTACTING THE EDITORS
Although every effort is made to
provide accurate information, we
live in a fast-changing world and
would appreciate it if readers
would call our attention to any
errors or outdated information
that may occur by writing to:
**Insight Guides, P.O. Box 7910,
London SE1 1WE, England.
Fax: (44 20) 7403-0290.
e-mail:
insight@apaguide.demon.co.uk**

www.insightguides.com

This guidebook combines the
interests and enthusiasms of
two of the world's best-known information providers: Insight Guides,
whose titles have set the standard
for visual travel guides since 1970,
and Discovery Channel, the world's
premier source of nonfiction television programming.

The editors of Insight Guides provide both practical advice and
general understanding about a destination's history, culture, institutions and people. Discovery Channel
and its popular website, www.dis-
covery.com, help millions of viewers
explore their world from the comfort
of their own home and encourage
them to explore it firsthand.

Insight Guide: Bahamas is structured to convey an understanding of
the islands and its people as well

as to guide readers through the
sights and activities:

◆ The **Features** section covers the
culture and history of the islands in
a series of informative essays.

◆ The main **Places** section is a
complete guide to all the sights and
areas worth visiting. Places of special interest are coordinated by
number with the maps.

◆ The **Travel Tips** listings section
provides a handy point of reference
for information on travel, hotels,
shops, restaurants and more.

The contributors
This updated edition of *Insight
Guide: Bahamas* was edited by
Lesley Gordon, a London-based
Insight Guides editor. **Sara Whittier**
produced the original edition.

The team of talented writers

enlisted for this edition includes **Deby Nash**, author of *Pocket Guide Bahamas*, who updated her feature *The Bahamians*, and supplied updates for: *Luxurious Lifestyles*, *The Underwater Bahamas* and *Hooked on Fishing*, and also for several Places chapters including *Nassau, New Providence Island, Paradise Island, Grand Bahama, Freeport, The Berry Islands, Cat Island, Long Island, The Southern Islands* and *Travel Tips*, originally compiled by **Holly Henke**.

New York writer **Rachel Christmas Derrick**, a regular visitor to the Bahamas, updated *Obeah, Superstition and Folklore*, as well as *The Out Islands* introduction, *The Abacos, Eleuthera, Harbour Island and Spanish Wells, San Salvador* and *The Exumas*. Derrick also provided new material on Bahamian cuisine,

the Exuma Cays Sea and Land Park, Lyford Cay and a profile of the artist Amos Ferguson.

Jill Hartley, a travel writer whose work regularly appears in British newspapers, wrote text on the legend of the lost city of Atlantis and also updated *The Bimini Islands*, originally written by Sara Whittier.

Gail Saunders, a notable historian at the Bahamas Archives in Nassau, produced the history chronology and assessed the history section of the book, produced by **Daniel Max**. Saunders is also the original author of the chapters on New Providence Island and Nassau.

Travel photojournalist and TV producer, **Juliet Coombe**, updated *Andros* and supplied material on the sponge industry, Androsia textiles, bonefishing, James Bond in the Bahamas, bush medicine, swimming with dolphins, the modern music scene and Bahamian arts. She also contributed additional photographs.

A Grand Bahama radio personality, **Paul Frances**, wrote the authoritative music feature, *Bahamian Beats*.

Nassau-based journalist **Jessica Robertson** updated the modern history chapter, *A New Nation*.

Contributors to the original edition whose text is used in the present edition include: **Deborah Williams, Timothy McCartney, Peter Barratt, Fred Sturrup, Donald Gerace, Anthony Forbes, Roderick Attrill** and **M.A.V.B. Whittier**.

The work of the main photographers, **Ping Amranand** and **Andrew Ammerman,** is supplemented by **Dave Houser, Wolfgang Tins, Catherine Karnow** and **Tony Arruza**. Thanks to **Julie Angove** and the Bahamas Tourist Office staff in London and the Bahamas.

Map Legend

— ‥ —	International Boundary
—‥●‥—	National Park/Reserve
– – – –	Ferry Route
✈ ✈	Airport: International/Regional
🚌	Bus Station
ℹ	Tourist Information
✉	Post Office
✝ ✝ ♱	Church/Ruins
✝	Monastery
☾	Mosque
✡	Synagogue
🏰	Castle/Ruins
🏛	Mansion/Stately home
∴	Archeological Site
∩	Cave
𝙸	Statue/Monument
★	Place of Interest

The main places of interest in the Places section are coordinated by number with a full-color map (e.g. ●), and a symbol at the top of every right-hand page tells you where to find the map.

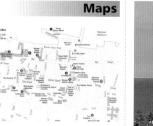

INSIGHT GUIDE
Bahamas

CONTENTS

**Boats
docked in
Hope Town
Harbour**

Information panels

Places

A WONDROUS PLACE

Pirates, pop stars and presidents have all been to the Bahamas.

And the population is as diverse as the visitors

> *Look from your door, and tell me now*
> *The colour of the sea.*
> *Where can I buy that wondrous dye*
> *And take it home with me?*
>
> —Bliss Carman

Bliss Carman is not the name of a rock group, but of a 19th-century poet who visited the Bahamas and memorialized it in enthusiastic verse. But the Beatles did vacation here, as have Richard Nixon, Winston Churchill, and many other, less celebrated, souls. In the 17th century the Spanish called the archipelago a "receptacle for all rogues", but the first visitor – Christopher Columbus – wrote that "there came from the land the scent of flowers or trees, so delicious and sweet, that it was the most delightful thing in the world." The Bahamas is a nation that can seem as simple as Carman's "wondrous dye", but that in reality is as complex, thorny and full of life as the many coral reefs that lie beneath its shallow sea.

The country's history (which began as the Lucayan Indians, pursued by the Caribs, migrated north from the Greater Antilles, then burst into worldwide prominence with a sailor's cry, *"Tierra, tierra!"* from the *Pinta* in 1492) is a good place to begin. Forming a wide chain between the south coast of Florida and Cap-Haïtien (Haiti), the Bahama islands lie at the crossroads of what for several centuries was one of the hubs of the world. Piracy, slavery, revolution, religion, smuggling and independence have all made their marks. And they have brought to the Bahamas an immensely diverse population.

Expatriates, descendants of freed Africans, of slaves and of plantation owners, and over 4 million visitors a year share the Bahamas. Some call the country "confused", but in this guide you will find a celebration of its diversity.

Finally, of course, there are the sights themselves – the "undiscovered" coves everyone knows about, and the ones nobody does; blue holes; sunken ships; homes with limestone walls, or wide verandahs or tin roofs; bright Junkanoo masks; pink stucco schools and white churches. The Places and Features sections in this book will introduce readers to these sights and sounds – in some depth or with a tantalizing glimpse – and whet your appetite to explore.

So, take to heart the words of Columbus when, following his first voyage, he wrote to the "catholic kings" of Spain (Ferdinand and Isabella), who had sent him. Entranced by the many marvels and wondrous things, he concluded "even the singing of little birds is such that a man could never wish to leave this place." ❑

PRECEDING PAGES: cay in the Exumas; fish swimming through a shipwreck; Bimini harbor; palmy twilight in George Town, Exuma.
LEFT: alone at Gillam Bay in Green Turtle Cay, Abaco Island.

INSVLÆ AMERICANÆ
IN OCEANO SEPTENTRIONALI,
cum Terris adiacentibus.

FLORIDA.

NOVÆ HISPANIÆ PARS.

Golfo De Mexico.

YVCATAN.

HONDVRAS.

NICARAGVA.

MAR DEL ZVR.

Ampl.mo Prud.mo Doct.mo Viro
D. ALBERTO CONRADI VANDER BVRCH,
I. C. Reip. Amstelodamensis Senatori, Collegii
Scabinorum Præsid. Societatis Indiæ.m.quæ
ad Occidentem militat assessori, et nuper
ad Magnum Moscoviæ Ducem Legato,
tabulam hanc inscribit
Guilielmus Blaeu.

Decisive Dates

EARLY SETTLEMENT AND COLONIZATION

AD 500–600 Traveling from Cuba and Hispaniola, Taino Amerindians settle the Bahamas.

AD 600–800 The Lucayan subculture develops in the Bahamas.

1492 Christopher Columbus, Genovese sailor and cartographer, lands on an island called Guanahani, which he renames San Salvador (Holy Saviour).

1625 France makes several unsuccessful attempts to colonize the Bahamas.

1629 England's Attorney General, Sir Robert Heath, is granted the Bahama Islands by King Charles I.

1648 The Eleutheran Adventurers, led by Captain William Sayle, form a settlement in north Eleuthera.

1670 Six of the Lords Proprietors of the Carolinas are granted the Bahama Islands by Charles II. Hugh Wentworth is appointed first Proprietary Governor but he dies on his way to the Bahamas.

1671 John Wentworth, brother of Hugh Wentworth, is appointed governor.

1695 Governor Nicholas Trott lays out Charlestown and renames it Nassau, in honour of the Prince of Orange-Nassau (William III of England). Fort Nassau is constructed on the site now occupied by the British Colonial Hilton.

BY ROYAL APPOINTMENT

1717 A former privateer, Woodes Rogers, is appointed the first Royal Governor of the Bahamas.

1718 Woodes Rogers arrives in the Bahamas. He expels the pirates, restores order, repairs Fort Nassau, organizes a militia and cleans up Nassau.

1729 The House of Assembly is convened.

1776 The fledgling United States Navy captures New Providence, occupying the island for two weeks. The Americans invade again in 1778.

1782 The Spanish invade New Providence and occupy it for nine months.

1783 The Bahamas is restored to Great Britain by the Treaty of Versailles. Andrew Deveaux recaptures New Providence, unaware of the treaty terms.

FROM SLAVERY TO EMANCIPATION

The Loyalist influx during the late 18th century included many enslaved people. The migration of American Loyalists to the Bahamas doubles the white population and trebles the black. Attempts to make cotton a staple crop end in failure.

1807 Abolition of the slave trade in Britain.

1808–60s About 6,000 liberated Africans captured by the Royal Navy and are settled in the Bahamas.

1834 Slavery abolished in all British Colonies. The Apprenticeship system is introduced, which maintains a form of slavery until 1838.

RECONSTRUCTION

1847 The Nassau Public Library and Museum is established.

1861–65 Nassau is used as a transshipment port by the Confederacy during the American Civil War.

1863 The Royal Victoria Hotel opens.

TOURISM, WARS, PROHIBITION AND PROTEST

1898 The Hotel and Steamship Act is passed and a contract made for the Florida East Coast Hotel Company to construct and operate the Hotel Colonial. The company purchases the Royal Victoria Hotel, marking the beginning of Nassau's development as a winter resort.

1915–17 The Bahamas raises its first World War I contingent known as the "Gallant Thirty". About 700 Bahamians participate in the war, and 37 die.

1919–33 During Prohibition in the US, the Bahamas become an entrepôt where liquor is bought and smuggled into North America.

1939–40 The Bahamas Defence Company and the North Caribbean Force participate in World War II. Bahamians serve in the British, US, and Canadian allied forces.

1940 Military bases are established on some Bahamas islands. The Duke of Windsor, formerly King Edward VIII of England, serves as Governor of the Bahamas until 1945.

1942 A riot in Nassau: thousands of laborers, working on two air-bases, storm Bay Street.

1943 The Bahamas sign an agreement with the US government known as "The Contract" or "Project", allowing Bahamians to work as agricultural laborers in America. It operated until 1966. Sir Harry Oakes, a multi-millionaire who invested heavily in the Bahamas, is murdered.

POLITICAL PARTIES AND REFORM

1953 The first Bahamian political party, the Progressive Liberal Party (PLP), is established.

1955 The government and the Grand Bahama Port Authority sign the Hawksbill Creek Agreement, paving the way for the development of Freeport/Lucaya as the second city.

1958 The United Bahamian Party (UBP) is formed, representing the majority of the House of Assembly, comprising mainly white Bay Street, Nassau merchants and lawyers. A general strike is led by labor leader, Randol Fawkes.

1959 Male suffrage is introduced, granting the right to vote to all males over 21 years of age.

1960–61 Women granted the right to vote and to sit in the legislature.

1964 A new constitution introduces the ministerial system and internal self-government. The late Roland Symonette is named Premier and the late Lynden Pindling leader of the opposition PLP.

1966–67 The first bridge connecting New Providence to Paradise Island is constructed.

1967 The PLP wins the election, majority rule is introduced. Lynden Pindling is appointed Premier.

1968 The PLP wins a landslide election victory. Establishment of the Bahamas Monetary Authority.

1969 The Bahamas becomes part of the Commonwealth. Lynden Pindling becomes Prime Minister.

1971 The Free National Movement (FNM) forms.

1972 The PLP wins a landslide victory. A white paper on independence is issued.

TOWARDS INDEPENDENCE

1973 The Commonwealth of The Bahamas gains its independence on July 10. The Bahamas becomes the 138th member of the United Nations.

1977 The PLP wins the general election. State Visit of Queen Elizabeth II – the first Monarch to deliver the Bahamian Throne Speech in person.

1978 Creation of the Bahamas Development Bank.

1982 The Bahamas becomes a member of the Organization of American States (OAS). The PLP win the election again. Lynden Pindling is knighted.

WINDS OF CHANGE

1992 The FNM, led by Hubert A. Ingraham, wins the election, ending 25 years of PLP dominance.

1995 The Atlantic Paradise Island Resort and Casino opens. Later called the Atlantis Resort.

1996 The Women's 4 x 100 meter relay team wins the silver medal at the Atlanta Olympics.

1997 The FNM, led by Hubert Ingraham, returns to power for a second term on March 14.
Italia Johnson is appointed the first female Speaker of The House of Assembly. The Freeport Container Port in Grand Bahama officially opens.

1998 The second bridge linking Nassau to Paradise Island is completed.

1999 The Securities Industry Act paves the way for the creation of the Bahamas International Securities Exchange (BISX).
Hurricane Floyd hits the Bahamas.

2000 Legendary politician Sir Lynden O. Pindling and labor leader Sir Randol Fawkes both die.

2001 The Bahamas welcomes its 4 millionth visitor. The Nassau Straw Market is destroyed by fire. ❏

LEFT: the Amerinidians did not survive colonization.
RIGHT: the Bahamas Coat of Arms.

THE PEACEFUL LUCAYANS

The Amerindians enjoyed a harmonious life free from conflict until the Spanish arrived. This sounded the death knell of their civilization

It is customary today to regard Christopher Columbus as the discoverer of the New World, though this is not true. When Columbus and his crew struck land on October 12, 1492, one of the first things they found was that there were already plenty of human beings living there. The Lucayans, Amerindians who inhabited most of what we call the Bahamas, were no newcomers to the area either. They had been in the Bahamas for somewhat longer than 500 years, and it is one of the great shames of European history that, once discovered, they would last out only another 25.

A simple way of life

The Lucayans were, according to the few accounts that survive from the time, a peaceful, graceful, docile people. They went about naked or with only a small cotton cloth hanging from their waists, adorning themselves with paint and earrings. They introduced to the Western world the hammock. Believing that broad foreheads were a sign of beauty, they practiced the ritual flattening of them.

Having only rudimentary tools, they lived primarily off the sea. They were skillful fishermen and expertly paddled the long and dangerous distances between islands in large ocean-going canoes.

Their diet was much like that of the modern Bahamian in so far as the sea was concerned – a variety of local seafood, such as shellfish, lobster, mollusks and a great deal of conch, still the mainstay of Bahamian cuisine. They also made bread from the roots of the local plants and practiced some primitive agriculture.

Modern archeological discoveries indicate that the Lucayans were a ceramic-using people. Fragments of their pottery have been found on several islands and has been used by archeologists to date the earliest inhabitants' presence on the Bahamas. Important historical finds have

been made on Grand Bahama and elsewhere. Research suggests that people in early Lucayan societies lived in loosely structured social communities made up of several family groups, were treated equally and were usually ruled by a *cacique* or chieftan. Although knowledge about the islands' first settlers is limited, an

enduring Lucayan legacy survives. The balanced diet of fish and ground provisions, such as corn, manioc and sweet potato is enjoyed by Bahamians today. And commonly used words, including hammock, hurricane, barbecue and canoe, are believed to originate from an Amerindian language.

Where the Lucayans came from is open to dispute, as are the origins of most of the Amerindians that spread out across the Caribbean in early modern history. The most often mentioned hypothesis is that the Lucayans originated on the northern coast of South America, the Spanish Main, but fled north before the deadly attacks of the Caribs. Although the Lucayans

LEFT: Lucayan hunters.
RIGHT: the Lucayans paddled their canoes long distances between the islands.

possessed spears they were not warriors and not adept at using them for defense.

But whatever damage the Lucayans may have suffered at the hands of the Caribs was paltry compared to what lay ahead that long-ago October. When the Spanish arrived, the innocent Lucayans greeted them as gods, perhaps mistaking their complicated clothing and light skin for some figure from their mythology. They offered the Spanish all kinds of gifts, and Columbus reported that "They

> ### LINGUA FRANCA
>
> Words originating from the Amerindian language are still used today: hurricane derives from *huracan*; hammock from *hamaca*; tobacco from *tobaco* and canoe from *canaua*.

are so ingenuous and free with all they have that no one would believe it who has not seen it. Of anything they possess, if it be asked of them, they will never say, 'No.' On the contrary, they invite you to share it and show as much love as if their hearts went with it."

Yet the Spanish in their hurried exploration had no time to dawdle – the small, mostly barren island was not what they had come for. In fact, it was not for several years that the fate of the Lucayans was sealed, and primarily by the accident of being too close to the island of Hispaniola – present-day Haiti and the Dominican Republic.

Cruelly enslaved

The Spanish, in their crazed search for gold, had established mines on the large island of Hispaniola. Quickly, they worked the native Taíno of the island to exhaustion, and, panicking as their labor force dropped dead at a remarkable rate, hit upon the idea of transporting Lucayans to take the Taínos' place.

Whether the Lucayans understood what was happening is not certain. Some resisted rather than permit themselves to be led away to the boats. A great many died on the sea crossing. Many others perished from the unfamiliar European diseases against which they had no protection; the rest died from homesickness and overwork in the mines. Within 25 years, the Lucayans – once perhaps 40,000 strong – were gone.

But their disappearance, though horrifying, is just one small episode of the Spanish genocide in the New World. No one has any idea how many perished through similar circumstances from South America to Florida – the number is certainly in the millions – but few peoples were wiped out as ruthlessly as the Bahamas' first residents. By the early 16th century, the Spanish were searching in vain for additional Lucayans to enslave, and the Bahamas was left depopulated and neglected by its cruel and casual conquerors. ❑

A LUCAYAN LEGACY

Most information about the Lucayans, a group within the larger Taíno Amerindian population, has been gleaned from old Spanish records. However, archeological digs on the Bahamas have unearthed valuable artifacts.

In the grounds of Lucayan National Park, near Freeport, Grand Bahama, are two large caves that connect to a vast underwater cavern. It is within this cavern that the skeletal remains of Lucayan Amerindians have been discovered in 6 ft (2 meters) of water. And at Deadman's Reef, in western Grand Bahama, animal bones and pottery shards dating to AD1200–1300 have been found at the beachfront dig there.

LEFT: many of the Lucayans who were transported to neighboring islands were worked to death.
RIGHT: Christopher Columbus lands in Guanahani in 1492 and is welcomed by the Amerindians.

Engraved for Middleton's
Complete System of Geography

The first Interview of Christopher Columbus
with the Natives of America.

DISCOVERY AND EXPLORATION

Europeans had ignored the Bahamas for years – after all, there was no gold.
The Spanish stumbled on the islands while searching for the Far East and its riches

It is a quoted fact that Columbus's discovery of the "New World" was an accident. When he spotted the island of San Salvador on a late fall evening, he expected to find the East Indies, for he had come looking for a shorter route to the riches of China and the Far East. He knew, as did many of the intelligent men of his time, that the earth was round, but, unfortunately, he vastly underestimated how large it was.

A stubborn man, Columbus found a group of nearly-naked Lucayans paddling out to him in their oversized canoes. He did not give up. He had simply found, by his reckoning, a barrier island – China was just round the corner.

Perhaps this explains the Spanish behavior on that first voyage to an unknown world. Barely had the Lucayans had time to proffer gifts than Columbus and his weary crew weighed anchor and set off in search of the Chinese trade routes. They thought they were so close that in a matter of days they would succeed.

But it was not to be. The intrepid mariner and his crew bounced around the Northern Caribbean, touching on Rum Cay and Long Island which he named, respectively, Santa Maria de la Concepción and Fernandina, after his royal patron. After only 15 days in the islands, the three ships swung down to Cuba, then to Hispaniola. Here the *Santa Maria* hit a reef and sank. Several crew members were put ashore until they could be picked up on a future voyage. When Columbus returned with a larger flotilla in September 1493, they were dead.

A significant discovery

It seems strange that the Spanish had so little sense of the immensity of what they had found, that they so pragmatically set about the business of continuing the search for China, as if missing the significance of their discovery. One explanation is that the Spanish were on a mis-

sion whose sole purpose was economic. And the only economic purpose that might have made them halt in Bahamas was gold – gold to trade, gold to carry away and gold to steal. But the Bahamas, being a mostly barren limestone chain, has no gold at all. Sensible men of business, the Spanish kept on sailing. They would return only to enslave the Lucayans and carry them off to Hispaniola, where they had found gold, though very little compared to the riches awaiting them in Central and South America.

The Spanish attitude toward conquest – more like a sack than a political occupation – is extremely important to the history of the Bahamas, because once the islands were emptied of the Amerindians, there was simply no reason for the explorers to go there.

While the exploration and despoliation of Mexico and other Central American countries continued at a furious pace, the Spaniards completely forgot about the islands they had first found. As a result, for more than a hundred

LEFT: Columbus giving trinkets to the Lucayans, as noted in an 18th-century engraving.
RIGHT: San Salvador, where Europe met the New World, as depicted in *Descriptions d'Universe*, 1686.

Admiral of the Ocean Seas

Christopher Columbus set out to look for China with three ships and a total crew of 90 plus about 200 more "friends of the King" and their servants. There were no priests and no women on this voyage. There was a *Converso*, a Spanish Jew converted to Christianity, who was versed in Hebrew, Chaldean and Arabic, brought along to act as their translator.

Cristóbal Colón, as he was known in Spain, had

spent six years trying to get backing from King Ferdinand and Queen Isabella for his "enterprise of the Indies." By April 1492 they had granted Colón two armed caravels for two years "to go to certain parts of the Ocean Sea on some errands required of our service." By allying with the Pinzón family of the Palos, Columbus saw that three boats were prepared. Daily rations per man were one pound of biscuit, two-thirds of a pound of meat and two liters of wine. The voyagers also carried cannon shot, stone and lead, also used for ballast, and trading items of beads, mirrors, little bells, pins and needles and bonnets.

Martin Pinzón and his brother Vincente Yanez Pinzón commanded the *Pinta* and the *Niña*, Colum-

bus the flagship *Santa Maria*. Calculating that he was at the latitude of Cipangu (Japan) and Cathay (China), Columbus sailed west.

Ferdinand and Isabella had offered a bonus of 10,000 maravedis to the first sailor to sight land. When, after four weeks at sea, birds were sighted, the watch for land intensified. Finally, a simple man from Palos saw land. "*Tierra, tierra!*" rang out, and the New World was discovered by the Old.

All three ships arrived at the island the Amerindians called Guanahani (renamed San Salvador by Columbus) on October 12, 1492. The Lucayans watched these pale strangers come ashore in skiffs, probably wondering at their clothing and "tails" (swords). The innocent Amerindians were not prevented from grasping the swords. They recoiled with bleeding hands. While the Spaniards gave gifts, and took possession of seven men.

The Lucayans complained that these visitors were no better than "Caniba," a fierce tribe to the south. "Caniba" meant Khan to Columbus, and when told that gold might be found in "Cubanacan" (Cuba-middle) he thought he heard "Kublai Khan." So he sent men off to the interior of Cuba.

Martin Pinzón then took off in the *Pinta* in search of gold. The *Santa Maria*, meanwhile, ran aground on a reef on Christmas Day and sank. The Amerindians used their solid mahogany canoes to rescue the crew and their provisions. Columbus left 39 men in the Dominican Republic, in a fort with provisions, and assurances of their protection by Chief Guacamagari.

The end of 1492 saw Columbus established on the *Niña*, preparing to sail east. He encountered Pinzón in the *Pinta*, admonished him for abusing the Lucayans and violating the rules for searching for gold, but spared his life. The two caravels were separated by storms on their way home, but eventually Columbus landed at the Azores for repairs, at Lisbon to send word to Isabella and Ferdinand, and finally at Palos just a day before Pinzón.

At the grand reception in Barcelona, Amerindians with gold bracelets and parrots on their shoulders marched with the new "Admiral of the Ocean Seas." In this moment of honor, as he accepted the title and a cash reward of 335,000 maravedis, Columbus also claimed the 10,000 maravedi prize for the first man to sight land. The sailor who had actually first shouted "*Tierra! Tierra!*" from the crow's nest left for Morocco, discouraged. ❏

LEFT: "There is no better people in the world," wrote Columbus of the Lucayans who welcomed him.

years after the Spanish bumped into them, the Bahamas would remain deserted.

Treasure hunters

No one came, except for the occasional ocean voyager, that is, most of whom knew enough already to live in terror of the tricky currents, hidden shoals and shifting winds of the islands.

The most colorful of the visitors to these waters was the peripatetic Ponce de León, that improbable figure of 16th-century Spanish history, who sailed through the islands in search of the fabled "fountain of youth." Like an extra in the wrong play, he wandered onto the scene make the long journey home. It was their misfortune to end up in a watery grave which, to this day, makes the Bahamas a mecca for treasure hunters.

English disinterest

English interest in the Bahamas, which resulted in three hundred years of rule, came about only through the accident of the puritan religious revolution. Those English adventurers who did visit the islands did so for private reasons, on slave-trading or privateering runs. English settlement in the New World didn't begin in earnest until early in the 17th century.

in 1513, explored several of the smaller islands including San Salvador, found the Gulf Stream, that fast-moving northern warm current, and cruised up the coast of Florida before bouncing back down to the Bahamas again. No fountain, and certainly no eternal youth.

Besides Ponce de León, other Spanish captains seem to have made a specialty of passing the islands by, their galleons laden with treasures on the way back to Spain. Certainly, the treacherous reefs did little to increase their appetite for the islands. Dozens of ships didn't

ABOVE: a 19th-century romantic interpretation of Christopher Columbus.

Until Charles I granted the islands to his Attorney General in 1629, as a throw-away with the Carolinas, the islands weren't officially claimed by anyone. Plenty of nationalities sailed through them – the Spanish of course, English, French and Dutch – but none with an eye to conquest. And even after the English claimed the Bahamas, they showed a remarkable lack of interest in pursuing and investigating the claim. Compared to the aggressive behavior of commercial England in India and elsewhere, the next hundred years stand as a monument to neglect – a neglect that determines a good portion of their history under the proprietary lords. ❑

PIRATES AND LORD PROPRIETORS

English settlement began with the Puritans, who came to the islands in search of religious freedom. Then came the pirates and privateers looking for riches

As time passed and the Caribbean grew more crowded, Britain finally woke up to the importance of the Bahamas, albeit in a small way. In 1629, Charles I granted proprietary rights to all the land from the Carolinas to the Bahamas to his attorney general, Sir Robert Heath. Proprietary rights seem to have counted for very little. Technically, they entitled Heath and his heirs to be tenants on the islands, with the Crown having a right to a healthy share of whatever Heath could produce there, which in 1629 must not have been very much.

But it is one thing to claim a 600-mile (960-km) wide island group and another to prove a right to it. Four years later, France included several of the previously-granted islands in a grant to a favorite of the king – with an equal lack of concrete results. And Charles I, caught in the growing Puritan revolt, must have thought little about his stillborn claim to the islands. In fact, in 1649, he would lose his head, and Robert Heath, titular head of a good chunk of the New World, would flee to exile in France.

Religious freedom

The same religious war that cost Charles I his head netted the Bahamas its first permanent settlement. The religious dispute of the early 1600s in England was between the Anglican Church, which the king of England headed, and the Puritans, who acknowledged no higher power than the Bible and God. The political divisions that resulted not only split England apart, but sent Puritans fleeing to colonize the New World, from Plymouth Rock to Bermuda.

In Bermuda, meanwhile, the religious intolerance of the old world was already infecting the new. In the early 1600s Bermuda, too, was split between supporters of the established church and Puritans, with it becoming clear to many Puritans that the time had come again to

move on. To find a suitable new home in the wide-open New World, the Puritans outfitted and sent off two ships. One disappeared without a trace and one came back without success.

Unfazed, William Sayle, a Puritan former governor of Bermuda, collected a party of brave settlers. After much fanfare, fund-raising

and declarations of principle – including the guarantee of religious freedom and a proclamation of the intent to form a representative assembly in their new home – the settlers set out. Had their government succeeded, its assembly would have been by far the oldest in the New World.

Some 70 in all, mostly farmers and fishermen, and many experienced in the travails of the New World, undertook the journey. Not unlike the Puritans who landed at Plymouth Rock, Sayle's Adventurers dreamed of founding a community that would be perfect in the eyes of God. But the sea, that harsh backdrop to Bahamian history, was particularly cruel to the men and women aboard the *William*. Their main

---

LEFT: the British laid claim to the Bahamas, from as early as 1629.
RIGHT: Anthony Lord Ashley, the most powerful and prominent of the six proprietors appointed in 1670.

vessel struck a reef off the north coast of Eleuthera. One man was killed and all supplies lost as the boat sank. They were suddenly alone.

The settlers, who became known as the Eleutherian Adventurers, were not complete amateurs, and they managed for the next few months to get by on the fish and fruit that the island threw their way. There is a cave on North Eleuthera called Preacher's Cave, where the Adventurers are said to have gathered for prayer.

ELEUTHERA'S SETTLERS

The name Eleuthera is taken from the Greek word meaning freedom. Some of the island's first settlers were Puritans who attempted to escape religious persecution by fleeing 17th-century Bermuda.

Sayle was both practical and religious, however, and he knew that death was just a matter of time if no effort were made to get new provisions. In the small boat (a shallop) that remained, he and eight other men set out for Jamestown, Virginia, home of fellow Puritans. Miraculously, they arrived, and word of their distress prompted the residents to dispatch several boatloads of food and provisions.

But relief was only temporary, as the Puritans learned that farming and the Bahamas don't mix. In contrast to the lush volcanic islands to the south, the Bahamas is made up of thin topsoil on a coral foundation, a dreadful base for agriculture. Try as they might, they could not get the poor land to produce enough.

After two years, little progress was made and many Puritans began to ship back to Bermuda. Life was intolerably harsh in Eleuthera, which comes from the Greek word for "freedom," but freedom, alas, was not filling their stomachs. Other Puritans continued to come to their aid. Those of Massachusetts raised a large sum and dispatched it to the Bahamas. In gratitude, the Bahamian Puritans shipped back a great quantity of native wood, the money from the sale of which would be used in the construction of Harvard College.

The experiment continued to teeter on the edge of failure. By 1657, even William Sayle had returned to Bermuda. Still, the colony kept growing, attracting everyone from new Puritans to freed slaves in search of a home.

During one of his tireless voyages on behalf of the colony, Sayle sought refuge from a fierce storm in a particularly fine harbor. The island, which residents named in his honor, is today better known as New Province (Providence). Its main city is, of course, Nassau, today the economic and political capital of the Bahamas.

Island lords

At the same time that the Puritan Adventurers were fighting the unyielding elements, Charles II was granting proprietary rights to the Bahamas, this time to several powerful lords. Whether he forgot or simply chose to ignore the government of the Puritans is not clear.

These lords, cognizant of the value of their new possessions, moved quickly to appoint a governor to run the settlement in Nassau. The fine harbor and the slightly more productive soil

was attracting a small number of settlers, including Bermudan Puritans, who were apparently uneasy with the difficult life on Eleuthera.

The governor that the proprietary lords chose was Hugh Wentworth, who died on the way to his post from Barbados. With this none too reassuring start began the long and harried struggle of the British to rule the Bahamas.

Whereas Eleuthera sprung from high-minded principles of religious freedom, Nassau seems to have been developed with a complete lack of principle at all. While there were certainly some farmers and solid merchants in Nassau, from the very beginning the island was the home of shiftless and seedy residents who squabbled with each other, cheated the proprietary lords of their fair cut, and exiled, badgered and wore down one governor after another.

New Providence continued to develop throughout the 17th century, despite a manifest lack of respect for law and government. The low road was apparently the best road, however, for Nassau quickly outstripped the other islands in importance and prosperity.

There was farming, of course, which seems to have provided only the most pious and diligent with a livelihood. For most, the ways of earning a living were decidedly less honest. Prime among these was the salvaging of wrecked

ships. Thousands of ships of all sizes went down in the tricky Bahamian waters, which through the 19th century were ill-charted, subject to vicious wind and currents, and without adequate lighthouses. Time and again word would spread that a boat had run into a reef, sending the locals out to salvage what they could.

The laws governing this salvage operation, called "wrecking," provided, first and foremost, for the rescue of survivors. But the order was not always followed. In the rough world of the

LEFT: a stone tower outside Nassau, said to have been used as a lookout by the notorious Blackbeard.
ABOVE: Anne Bonney, a notorious pirate.

wreckers, it can be assumed that not a few sailors were allowed to perish while coins, biscuits and rigging were saved. Stories have even been told of wreckers deliberately misplacing shore lights to lure hapless boats onto the rocks.

Rogues and ruffians

Wrecking, when the boat is not yet in trouble, goes under the stiffer name of piracy, and Nassau could claim its fair share of ruffians involved in this nefarious business. Much of the Caribbean at the time was a pirate refuge, with whole towns succumbing to pirate anarchy, including Nassau, where the governor served his term at the pleasure of the town's rougher elements.

The pirates are the most colorful figures in Bahamian history, and though they did not last long, their mark is significant. Many pirates – Edward Teach (also known as Blackbeard), Mary Read and Anne Bonney (notorious female pirates) – were incomparably cruel, and executions, murders, wholesale slaughters of captured crews and general heinous acts of mischief occurred. No doubt, though, the average life of the pirate resembled that of any other seaman. Much of what we know of their life comes not from their own accounts, of which they left few, but from the talented romantic musings of Daniel Defoe, the author of *Robinson Crusoe*.

Piracy against the vessels of a hostile nation was perfectly legal. Privateering, as it was called, was another major industry for Nassuvians. Several wars of this period – the War of the Spanish Succession and the War of Jenkins' Ear – provided ample opportunity for the ambitious pirate to turn privateer and do himself and his country a favor by sacking gold-laden Spanish galleons on their way back to Spain.

Predictably, all this wrecking and privateering tried the patience of the Spaniards; they attempted to recover their own wrecks, for privateering cost them a great deal of money. In reprisal, they sacked Nassau four times in 25 years, burning it to the ground and causing its inhabitants – pirate and merchant alike – to flee.

But Nassau was just too good to leave alone, and after each attack, the town would fill again with criminals, marginal men and solid citizens. Reports of the conditions of the town under the proprietary governors forced the Crown to act. The arrival of Woodes Rogers as the royal governor of the colony finally brought the Bahamas under the direct control of England. ❑

RULE BRITANNIA!

While the British hold on the Bahamas remained steadfast, the influence

of the American Loyalists profoundly changed the face of the islands

The problems of governing the Bahamas must not have weighed too heavily on the King's ministers in the early 1700s – the number of England's possessions far outstripped its ability to govern them – but sooner or later the Crown had to come up with a solution. The solution was to make the Bahamas into a royal

government meant business this time, and Rogers was renowned for his military skills, but after all Nassau was Nassau. Wisely, Rogers first offered pardons to the pirates, not least because he needed help in defending the islands against the Spaniards. When only *some* pirates accepted his offer, he sweetened the deal with a

colony. A royal colony meant a royal governor, and a royal governor meant guns and forts.

The Royal Governor

The man selected to transform the Bahamas into a sedate colonial seat was Woodes Rogers, a salty veteran of innumerable European naval wars. To him the Bahamas owes a great debt, so great that his own description of his tenure has become the motto of the nation: *Expulsis Piratis – Restituta Commercia* ("He expelled the pirates and restored commerce").

Naturally, when Rogers first arrived in 1718, the pirates were none too eager to be expelled. Rumours had reached the islands that the

good bit of public hanging. The remaining pirates either fled or quickly turned law-abiding.

But pirates were one problem, the Spaniards another. Rogers set about improving New Providence Island's still rudimentary fortifications, and the next time the Spanish sailed in, as part of yet another European war in 1720, a volley of cannonballs convinced them that they were not welcome. For the first time the Bahamas had repulsed an attack.

In domestic affairs, Rogers was, alas, less successful. He poured all his own money into farming schemes that the unforgiving soil would have none of, and when he was recalled to England, he was thrown into debtor's prison.

Besides cleaning up the pirates, Rogers also left one other contribution. In 1729, he convened an assembly of Bahamians. From that date on, the assembly rarely missed a session, making it one of the longest continually meeting assemblies in the New World. The contribution of the assembly through the years was a decidedly mixed one. It quickly became the repository of local political power, often acting with more self-interest than wisdom. The assembly began in opposition to the governor, and so it continued nearly to Independence in 1973.

So it is that an apparently democratic legislature fast became one of the more troublesome factors in Bahamian life, wearing out governor after governor, withstanding Crown reforms and 20th-century liberals with its scrappy ability to survive. Only the rising forces of nationalism later would dethrone the oligarchy Woodes Rogers first summoned into being.

For the next 40 years after Rogers' departure, until events on the American mainland would flush the Bahamas with new vigor, the islands muddled along with a mixture of subsistence agriculture, over-aggressive wrecking, a fair bit of piracy and privateering, turtle trapping, whale hunting, and salt farming – a mocking name for the only kind of farming that ever succeeded in the Bahamas, the evaporation of water from shallow ponds to collect the salt left over.

The 1760s saw Nassau rally under Governor William Shirley. A former governor of Massachusetts, Shirley brought a dose of Yankee order and ingenuity to ramshackle Nassau, ordering the town surveyed, swamps filled and straight new streets laid out. But big events were brewing as the 1770s rolled around, and when the Thirteen Colonies (which became the US) declared open rebellion against Britain, the effect on the Bahamas was immediate and profound.

American invasion

It is important to realize the degree of interrelatedness between the British Atlantic possessions. The original proprietary grant lumped the Bahamas with the Carolinas; the relationship was much more than nominal. Trade with America was vital, relations casual, families interconnected. Nassauvians and Bostonians

fought the same enemies of the British Crown. All that changed with the American rebellion.

The Bahamians probably did not feel any desire to join the rebellion, but there was considerable sympathy for the cause among some Bahamians. We know this, paradoxically, because America's fledgling Continental Navy attacked the Bahamas in 1776.

The action in which the Americans easily overran the hapless British defense of Fort Montague and proceeded to occupy the capital city was one of the first US naval actions ever. What the marines were seeking was not more sympathizers, but the gunpowder the British

had hidden away in Fort Nassau. The incompetent British governor did only one thing right during the attack – he got the gunpowder safely away. When the Americans arrived at Fort Nassau they found little of military value left.

The Americans stayed for a couple of weeks anyway, after assuring the Bahamians of their safety. They enjoyed themselves, and when they left, taking the governor with them, there seems to have been genuine regret on all sides.

The Americans came once more, in 1778, sneaking into Nassau Harbour at night. When the residents awoke in the morning, they found the American flag flying over Fort Nassau and the cannons trained on the town.

LEFT: Woodes Rogers, who expelled the pirates from Nassau, in a scene of domestic tranquillity.
ABOVE: Royal Governor Rogers in a fighting pose.

The Spanish arrive

Alert to Britain's problems in the north, the Spanish attacked Nassau in 1782 and conquered it easily – not surprising, considering they brought more sailors than the island had residents. The Spanish were kinder when bent on occupation than when they were just out for revenge, and many islanders stayed on under their rule. For almost a year the Bahamas was under a foreign flag, the only interruption in its long allegiance to Britain.

It was a loyalist American named Andrew Deveaux who recaptured the Bahamas for Britain. He set sail in 1783 with 200 men and more valor than good sense. Knowing the Spanish soldiers on the island far outnumbered his men, he picked a point offshore from which to ferry his troops. As the Spanish watched they saw long boat after long boat laden with men make the ferry run between Deveaux's ship and land. They must have imagined a veritable horde was about to attack. What they did not know was that the same men who were being ferried in were lying down in the bottom of the boat and being ferried back out again, only to stand up for the return trip. Outsmarted and probably none too eager to lose their lives on an island they were finding inhospitable anyway, the Spanish surrendered and set sail for Cuba.

But the final irony is that Andrew Deveaux's daring and romantic raid was unnecessary. The British had already recovered the islands by the Treaty of Versailles of 1783, by which the American colonies gained their freedom. The British had traded Florida for the Bahamas.

Planters versus Conchs

The next 10 years were formative for the Bahamas as American Loyalists, terrified at the prospect of remaining in the independent colonies, fled the mainland. Many went to Nova Scotia or Florida, others to the Bahamas.

The old Bahamians were a practical people, who did business with anyone. The Loyalists – the Colonies' most distinguished residents, gentlemen farmers and prosperous merchants – didn't see things that way. Within months, they and the old residents, whom they disparagingly called "conchs" after the lowly mollusk, were at each other's throats. The Loyalists sought a say in how things were run, representation, and land grants from the Crown. The old Bahamians wanted mostly to leave things alone.

Despite local opposition, the Loyalists managed to alter the economy profoundly during their short stay. Using hundreds of enslaved men and women, they built plantations reminiscent of the American south and successfully planted acres of cotton.

Within a decade, however, most of the plantations had failed, victims of cotton bugs and erosion caused by overplanting and deforestation. Loyalists began to look elsewhere, trying out other islands or moving back to the US.

Loyalist legacy

The Loyalists left an important legacy to the Bahamas. They changed the racial composition of the islands, increasing the number of black people and accentuating a system of discrimination and inequality. Today, many whites and blacks bear the names of well-known Loyalist families. At the same time, the Loyalists left their architecture and their concern for public and civic buildings. Lastly, those who did stay joined the old establishment as prosperous and powerful Nassauvians.

Slavery as an institution was doomed in the British Empire. In 1772, English agitation outlawed its practice at home. In 1807 the slave trade was prohibited throughout all British possessions and on British ships. Many enslaved people became freemen and found a home in the Bahamas, in settlements like Adelaide and Carmichael on New Providence Island, and on several Out Islands. In 1834, enslaved people throughout the British Empire were emancipated. In the Bahamas, they were subject to a period of apprenticeship before total freedom was obtained. In practice the freeing went smoothly in the islands, in marked contrast to the US.

Why did the Bahamas have less trouble adjusting to a system of freedom? To start with, Bahamian slave holders had less to lose. The plantation system had already collapsed. For many failed planters, freeing slaves was cheaper than having to feed them. Thus the racial battles of Haiti, Jamaica or the US were avoided.

Free though they were, black and mulatto Bahamians still had a difficult road before they would have either political power or equal rights. And progress on this front would have to wait nearly another century. ❏

RIGHT: Colonel Andrew Deveaux, a fervent Loyalist from South Carolina, became a Bahamian hero.

THE ROYAL VICTORIA HOTEL, AS SEEN FROM PARLIAMENT STREET.

SCENES IN SUN-LANDS.

GENERAL IMPRESSIONS OF NASSAU.

NOT the least attractive feature of Nassau is the Royal Victoria Hotel. This imposing establishment is situated in a charming pleasaunce "bosomed high in tufted trees." The lawn, sacred to croquet and to those who revel in their far niente, is a sweeping carpet of the greenest grass, fringed with ribbon-borders of flowers that glow in color-glory beneath the amorous rays of the glittering sunlight. In the centre of this "bit of Eden" stands a superb specimen of the forest king, whose branches, spreading far and wide, afford a cool and refreshing retreat for coquettish nursemaids; children whose toilets are veritable poems in lace and muslin; invalids whose sole occupation would seem to lie in the reading of word-painted novels, and for the delectation of the stereotyped "whispering lovers." A balcony or gigantic nest has been constructed in one of the forks, approachable by a wooden staircase, and in the wide world there is not a more delightful coigne of vantage wherein to enjoy a favorite author, a cooling beverage, or a reverie. The western semi-detached portion of the hotel was formerly the King's College School, in connection with the King's College, London. The piazzas are much utilized by invalids, who, unable to undergo the fatigues of out-of-door exercise, move about here languidly enjoying the charming scenery and the refreshing breezes. On the summit a roomy glazed cupola, with a gallery, affords a bird's-eye view of the entire of New Providence. To lean over one of those balconies and gaze at the glories of the tropical vegetation below, at the gay-attired groups gossiping 'neath the trees, at

TYPES OF THE NATIVE REGIMENT.

the well-appointed equipages as they flash to and fro, at the gambols of pleasome children, or to attend the glance and take in the blue belt of the broad Atlantic, the City of Nassau and harbor and adjacent islands, the eager will find a series of tableaux, unique, refreshing, satisfying.

A STREET IN NASSAU.

To the lovers of the picturesque, of vivid contrasts and bizarre effects, a street in Nassau is "a thing of beauty," and, as a consequence, "a joy for ever." The natives in their quaint costumes, the open bazaars, the delicious tone-poems in color; the houses of every hue of the rainbow, so trying to the aching eyeballs of those not to the manner born; the curiously shaped vehicles, the strangely constructed buildings, the tropical vegetation, the neat, yet clumsy, attempt at the recent and modern, as witness the solitary street-lamp in our illustration, tend to form a coup d'œil, a veritable treasure-trove, to the appreciative artist. At every corner lounges a group in attitudes worthy of the Farnese rooms, some but scantily attired, others in bright particular effulgence—all picturesque. The women, after the fashion of the women of Spain, carrying baskets upon their heads laden with country produce for the market, not unlike gigantic lobster-salads, lounging lazily along or tarrying beneath the friendly shade of the banyan for the interchange of mutual courtesies; the men talking oranges and pine-apples and cocoa-nuts, under their yellow-leafed hats; the drivers of nondescript vehicles creeping slowly by the way, glad of any excuse for a pull-up; children squatting in corners munching sugar-cane; and above, the blue sky—blue as that of Italy; below, the yellow-white roadway; on all sides, rainbow tinted buildings. A

VIEW ON BAY STREET, THE PRINCIPAL BUSINESS THOROUGHFARE.

SCENES IN SUN-LANDS.—INCIDENTS OF A TRIP FROM NEW YORK TO NASSAU AND HAVANA—SKETCHES OF NASSAU, NEW PROVIDENCE.

FROM PHOTOGRAPHS BY J. F. COONLEY AND SKETCHES BY WALTER YEAGER.

FORT MONTAGUE AND BATHING-PLACE.

THE QUEEN'S STAIRCASE.

THE GREAT SILK-COTTON-TREE.

THE LOOKOUT AT FORT CHARLOTTE.

A COCOA PALM GROVE.

SCENES IN SUN-LANDS.—INCIDENTS OF A TRIP FROM NEW YORK TO NASSAU—STREET SCENES IN THE TOWN OF NASSAU, NEW PROVIDENCE.
FROM PHOTOGRAPHS BY J. F. COONLEY AND SKETCHES BY WALTER YEAGER.—SEE PAGE 239.

BOOM AND BUST

*Blockade running brought great wealth. When that bubble burst, the Bahamians
set up a fledgling tourist industry, capitalizing on the year-round sunny climate*

The days of sneak invasions under cover of night, of pirates bearing down on unarmed merchants swearing to take them all to hell, of castaways on sun-drenched isles, began to fade away. The world of the Caribbean by the 19th century had grown considerably smaller and grubbier. The colonial system had

the Bahamians eked out a living much as they always had. Wrecking was still a profitable enterprise, though not nearly as much as it once had been. Better maps and the gradual construction by the British of lighthouses – with no great enthusiasm on the part of the Bahamians – had taken its toll on the wreckers' living.

its finest hold, explorers had nothing left to explore, and the merchants and farmers of the Bahamas did their level best to make money and maintain respectability.

The Bahamas has consistently benefited from the misfortunes of others. Wars in Europe guaranteed privateering spoils; a ship impaled on a reef was a windfall for the islanders. This pattern was repeated in the 19th century, when the only real economic stimulus the Bahamian economy would have was the sanguinary tragedy of the American Civil War. After 1861 and then 1865, the Bahamas enjoyed a boom that would not be matched for 60 years.

With the exception of the Civil War period,

Agriculture and fishing began to make their marks as the transport of materials between the Bahamas and the mainland grew more reliable. Fruits such as pineapples and oranges were in demand. But again and again it was only a matter of time before the United States responded to domestic pressure and imposed ruinous tariffs on these imports, freezing the burgeoning industry in its tracks.

One bright note throughout was the sponging industry, which at times was the country's largest money earner. Sponges, growing naturally on the sea bottom, could easily be collected and brought to market, employing in the process thousands of Bahamians.

Boom times

Into this picture came the unexpected boon of the American Civil War. It is, of course, ironic that the Bahamas, by now a predominantly black country, should work so hard to support the South, but it is not an unusual irony for the time. The British leaned toward the South, and the Bahamas, as they did in so many areas, followed suit. The economics of the situation predominated. The Bahamas' good luck came about because President Lincoln believed the South could be blockaded, starved into submission.

At first the idea was regarded as laughable, and when Bahamian boats ran the blockade to springing up along the harbor. Out Islanders crowded in to Nassau to get a piece of the enormous earnings that smuggling was producing.

The most splendid product of this smuggling paradise was the Royal Victoria Hotel in Nassau, which was destroyed by fire in 1990. This tremendously opulent structure was built at great cost and fast became the business center of the smuggling trade. Everyone from sea captains to Union spies to cotton buyers crowded in the impressive hotel to get wind of which ships were leaving and what they would carry.

But it was a false bountiful summer that Nassau was enjoying. When the war between the

nearly all the southern ports, there was little resistance. But as the war wore on, the North began to succeed in sealing off portions of the coast and the Bahamians had to use faster, quieter boats to elude their grasp. The Bahamians reaped incredible fortunes, bringing in food supplies and carrying away bales of cotton.

All this was good news indeed for Nassau. The island experienced an unparalleled building boom, with warehouses, piers, houses and stores

---

PRECEDING PAGES: in 1872 a visitor to the Bahamas dispatched reports to this New York newspaper.
LEFT: unloading cotton *circa* 1865.
ABOVE: the Royal Victoria's lobby in 1868.

States came to an end, so would the Bahamas' prosperity. But the tomorrow-we-die mentality and the boom went on without concern for its inevitable end.

When the end did come, with the peace signed at Appomattox in the spring of 1816, the effect was quickly felt in the Bahamas. Whole streets became ghostly. A tremendous hurricane swept through the next year as if in divine warning. But the message was clear enough, as Nassau found itself with a huge labor force with nothing to do beyond the old standbys of wrecking, sponging and growing citrus fruits. These could never be long-term economic solutions, for wrecking was gradually coming to an end with maps and steamships taking the terror out of ocean travel. Sponging would also be gone by 1938.

Alone again

For all the hundred years of toil, the post Civil War Bahamas was remarkably close to the one Woodes Rogers left: a quiet, marginal society with a great deal of manpower controlled by a small, powerful group.

As the century wore on, many Bahamians became immigrant laborers, moving to the United States, especially Florida, to work in the citrus industry and the building boom that the Bahamas had never been able to sustain for

long. Immigration to the States persisted right through to World War II, and came to an end only with the tourist boom. The Bahamian emigration to the more promising world of Florida was especially marked in the Out Islands, and the loss of population was significant.

If the Bahamians were far poorer than the English, they were no less proud or patriotic. The outbreak of World War I, in 1914, though half a world away, brought a resounding response from all levels of Bahamian society. Notions of anti-colonialism like the ones that developed after World War II did not exist in those days, and if the mother nation were imperiled, it was thought every citizen's duty to

defend her. Hundreds of Bahamians, black and white, volunteered for the Canadian and British West Indies forces, which were sent to Europe. Many Bahamians gave their lives. Those who remained at home raised copious amounts of money and sent the proceeds off to England. Armistice Day was a triumph for the people of the Bahamas as well as the rest of the Empire.

Such spirit is all the more remarkable considering that the Bahamas had no real contact with the German or Austrian enemy. The closest the Bahamas came was the sighting of a single German warship, which was chased by a British cruiser.

Sun-drenched holiday

The concept of the tourist is an old one in the Western Hemisphere, but it really only gained its modern meaning as the 19th century came to a close. By this time, the habit of rich people departing for warmer climates was well established. The Europeans had their Riviera and countless Italian and German watering holes, and the Americans began to take more notice of Florida. The result was a great amount of publicity about the healthy effects of vacationing in warm climates, and a building boom began in the Sunshine State. This washed off on the Bahamas, for from the Civil War on there was a small but consistent trickle of Americans wintering there.

Intermittent attempts were made to establish a regular steam boat service between Florida and the Bahamas. Most notably, Henry Flagler, who did much for Florida's tourist industry, built a hotel in Nassau and pioneered the Miami–Nassau steamship service, but both failed. World War I caused a steep drop-off in the number of visitors, and the volatile nature of the business of entertaining foreigners was no doubt reaffirmed.

The notion of leisure time for the working and middle classes would have to become entrenched, the cult of swimming and tanning would have to be sold to Americans before the Bahamas could hope to siphon off any but the richest of Florida's visitors. But, with a little patience, the Bahamas was finding its way to the most successful industry it had ever known. ❏

LEFT: blockade runners rest in Nassau Harbour.
RIGHT: the uniform of the British West India regiment, unique among British military costumes.

RUMRUNNERS AND BOOTLEGGERS

Profits were high as a result of the American Civil War, and higher
still from Prohibition. Then World War II helped foster a modern tourist industry

The Bahamas may not have known in advance the good news that the 18th Amendment to the United States Constitution would mean for them, but they soon found out. To look for a comparable piece of luck, you would have to go back to the Civil War, when the Bahamas became the major entrepôt for the southern United States. While the profits from the Civil War were enormous, those from Prohibition may well have been higher.

It did not take long for the Bahamian fleets to spring into action. The United States was unprepared when it came to defending its coasts from smugglers, and soon Nassau was a great open liquor market, with thousands of gallons of alcohol destined for the great "Rum Row" from New Jersey's coast to the hidden coves of Florida. Slowly, the US Coast Guard became more adept at policing the endless American coastline, but it was impossible to stop the torrent rushing up from the Bahamas, where smuggling became virtually a national industry.

The local economy grew fat on profits, with new hotels and harbor improvements built with the assistance of the flush treasury. A gambling club – the islands' first – was opened, and gangsters and society dandies down for the winter rolled craps side by side. The Bahamas was becoming a gangster paradise.

But paradise couldn't last forever, and when repeal came in 1933, the Bahamas was caught short. Overnight the clubs, elegant hotels and expensive stores emptied, streets filled with loafing, idle men. The Depression overlapped with the end of the Prohibition era, leaving the Bahamas out of one job and unable to find another.

By this time, the oligarchy of powerful merchants and lawyers known as the "Bay Street Boys" was firmly entrenched in power in Nassau. They controlled the assembly, which was openly hostile to the King's governor and which disbursed all treasury funds.

This oligarchical political arrangement prospered, keeping the far more numerous blacks virtually out of power and controlling a remarkable amount of the island's economy.

Greater events overshadowed the economic woes of the Bahamas by 1940. World War II broke out in Europe and the Bahamas once again raised an impressive number of volunteers. But this time the naval war would truly be international in scope, and as a result the Bahamas gained both military and tourism industry.

A royal presence

Into this small scene steps the larger-than-life figure of the Duke of Windsor, the former King Edward VIII of England. Why a man who had ruled millions was assigned to a small colony is not certain. Given the reputation of the Bahamas at the time and the degree to which official England disapproved of the former king, it is the theory of more than one historian of the time that it was a kind of punishment. Whatever the motive, the duke's arrival immediately put the Bahamas back in the spotlight. For his part, the duke seemed an able man, intent on righting the economic miseries of the country and countering the backward policies of the Bay Street Boys.

Agricultural reform remained elusive, but a piece of wartime good luck still serves the Bahamas well to this day.

The British and American high command chose a deserted section of the western part of New Providence to construct an enormous pilot training center.

Despite the Duke's good efforts, the building of the ai base was the cause of a major riot, the closest thing to racial strife that the Bahamas has ever known. Black construction workers on the air base were

RIOT ON BAY STREET

Laborers from two air bases took to the streets in a rare moment of unrest. The men stormed Bay Street, dissatisfied with political, economic and social conditions and racial discrimination.

looted. It took several days for the riots to quieten down, and black wages were quickly raised. The airbase that was eventually built went on, after the war and modernization, to become Nassau International Airport, opened with great ceremony in 1959.

Harry Oakes

Violence of a more direct kind woke the Bahamas in 1943. Sir Harry Oakes, a Canadian-born gold magnate and one of the richest men in the British Empire, was found brutally murdered

offered a wage which was in accord with local rates but unconscionably low. Avenging years of poverty and racism, they rioted, sacked and looted Bay Street, the long-time seat of entrenched white power. The police and Company of Cameron Highlanders then in garrison were only able to force them back "over the hill," to the area of black townships away from the harbor. There, several men were killed in clashes, the police station and other official buildings were burned, and bar rooms were

LEFT: a royal welcome for the Windsors.
ABOVE: cases and barrels of whiskey on the Nassau quay, destined for Prohibition America.

on 8 July, 1943. One of the Bahamas' distinguished philanthropists, the builder of its only pre-war airport and a personal friend of the Duke of Windsor, Sir Harry's murder sent shock waves around the world. Everyone in society and out was suspected in the frenetic hunt for his killer. Eventually, Sir Harry's son-in-law was arrested and tried, but acquitted.

No one knows, to this day, who the murderer was. But Sir Harry is important for more reasons than his death, for his move to the Bahamas was an early sign that a new industry lay within reach of these sunny islands – providing recreation for the exhausted Americans who would be enriched by the post-war boom. ❏

THE ROAD TO INDEPENDENCE

Tourism and banking bolstered the Bahamian economy, and nothing could stop
the people's political and social progress as they marched toward nationhood

In the aftermath of World War II, one can imagine Bahamian pundits gathering to ponder what to do with the nation's ever-lackluster economy. Besides small industries like salt farming, there was the export of workers to the United States to do blue-collar jobs and the possibility of a revival of the fledging tourism industry. But stricter American immigration rules and improved home economic conditions would make the export of workers obsolete – the way to the future for the Bahamas was clearly through tourism.

The Bahamas before World War II was certainly not unknown to tourists, especially wealthy Americans and Canadians on winter retreat. But this was clearly an embryo industry, and a highly unstable one at that.

The new economy

It took a man of unusual ability to make the development of the Bahamas a full-time job. That man was the controversial Sir Stafford Sands, who in the 1950s strengthened and mobilized the Development Board to concentrate on the Bahamas' economic problems. The board promoted the Bahamas as a vacation spot for North Americans. Tremendous advertising, the opening of new hotels and year-round tourism put the Bahamas on the map.

The jet engine shortened flight times to the Bahamas. Nassau harbor was dredged to provide docking for even the largest ships in the expanding Caribbean cruise market.

Who reaped the profits from the new economy of tourism, profits that included the vacation dollars of more than 1 million people a year by 1970? Certainly, in grand measure, it was every Bahamian, for hotels and shops provide nearly all the employment in the Bahamas today. Yet the truly huge fortunes were limited to the insiders in government and industry.

Sir Stafford and his friends did not rely only on the goodwill of American tourists; they also set up the Bahamas as a corporate tax haven. A web of secrecy laws comparable to Switzerland's, the lack of corporate income taxes, and the government's constant hand in assisting in construction and the launching of new ventures, has made

banking and allied business the country's most important source of income after tourism. Banking, too, provides a huge number of jobs for local residents – the government enforces employment laws that restrict the number of positions open to non-Bahamians. Through these laws and the healthy banking industry, a whole new professional middle class now bustles in the once languid islands.

Thus, while a few men have grown extremely rich, many have become at least reasonably well-off. It took a great deal of foresight to make tourism and banking the twin industries of the second half of the 20th century in the Bahamas islands.

PRECEDING PAGES: Nassau's toney little racetrack, Hobby Horse Hall, in 1948.
LEFT: the opening of legislature in 1962.
RIGHT: under the eyes of the Queen Victoria statue.

Party politics

The end was nearing for the Bay Street Boys. The affluent, mostly white, power brokers who had run the Bahamas for most of the 20th century began to come under public scrutiny in the late 1950s thanks to the rise of party politics.

Before the formation of the Progressive Liberal Party (PLP) in 1953, Bahamians of African descent had little say in government. There were some black representatives in the assembly, and some wealthy black businessmen, but with the rising tide of nationalism in the region, the division of the profitable pie was bound to change.

This was clear to almost everyone but the

cratic constitution was drawn up in 1963. It diluted white assembly power and turned the legislature into a more representative body. The UBP, led by Roland Symonette, with Stafford Sands as Minister of Finance and Tourism, ruled under this new constitution after the UBP beat back the PLP in nationwide elections.

They certainly brought times of prosperity and growth to the country, not least in the miraculous development of the enterprise zone of Freeport. But the PLP had larger forces working on its side. The black Bahamas had only to see what was going on in the American civil rights movement of the 1960s to see that there

Bay Street Boys, who joined with other establishment groups to form the United Bahamian Party (UBP) in 1958. The battle between the UBP and PLP was a long and bitter one. A great step towards black rule was the General Strike of 1958 that accompanied the opening of the new international airport, a strike over who would carry passengers to the hotels. What began as a small, unpolitical issue soon spread to other industries, causing a nationwide show of black labor strength in alliance with the PLP rather than the establishment UBP.

It was now clear to even the Bay Street Boys that times were changing, and with the assistance of the British government, a more demo-

was power in solidarity. Lynden Pindling, leader of the opposition PLP, began to play a significant role. He and his party leaders practiced a form of disobedience in the assembly on Black Tuesday in April 1965. They staged massive demonstrations over the Boundaries Commission and Pindling hurled the Mace out of the House of Assembly, reminding everyone that the PLP was a force to be reckoned with.

Finally, after a PLP boycott and revelations of corruption against the governing party, an election was called in January 1967. This election, with the largest number of voters ever enfranchised, ended in a near tie, but when two independent parties dramatically threw in their seats with the PLP, Pindling's party triumphed over the UBP and took power. There it would stay for the next 25 years. Blacks had at last achieved real political power in their own Bahamas.

It is worth reflecting on this truly remarkable chain of events. In contrast to other countries, the black majority had peacefully and democratically taken control of the instruments of government. A new generation of majority rulers now ran the government. Not less remarkable is the realization that all these events occurred over little more than ten years. Through the early 1960s the general idea had been that blacks would benefit from a prosper-

Toward independence

A new constitution was put together in London in 1969, turning over responsibility for internal matters and many other areas of authority to the Bahamas. By this time, the British Empire was largely dissolved, and other nations had moved toward independence. The Bahamas could have independence whenever it desired.

But as the 1970s began, it was not at all clear whether the Bahamas wanted independence. As the party of the black Bahamian, the PLP naturally urged it, while the UBP, now allied with disenchanted elements of the PLP and several splinter parties and calling itself the Free National

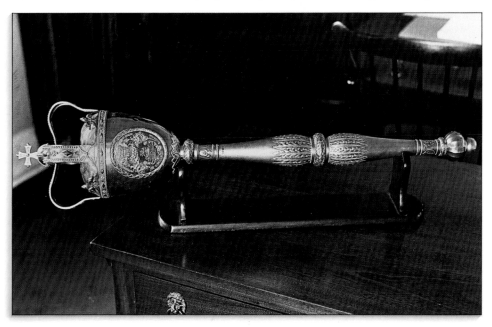

ous economy run by whites. There was little discussion of the realistic possibility that things would change; the assumption, among other rationalizations, was that American tourists and bankers would not feel confident dealing with a black government. After Pindling's rise to power, this fear of white flight was proven untrue. Investments and tourism were high on Pindling's list of priorities, dispelling fears that white confidence in business and tourism would be lost.

LEFT: assemblyman Arthur Hanna, expelled from the House of Assembly in April 1965.
ABOVE: Lynden Pindling defiantly threw the Speaker's mace out of the window, also in April 1965.

Movement (FNM), argued that the Bahamas had more to lose than to gain by independence.

The extent and duration of the ties to England were relevant. Everything from language to laws are English. Many felt that with things going so well and the cost of being in the Commonwealth so low, independence could be achieved later.

But the issue was decided by the general elections of 1972, when Lynden Pindling's government party thrashed the FNM. Accepting the inevitable, the FNM cooperated in negotiating the terms of the nation's first independent constitution. A sovereign Bahamas was now a certainty. The people prepared for the day when the Bahamas would become a nation. ❑

A NEW NATION

*Independence issued in an era of political change, while the economy adjusted
to multi-million dollar investment and the demands of tourism*

O n July 10, 1973, after 250 years as a
colony and possession of Britain, the new
nation of the Bahamas was born. For the
British the moment was one more in the long
retreat from imperial power, but for the young
Bahamian people it was the fulfilment of a long
and steady march toward self-governance.

It was a thrilling sight for thousands of
Bahamians who assembled at Fort Charlotte,
awaiting the hour when the British flag would
be lowered for the last time. At the stroke of
midnight the new flag of the Bahamas was
raised, beginning a new day.

Business as usual

In truth, the Bahamas had shown that it was
ready for independence. All the systems of
government were long in place, trained ministers prepared, and national and domestic strat-
egy stable and well thought out. To lead the
Bahamas, there was the familiar figure of
Lynden Pindling, a charismatic, energetic man
and prime minister of the Bahamas until 1992.
Whatever the political opinions – and the
Bahamas is full of dissenters and gadflies – for
a long time there was a certain comforting
familiarity in the presence of the man who had
brought himself and his party so far.

During Lynden Pindling's leadership the situation in the Bahamas stayed pretty much the
same. The economic policies set in place by the
United Bahamian Party (UBP) had been fine-
tuned but continued more or less unchanged.
Tourism, banking and the provision of luxury
homes for foreigners were still important to the
economy. Pindling's government allayed the
flight of white capital following independence
and, as a result, the Bahamas did not have to
significantly alter its banking policy until the
Organisation for Economic Cooperation and
Development (OECD) included the Bahamas on

a list of countries not cooperating fully with
those trying to curtail money-laundering.

Then, on August 19, 1992, the opposition
party, the Free National Movement (FNM),
under the leadership of Hubert Alexander
Ingraham, celebrated an overwhelming victory
over the Progressive Liberal Party (PLP), there-

by putting an end to Pindling's 25-year-long
era of power. It was a major change that many
Bahamians had anticipated for quite some time.

Pursuing the dollar

In tourism, the Bahamas has sometimes taken a
battering from other Caribbean nations waking
up to the example of this early bloomer. The
country faces the constant task of remaining
attractive to tourists, as other Caribbean nations
have increased their appeal to Americans.
Florida itself, with lower airfares and a highly
developed industry, has been a tough competi-
tor. But the Bahamas is experienced and professional in dealing with these problems. The

LEFT: Lynden Pindling and Prince Charles, representing the new and old at the independence ceremony.
RIGHT: the Honorable Sir Clifford Darling, Speaker of
the House of Assembly.

tourism industry received a much needed boost when the FNM government sold all but two state-owned hotels to private investors. But undoubtedly the most significant single contribution to the resurrection of the Bahamas as a tourist destination was the arrival of Sun International. Sol Kerzner's South Africa-based company bought and overhauled two Paradise Island hotels, and then expanded, spending more than $1 billion in the country.

Gradually, the government turned its attention to the less developed Out Islands, with the dual goals of speeding their growth as tourist destinations and arresting the steady migration of Bahamians to Nassau in search of work. With thousands of Bahamians directly dependent on tourism and tens of thousands more indirectly dependent on it, tourism is no casual matter for the government but a number one economic priority.

The Hong Kong-based company Hutchison Whampoa has invested millions to revive Grand Bahama's struggling tourism industry. The island has been developed as the country's manufacturing and industrial center, with attractive business incentives luring foreign investors including Polymers International and Hemisphere Container Repair.

PINDLING: A NATIONAL HERO

In 1967, a young man named Lynden O. Pindling made history, becoming the first black Bahamian premier. He inked his name in the history books again in 1973, when he led the small island nation to independence from England. Pindling's policies helped create a large black middle class by broadening educational opportunities for the country's entire population.

Pindling led a colorful and often controversial political life. Knighted by Her Majesty Queen Elizabeth II in 1983, he was cleared only one year later by a Royal Commission of Inquiry of drug smuggling charges.

Sir Lynden Pindling's 25-year reign as Prime Minister of the Bahamas ended when his Progressive Liberal Party (PLP) lost the 1992 election to Hubert Ingraham and the Free National Movement (FNM).

Sir Lynden served one term as leader of the official opposition and then, in 1997, retired from front-line politics, telling Members of the House of Assembly: "When all I did for good is put in the balance against all I did for ill or failed to do at all, I hope that future generations will not find me sorely wanting."

In August, 2000 at the age of 70, Sir Lynden died of prostate cancer. At his funeral, which was attended by thousands, Sir Lynden was recognized as a national hero.

The Bahamian economy has remained one of the strongest in the region, but attempts to develop agriculture to help keep valuable foreign exchange from slipping out of the country to pay for imported food have all but failed.

Fish farming has been started on several islands, and prices are guaranteed for Bahamian-grown fruits and vegetables, but still, the vast majority of all food consumed in the Bahamas is imported, mainly from the US and Canada.

Unofficial industry

While the Bahamas' location has been a boon for its tourism industry, it has been a key factor tions for smugglers, that same proximity – plus the fact that it consists of hundreds of islands and cays, many uninhabitable and most unpatrollable – makes it a haven for illegal immigrants. Every year, thousands of Haitians flee their home island in search of economic, political and social stability.

Bahamian Defence Force and immigration officers are faced with the never-ending task of detaining, processing and repatriating the immigrants of various nationalities. Over the years, however, many thousands more have made it into the country undetected and now call the Bahamas home.

in the development over the years of two activities – drug smuggling and illegal immigration. In the 1980s and early 1990s, smuggling of narcotics, mainly South American cocaine, escalated, resulting in the sudden influx of dollars. However, the Bahamian government, working in close cooperation with the US drug enforcement agency, has been fairly successful in combating the drug trade. Just as the Bahamas' proximity to the US is a natural base of opera-

LEFT: Queen Elizabeth, flanked by Governor General Sir Gerald Cash and Sir Lynden Pindling at a banquet in 1985.
ABOVE: cruise ships and conch shells, Nassau.

In the world's spotlight

Even before the nationally and internationally welcomed change of government in 1992, the prestige of the Bahamas had grown. In 1983, despite considerable internal difficulties, Pindling was knighted by the queen as Sir Lynden O. Pindling, Knight Commander of the Most Excellent Order of St Michael and St George. The gathering of premiers and prime ministers in Nassau for the 1985 Commonwealth Heads of Government meeting undoubtedly boosted Bahamian self-esteem and the islands' international image. On a more homely level, the town of Hope Town, on Elbow Cay in the Abacos, celebrated its 200th anniversary in 1985, with speeches by local dignitaries, songs by school children, flags fluttering overhead, and the oom-pah-pahs of a small marching band. And, in 1992, the island of San Salvador took the spotlight during the half-century anniversary celebrations of the New World.

With 304,000 residents spread out on hundreds of islands, but with most gathered on a few, the islands present vistas of extreme loveliness – the kind of empty beaches that differ little from those the pirates used to see –

OLYMPIANS

The women's 4 x 100-meter relay team's gold at the 2000 Olympics, took the total medal tally to two, the equivalent of one medal per 154,000 – a better performance than that of many larger nations.

and the modern overcrowding of the medium-sized city. If Nassau seems to have embraced the 21st century, other islands seem to have changed far less. And even in Nassau, despite a large population busily engaged in making a living, the feeling of cordiality and relaxation is never far from the surface.

Onward together

The future for the Bahamas is both uncertain and inviting. Despite all its problems, the country seems confident and sure that it is on the right track. Tourism remains strong and continues to attract more than 3 million visitors to the islands each year, while the stridency and difficulty that so much of the developing world is experiencing has little counterpart in the Bahamas.

Just as its history is consistently different from that of larger island nations like Haiti and Jamaica, so has it avoided difficulties and strains that have made several islands in the Caribbean politically unstable. It is difficult to pinpoint how the Bahamas, from deepest poverty to the rumblings of majority power, has managed to maintain a balance.

Lynden Pindling resigned as leader of the PLP in 1997, following the FNM's landslide victory and return to government for a second five-year term. Beset by allegations of corruption while in power and fighting a battle against prostate cancer, the aging statesman who led black Bahamians to independence stood aside for his deputy, Perry Christie.

What has gone on in the Bahamas may be an accident of sorts, but the country has successfully weathered the kinds of difficulties that have beset much greater and more powerful nations. Whether this pattern will continue is impossible to predict. Equally impossible to foresee is how the tourist economy will fare in the coming decades, or whether the Bahamas will keep its position as one of America's pre-eminent vacation destinations. Whatever the result, one hopes and even expects that the Bahamas will make it through, as it has done for so long, remembering the nation's motto, "Forward, Upward, Onward, Together." ❏

THE GOLDEN GIRLS

Bahamas, the country, long known for its sun, sand and sea, began to make its mark in a much different arena – athletics. In the late 1990s and into the 21st century, the five members of the Bahamian women's relay squad stole the spotlight at the World Championships in 1999 and again at the Sydney Olympics in 2000. They were, known affectionately at home as "The Golden Girls," after the team won Olympic gold medals in the 4x100-meter relay, in Australia.

In 2001, it was the Bahamian men, led by quarter miler Avard Moncur who let it be known that the small nation's prowess on the track was more than just a fluke.

LEFT: gold medalist Chandra Stirrup crosses the line.
RIGHT: paying attention to detail on a cruise ship in Freeport.

THE BAHAMIANS

The islands are home to a pot pourri of people with a steely determination and a sense of fun; they are smart and savvy, with a ready welcome for any visitor

It's an early weekday morning, and on the main thoroughfares of New Providence there are wall-to-wall cars. (It has been estimated that there are almost 90,000 cars for a population on this island of about 212,000.) These cars are not old by any means. In fact, there is a preponderance of new cars: Mazdas, Mercedes Benzes, BMWs, Cadillacs, Lincolns and, yes, – even a Rolls-Royce or two.

On Bay Street, at the center of the commercial area, women strut in elegant clothes as if before an audience of sophisticated Parisians. Bahamian men look just as comfortable, and stylish, in their three-piece suits.

There are other Bahamians as well... or they may not be Bahamians but Haitians, or people from other West Indian islands, who have become part of the Bahamian community, hurrying along to their jobs.

The streets are immersed within a cacophony of noises – car horns, police whistles, laughter, and the cries of fruit and vegetable vendors or straw-workers, jostling for places in the new market and on the sidewalks. The *clomp! clomp!* of a horse and carriage blends with the roar of traffic. Tourists on motorbikes, with T-shirts proclaiming "It's Better in the Bahamas," try hard to stay on the left side of the road. From the many cruise ships berthed at Prince George Dock, whistles blast and hordes of tourists emerge like ants scurrying from an anthill.

Prospering by proximity

About 18 island areas (out of 700 islands and 2,000 cays) have been developed in the Bahamas, with the two major cities of Nassau, on New Providence, and Freeport, on Grand Bahama, home to 260,000 of the country's 304,000-odd people.

PRECEDING PAGES: clowning around after school in Alice Town, Bimini; chic Bahamian Sunday Best; a family reunion bringing together several generations.
LEFT: Garet "Tiger" Finlayson, a well-known Nassau entrepreneur.
RIGHT: a Bahamian smile, Green Turtle Cay.

The country isn't a Third World backwater. Indeed, the Bahamas is an extremely stable developing country, with a per capita income of over $15,000, considerably higher than most of its neighbors. (The high per capita income is helped, no doubt, by the fact that the Bahamas manages to capture nearly 15 percent of all of

the money spent by tourists visiting the Caribbean region.)

Given the compact size of the islands, it is not surprising that over 80 percent of Bahamians live within an urban area. And with that urbanity comes demographic statistics equal to any modern and highly-developed country. Birth and death rates are half that of the world average: life expectancy is over 70 years old for men (women, of course, have the edge at 76 years), and literacy is around 85 percent of the population. There is a telephone for every two persons.

Bahamians are, for the most part, an urban people whose labor force – nearly half of the population – is employed in government (30 percent), travel and service industries (30 percent), business (10 percent), construction/manufacturing (10 percent) and, at the bottom, agriculture, with less than 5 percent of the work force.

Providing about 2 percent of the GDP, land devoted to agriculture in the Bahamas is almost negligible at less than one percent, primarily given over to the cultivation of fruit trees. Indeed, agriculture has never played a substantial part in the life or the development of Bahamians. This lack of agricultural importance was most significant in the transition from slavery to emancipation.

Bahamians have largely been influenced by the islands' proximity to the American mainland. For several centuries, until as recently as 50–60 years ago, the Bahamas not only made a good living but had thrived on what some might consider to be the less proper of economies: piracy, slavery, bootlegging and smuggling.

Today, the economy is energetically – and not without considerable forethought – focused upon tourism, banking and shipping registration. By itself, tourism generates over 50 percent of the country's entire income, directly or indirectly employing about 50 percent of the total work force.

The legacy of slavery

The legacy of slavery in the New World has, as elsewhere in the Caribbean, left a majority population of blacks, who make up 85 percent of the Bahamas' population, with whites the remaining 15 percent. Over half the population is Protestant, mostly Baptist, with the remainder split between the Anglican and Roman Catholic churches.

Fortunately for the important tourism industry, the language of business and daily life is English, although a smattering of other Caribbean languages are also spoken, including some Creole among Haitian immigrants.

Since the 17th century, lifestyles of the

Razzmatazz streets

Between sunrise and sunset, thousands of sunburned tourists casually stroll along the sidewalks of Nassau and Freeport, the two largest and most well-known cities of the Bahamas. The loud shorts and ever-present cameras should – if sun-broiled complexions don't – give away the fact that a large number of tourists are most likely to be cruise ship passengers who have disembarked for a few hours.

And should you be one of them (or a solo traveler on a slow-boat ramble through the islands), be prepared to experience something other than what one might expect from a tiny island considered to be the "gateway to the Caribbean."

Certainly, the striking contrast between one's preconception of a tropical village and modern-day Nassau and Freeport leads one to reconsider stereotypes. Nassau and Freeport are true cosmopolitan cities, filled with the whirl and bustle of any urban metropolis. Thousands of people mill through the streets. The boutiques, jewelry shops and ethnic restaurants compare in quality with those of any major city in the world.

Fragrances, jewelry, gold and watches from around the world fill the stores, as do local and international fashion. Walking down Bay Street or through the International Bazaar is a feast for the senses. Both men and women in the

straight and proud, yet without arrogance. By the way they carry themselves, you'll probably be able to distinguish Bahamians from other Caribbean islanders. Theirs is a studied casualness. Even when there seems a need to hurry, if not to acknowledge an impending deadline panic, a Bahamian will most likely maintain their pace, with an acceleration (if at all) that is barely perceptible. It's somehow undignified and inappropriate to get concerned about speed, or at least to show it.

You'll notice it, too, in the traffic. Yes, the narrow streets are frequently jammed with new cars and overcrowded jitneys. But amidst the

Bahamas are extremely fashion-conscious, clearly seen in their sense of style.

Modern Nassau has come full circle from being a quaint, sedate fishing village to a fast-moving, razzmatazz city that still retains a distinctly Bahamian flavor. But you will notice that even on these busy streets the pace of the people is, well, different than what it first seemed.

Probably most striking is a certain presence that Bahamians have, a fluid and smooth movement in the way they walk. Their posture is

chaos, there is no blasting of car horns, nor epitaphs shouted in impatient anger. During bumper-to-bumper rush hours – and these are common in Nassau – Bahamian motorists are more likely to sit back, sing along with tunes on the radio, and patiently wait out the delay.

But don't let the easy pace nurture the wrong impression. Remember that the international banking community has, for many years, chosen the Bahamas as one of the offshore banking centers of the world. And don't forget that this tiny island nation makes more than $1.6 billion a year from tourism.

Bahamians take their time, but they do it with a stylish nonchalance.

LEFT: Fisherman, Jimmy Lowe, Abaco.
ABOVE: a Hope Town girl dressed for a pageant;
ABOVE RIGHT: beads and braids in Harbour Island.

Bahamian dialect

Though a visitor might not easily distinguish casually dressed Bahamians from their Caribbean or North American neighbors, both the Bahamian walk and speech will highlight the difference. Several centuries of foreign contact, not to mention contemporary tourism (tourists outnumber the Bahamians by 50 percent on any given day), have shaped their "familiar" appearance and lifestyle.

The Bahamian dialect, for example, lies somewhere between London and Miami, with a pinch of pure Caribbean. When Bahamians speak, listen for the lack of "-ed" in the ending of verbs in the past tense. A "v" works just as well as a "w," it seems, and you may note that "d" replaces "t" at the beginning of most words.

Finding the local style

Probably the only time you'll see working Nassuvians downtown during the week is between noon and 2pm – lunch time. Fast food franchises inevitably abound on the two most populated islands, but for a taste of the local, watch where many Bahamians go, what they order, and do likewise. Bahamians are very particular about their food, and are hearty eaters, too. You'll see that the waiters and waitresses in

ISLAND FLAVORS

Local cuisine eaten at an unassuming family-run restaurant, is the next best thing to having Sunday dinner at the home of an islander. For the most part, the fewer the frills, the truer the island flavors. While beef, pork and chicken are widely available, the home-style cooking here revolves around the sea. *(See Travel Tips, page 334.)*

The star of the culinary show is conch (pronounced "konk"). In testament to the popularity of this tasty mollusk, huge mounds of discarded conch shells stand at the edge of the water near boat docks everywhere. Bahamians claim that conch gives men "strong back," meaning that it can pump up the volume between the sheets. No wonder the

meat is transformed into so many local favorites. Served in most simple dining rooms, cracked conch is pounded until tender, battered, and deep fried. Among the other incarnations are steamed conch (cooked with sauteed onions, peppers, thyme, tomatoes, and maybe okra or carrots), conch chowder (a rich, spicy soup with vegetables), and conch salad (minced raw, marinated in lime juice, and mixed with chopped onions and peppers).

Fish, another staple, turns up for dinner, lunch, and even breakfast, with snapper and grouper being the most common. "Boil fish" (cooked with salt pork, onions, and green peppers) is a popular morning eye-opener, with grits.

most restaurants are Bahamians, not seasonal help brought in from outside. This is a good sign; you'll be hard pressed to find an even mediocre plate of peas 'n' rice, or an underdone chicken, or a fish meal without fresh herbs and just the right amount of tasty local seasonings.

Two other places to watch local life are at the bus stop and in a church. Much as cars crowd the slender streets, thousands of commuters from all walks of life take the jitney. School children punctuate the crowds with their distinctive school uniforms, especially between 3.30pm and 5pm when school is out.

Churches throughout the Bahamas are a real

their time and hospitality for visitors via the Bahamas Ministry of Tourism. A visit includes staying with a family, sharing a home-cooked meal and seeing the local sights. It's probably the best way to experience contemporary Bahamian lifestyle, whether in the countryside or amid the urban bustle.

Tourists typically go to see the casino show, at Marriott's Crystal Palace Casino, which offers world-class entertainment. You can see everything from magic acts and long-legged show girls, to acrobats and dazzling Las Vegas headliners. It's a fabulous visit to a world of bright lights, big city. Yet few of the performers

fashion show, with elegant hats on the women, frilly silk dresses with ruffled lace ankle socks for the little girls, and Parisian or Italian shirts and/or suits for the men.

Meet the people

Travelers with a penchant for getting a real feel of the country and its people should have their travel agent arrange a stay with a Bahamian family through the Bahamas "People to People" program. Members from a cross-section of Bahamian society have volunteered

and even less of the music can be considered truly Bahamian. The same is true of the audiences, who are mostly cruise ship or hotel guests; you'll be hard pressed to find any Bahamians at all in the audience.

The closest many visitors get to local entertainment is in the smaller bars and nightclubs in the larger hotel properties. Better are locally-owned places, such as the popular Baha Men's Culture Club (contemporary and Junkanoo music), and the Blue Marlin, a long-established restaurant and nightclub on Paradise Island, offering a local show, complete with not so Bahamian fire dancing and traditional rake and scrape music.

LEFT: in Nicholl's Town, Andros, the bride's side.
ABOVE: the groom and his groomsmen lined up.

With urban sophistication comes the requisite night crime and shadier aspects of city nightlife. It's a good idea for visitors to ask members of the hotel staff or a tour guide to recommend good spots for night activities.

Enviable position

Most Nassuvians and Freeporters are true city dwellers, and a nine-to-five work schedule results in little free time during the week. Socializing comes on weekends, when you'll probably find them on the beach, a basketball court, or on a soccer field.

The Bahamas are an archipelago with some

Arawak Cay, located along West Bay Street in Nassau, offers a more "organic" tourism experience. A few years ago some Bahamians, hankering for their parent's traditional island life, threw away their three-piece suits, set up some wooden stalls, and began selling the day's fresh catch of fish. The outdoor ambiance along the seaside, paired up with cold beer, cool music and soft drinks, have quickly turned Arawak Cay into *the* local hangout – and an ideal place to visit, even though its not on the official itinerary of the Bahamas Ministry of Tourism. This is one of the best places to sample authentic and delicious Bahamian food.

of the most beautiful beaches in the world. Bahamians are fortunate in having islands able to support more than 305,000 people through tourism, banking, light industry and agriculture and fisheries.

The proximity of the United States and Canada has placed the entertainment-hungry Bahamian in an enviable position; no other third world country has access to so many cable and satellite television channels. It's estimated that Bahamians have more satellite systems per capita than any other nation.

But there is a rural side to the Bahamas, should the tourist want to escape the resort or cruise ship tour.

Ask your taxi driver or your tour guide to take you to Arawak Cay. Everyone is welcome at this friendly local hangout. Bahamian families bring their children to the cay for outings, and it's not unusual to see anything from a jalopy to a Mercedes pull into the parking area so that the occupants can enjoy a quick cup of conch salad during their lunch break, or a fried snapper dinner on their way home from air-conditioned offices. There's no pretence or artifice, no need for "best behavior" by the visitor. In places like Arawak Cay, you'll get to see Bahamians at their best – laughing, singing, dancing, and exhibiting a relaxed charm that is quite infectious.

Off to the smaller islands

You can see dignity and pride towards work in the faces of the "family islanders" on the Out Islands, sometimes called the Family Islands, but more recently referred to by their original name. Unlike the cities of the more populous islands, where the streets are often empty after sundown and pretty much shut down at night, the outer islands are almost always both safe and neighborly.

A visitor on an out island is treated very much like a new neighbor. Although they only get a quarter million of the Bahamas' annual total of 3 million tourists, out islanders deserve

You'll discover that residents of the out islands have the savvy, a sixth sense of sorts, about whether you want to chit-chat or maintain privacy; no one will seek you out to hustle or charm. It's not uncommon to be invited to someone's home, and then leave several hours later with a fresh fish or warm loaf of bread under the arm. Many are the island visitors who make a friend for life, at the local grocery store or gas pump on an out island.

After some 60 years, Bahamians have brought the Caribbean's tourism industry to a sophisticated level, redefining in many ways how best to market a tropical resort destination.

their reputation for maintaining integrity, safety and the simple courtesies.

Another plus is that, unlike in downtown Nassau and Freeport, most of the people you'll see on the street and in the quiet shops will be local residents. Street life is for the local, not the tourist. Whereas the busy city shops sell international products for international tourists, the island settlement customers are, for the most part, Bahamians.

FAR LEFT: Anglican formality in George Town, Exuma.
LEFT: a Long Island man's private devotion.
ABOVE: a woman displaying a flag and letter of recommendation received from a British dignitary.

The "product" they serve up is arguably the best in the whole of the Caribbean. Tourism nourishes the islands, and whether in a rural or urban setting, you can be sure that as a hotel guest, a customer, or a casual pedestrian, you will be treated with courtesy.

By the same token, Bahamians have finely-tuned the distinction between service and servitude. Bahamians quite rightly expect the same courtesies that they give to any visitor or local Bahamian: that of an equal to an equal. Treated like the hired help, the Bahamian will advise, "Talk to me right. Make me feel like you know me." Follow their advice, and you will be treated as a friend.

The first Bahamians

The Lucayan Amerindians, also known as Arawak, were the original inhabitants of these islands. The Amerindians called themselves *Lukku-caire*, meaning "island people." This was later adapted by Europeans into the name "Lucayan." Dr Julian Granberry, in an article titled *The Lucayans* in the *1973 Bahamas Handbook and Businessman's Annual*, suggests that during the early years of the Christian era, the Arawak peoples of the Guianas, on the northeast coast of South America, began a lengthy migration up through the Antilles.

The Lucayans probably came north to the

Bahamas from the southern Caribbean to escape the reportedly warlike Carib Amerindians. Since the Lucayans were a peaceful, non-violent people, their very survival depended on staying as far as possible from the Caribs.

The Lucayans were evidently beautiful people. Two chroniclers, Christopher Columbus in 1492, and Peter Martyr in 1511, described them. Columbus recorded his impressions in his journal: "They (the Lucayans) go about naked as they were born, the women also…everyone appeared to be under thirty years of age, well proportioned and good looking. The hair of some was thick and long like the tail of a horse, in some it was short and brought forward over the

eyebrows, some wearing it long and never cutting it. Some, again, are painted, and the hue of their skin is similar in colour to the people of the Canaries – neither black nor white."

Although there were approximately 20,000 to 40,000 Lucayans living in the Bahamas when Columbus visited, a slaving expedition in 1511 reported that it found no Lucayans on the islands, despite having "searched with the greatest diligence."

The Lucayans had been captured and taken to Hispaniola, Puerto Rico and Cuba to work in the mines. A significant number were also taken to Cubagua, an island off the coast of Venezuela, to dive for pearls. Most of them died of overwork and cruel treatment, or through disease and suicide. It is alleged that when they no longer served any useful purpose, they were cruelly killed.

The population vacuum left by the decimated Lucayans did not last long. Seeking refuge from upheaval in England, persecuted groups began settling in the Bahamas, establishing small and fragile settlements. Into the early 18th century, settlers endured pirates, political corruption and epidemics.

Plantation slaves

The American War of Independence sent large numbers of royal loyalists and their slaves to the Bahamas. In 1789, the population of the Bahamas was estimated to be 11,200, of which 8,000 were blacks. By 1831, there were over 12,000 black people in the Bahamas, outnumbering the white population by three to one. Out of this majority, 3,000 of the blacks were free, some owning their own slaves.

The system of slavery, which became very important economically to the colonizers, differed somewhat in the Bahamas from that found elsewhere in the Caribbean and North America. The poor soil of the Bahamas allowed only a small amount of farming to flourish on the few inhabited islands. The immense plantations found in the American South, for example, did not exist in the colonial Bahamas.

In 1834, enslaved peoples throughout the British empire were emancipated. The majority of the population of the Bahamas – the blacks – were now, to all intents and purposes, free. An apprenticeship scheme followed, maintaining the bondage, but freedom eventually came. Because of the poor Bahamian soil, there was not much demand for agricultural labor. Hence there was no need after emancipation for imported labor to replace freed blacks, unlike elsewhere in the Caribbean, where Indians (from East India) and Chinese were brought in under contracts of indenture.

After emancipation

The post-slavery era heralded a growing population and with it the growing problems of colonialism, racism, social division and discrimination. The majority of people were black, yet the Bahamas was still ruled by a white power structure, a minority, in a hierarchy similar to the racial divisions in parts of the United States, especially the South.

Bahamian whites were, for the most part, descendants of pirates, buccaneers and American Loyalists. These whites were merchants and businessmen and, along with the British administrators, were members of the ruling class. Although the British had accepted some elements of the wealthy white Bahamians into the proper English social circles, the white Bahamians were officially classed as "colonials," a designation that placed them clearly below Englishmen in the social hierarchy. These whites were very sensitive about their heritage, and compensated by rigidly maintaining the "purity" of their society by setting up strict social and racial barriers.

For Bahamians – and it didn't matter whether you were black or white, or something in-between – becoming as much like the British as possible was the single most important prerequisite for attaining self-esteem and status.

This effort, therefore, encouraged black Bahamians to place less emphasis on their African heritage and more on that of their previous slave masters. During the post-slavery period and up until the late 1960s, Bahamians of all racial backgrounds tried to be as British as possible – culturally, politically, educationally and legally.

Black and white

The black Bahamian is more than likely to be the descendant of the African slave, the "field hand" and other imported, sometimes free, blacks. It is believed that the majority of

LEFT: a replica of a Lucayan hut in San Salvador.
RIGHT: straw weaving on Exuma.

Bahamian enslaved people came from the more northerly parts of West Africa, but no one has been able to find evidence of patterns of living or any strong African traits to point to any definite tribe or race of Africans. Most Bahamian historians suggest that the tribes which were plundered during the slavery trade included the Ibo, Yoruba, Mandingo, Nango, Congo, Fullah and Housa.

There were, however, free black families who owned extensive property, took part in politic life and were highly respected in the community. Some of these blacks could trace their ancestry directly to an African tribe, and many

Africans arriving in the Bahamas during slavery were from the elite of their communities.

During the slave trade, slave ships stopped first either in Bermuda or the Bahamas. As a result, buyers had first choice of the most healthy, robust and intelligent slaves. The relatively less brutal treatment of the enslaved Africans by Bahamian white and black slave owners accounts for the small number of slave uprisings witnessed on these islands. Eventually, when whites lost political power, the transition from white to black government in the Bahamas was peaceful.

When the Loyalists left the United States and came to the Bahamas, they brought with them the most intelligent, strongest and trusted slaves. Other black people arriving in Bahamas were runaway slaves, people of imagination and great courage landing in the islands as free people after British colonies were emancipated. Still other blacks were slaves on ships that were intercepted by the British and brought to the Bahamas as free men and women.

The minority whites are now considered to be politically insignificant, but still, unsurprisingly, form the mainstream of Bahamian economic life. Some have ventured into interracial social interaction if it suits their business or otherwise; yet old prejudices, unfortunately,

still exist. But discriminatory barriers have been broken down through time, with the exception of the last remaining "security" white vestiges – the yacht clubs.

Greeks, Chinese, Syrians and Jews make up less than 1 percent of the Bahamian population. These groups came to the islands in the early 1900s (some from Cuba, the United States and Hong Kong) and have made valuable contributions to the Bahamian way of life. They still tend to be clannish, and have maintained their language and other cultural customs. Greek women dressed in their traditional black dresses can still be seen walking towards Nassau's Western Esplanade during Epiphany.

Not black and white

There is an image that the foreign visitor conjures up as being typically Bahamian: not too white and not too black, just something in between. However, there is no such thing; no typical Bahamian.

There have been great strides in terms of interaction between social classes and between blacks and whites; and pressures from within and without by white and black expatriates, Haitians, West Indians, Central and South Americans have further diversified the "pot pourri" of Bahamian life.

The legacy of a slave system in the Bahamas, though far less brutal than that experienced by enslaved men and women north and south of this archipelago, has left its mark. First-time visitors are often pleasantly surprised to see that as citified as most Bahamians living in Freeport and Nassau may be, they will meet visitors without hostility or arrogance, but rather, with subtle interest. The Bahamian resembles neither the Jamaican rasta, nor the African-American gangsta rapper, and this is where the fascination begins.

There is something to be said for a country that achieved independence from Britain without the contribution of outside negotiators and without a single gunshot being fired. The Bahamas has enjoyed a continuous and peaceful democracy since 1973 – a predominantly black country governed by a predominantly black government.

The geographical position of the Bahamas, south of Florida and north of the Caribbean chain, has allowed it to play significant roles in world history as a haven for pirates, a station for slave ships, and a base for gunrunners and bootleggers.

Most importantly, however, is that the Bahamas has defined itself as the perfect destination to live or to visit, where the goal is not to look at one another as either black or white, but simply as people. Bahamians find comfort and security in their heritage; in the Bahamas, particularly in the Out Islands, this powerful institution shows little sign of waning. For the traveler, it is an elixir. ❏

LEFT: Bahamian hospitality and delicious seafood staple.
RIGHT: Bea and Amos Ferguson – his colorful paintings reflect the warmth of Bahamian family life.

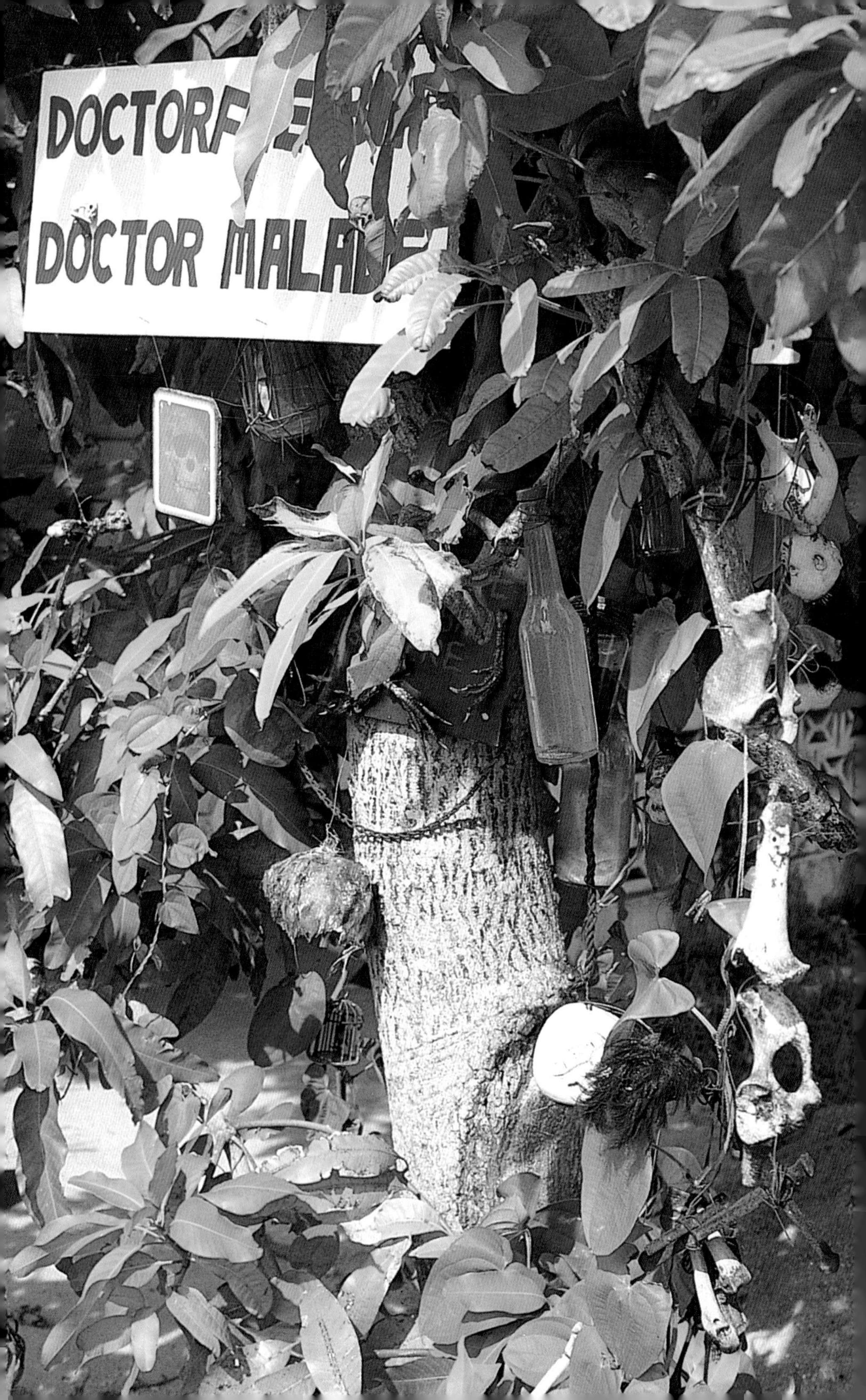
DOCTORF
DOCTOR MALAD

OBEAH, SUPERSTITION AND FOLKLORE

Belief in the supernatural isn't uniquely Bahamian, but what has been created here is a cultural cocktail shaped by both African and Western philosophies

People everywhere tend to have three fundamental things in common: family, religion, and folklore. In many cultures, the distinctions between these can be somewhat hazy, as are distinctions between religion, medicine and superstition. Factors including travel, immigration and the electronic media can muddy the waters even further.

Throughout Bahamian history, superstition and folklore have melded into a dominant and supernatural system called Obeah. Obeah is not unique to the Bahamas, and similar practices are found in much of the Caribbean. Haiti has voodoo; Trinidad has shango; Cuba, santeria.

Wherever enslaved Africans were brought, they naturally carried with them their religions, healing techniques and superstitions, not only to the Caribbean but also to parts of South America and the southern region of the United States.

The influence of Obeah

In the 1970s, several years after Independence, a Bahamian musician, then living in New York, suddenly burst onto the international and Bahamian music scene with songs all Bahamians could identify with: he was Tony McKay, a Cat Island-born Bahamian who called himself "Exuma, the Obeah man" *(see page 94). Kifaru Magazine* of Freeport said of him: "Everything is a bit mysterious about Exuma, from his outfits to his music, his paintings, his poems, his life. 'Exuma is one,' he has written. 'Exuma is three. One, two, three, they all can see.' Also, 'His time is short, his time is long. Exuma ain't right and Exuma ain't wrong.' Also, 'Exuma took his wooden hand and scorched his mark across the land.'"

Around the same time, Obeah had peaked in a revival in the Bahamas, and Exuma's rhythms

and songs not only highlighted a practice embedded into the Bahamian psyche, but also provided a meaningful cultural expression of African background relevant to a newly independent Bahamas.

Good and evil

Bahamian Obeah is supernatural. It renders evil or good, makes dreams come true and influences individuals holding either for their demise or in another's power. Its practice can bring wealth or poverty. It can bring on an illness (either physical or mental) or cure a problem. It can cause death, too.

Obeah is a type of spiritualism, surrounded by many tales of unexplained phenomena and superstitions, and with a catalogue of articles (fetishes), bush medicines, "signs" and specific directions to remove problems. Obeah, like other similar beliefs, is a blending of African religions and superstitions with those of western religion, especially Christianity.

One can also assume that Obeah originated from an African religion that had elaborate ceremonies with priests, saints, and special days. It has evolved into a form that is not, however, a cult or dogmatic religion. Today, there are no priests, collective rituals, gods or saints. It does not have ceremonies resembling those found in voodoo, shango or other beliefs in the region.

Interaction between the Obeah believer and society is one-to-one. An Obeah believer may chant, sing or go into a trance to give an impression, gain special powers, or to set the right mood, but there are no meetings, dancing, drum playing or collective singing. While there may be some Christian ministers practicing what closely resembles "Obeah" in the form of "White Magic," there are no "priests" or "ministers" in Obeah. (Theoretically, most Christian revivalist leaders in the Bahamas are not involved in the practice of Obeah; Obeah believers are, supposedly, evil persons engaging in magic. Nevertheless, the temptation for

PRECEDING PAGES: Junkanoo *Vibrations* by the Bahamian artist R. Brent Malone.
LEFT: a tree in Nassau hung with bottles and bones, a sign for an Obeah practitioner.

revivalist leaders to try their hand at Obeah is strong because of the requests made by followers; plus, of course, there is a profit to be made.)

African origins

The origin of Obeah and the word itself have never been carefully researched in the Bahamas, nor is there any comprehensive historical or current literature on the topic, except for Dr Timothy McCartney's book, *Ten, Ten the Bible Ten – Obeah in The Bahamas*. Most commentators agree, however, that Obeah was originally practiced by people of African heritage.

L.B. Powles, a circuit judge, wrote in the late

1800s that "the people here are very superstitious and what is called 'Obeahism' is very common among them. I have never been able to find out exactly what the 'Obeah-men' are supposed to do, further than that they are species of African magicians, who, for a trifling, will bewitch your enemies and charm your friends, so that any one stealing from them will be punished by supernatural agency without the intervention of the policeman or the magistrate."

In 1905, J.B. Shattuck observed that "at some of the islands we found hanging to various trees, fantastically draped bottles and sticks, which, we were informed, were charms to frighten away thieves and evil spirits. It is believed by the negroes that if anyone but the rightful owners should eat the fruit from a tree on which this spell has been placed, he will swell up and burst."

In the Bahamas, the clearly defined supernatural practices that originate from the African version – religion, medicine and superstition – are present. Many Obeah men and women possess all the attributes of religion, superstition and medicine. With regard to witchcraft and medicine, Bahamian practitioners appear to follow the tradition of Yoruba beliefs.

It is believed that in the Bahamas those Africans who were freed on arrival in the Bahamas – who were never enslaved and were therefore not exposed to the influence of Christianity – were the principal practitioners of these beliefs. While Obeah originated in Africa and may have had roots in some African religion or cult, it developed into an individual belief system, a type of sorcery that largely involved harming others at the request of clients by the use of

BUSH MEDICINE

The widespread use of bushes, barks and herbs for healing extends back to prehistory. Medicine from the earth, or bush medicine, is still an important part of Bahamian life. Most Bahamian herbalists have nothing to do with Obeah and use local bushes and barks strictly for preventive and healing purposes, sexual potency and longevity.

Particularly in the Out Islands, many Bahamians are well versed in healing ailments naturally. The leaves, bark, stems, roots, and sap of various plants are boiled for tea, eaten raw, ground to make salves, or slathered on as ointments. Lard, olive oil, kerosene, salt, port, onion, and garlic are sometimes in the mix. Chat with an older

Bahamian, and chances are he or she will tell you about the bush medicine they learned from a grand- or great-grandparent. You might hear about pawpaw milk, with a dash of sugar, used for getting rid of worms; jack-me-dark bush for colds and fever; pepper leaf for boils; rooster comb bush for burns and sores; soursop leaf for calming nerves; crab bush for stomach aches; or love vine for "loss of sex power," as Bahamians say. An excellent guide to local healing plants is *Bush Medicine in the Bahamas*, by Leslie Higgs. Though herbalists are not necessarily Obeah practitioners, the majority of Obeah men and women use bush medicine as part of their practice.

charms, shadow catching, and poisons. The Obeah professional performed Obeah practices and was paid by his clients. Many European superstitions and practices – white magic, for example – were incorporated into Obeah. Eventually, healing by bush medicines also developed.

Cat Island and Andros have strong historical Obeah roots, and the most powerful and renowned of the Obeah practitioners lived on these islands. Obeah beliefs are also strong in the Exuma Cays, Acklins, Mayaguana, South Eleuthera and Crooked Island. Each island has its Obeah center. On Cat Island it's The Bight; on San Salvador it's Breezy Hill; on Andros it's North Andros; and on New Providence it's Fox Hill. Most of the older Bahamian practitioners are Bahamian-born, but there is an increasing number of Haitians, Haitian-Bahamians, Jamaicans and others who also have lucrative Obeah practices.

There appears to be a remarkable belief in Obeah among many West Indians who do not have a strong Christian faith, but believers typically think that the magical practices of a neighboring or distant island are always more powerful than one's own. Bahamians believe that Haitian voodoo is more powerful than Bahamian Obeah. The influx of Haitian immigrants with their different language and reputation for the supernatural, to the Bahamas, has enlarged this belief. Anytime there is an election, it is rumored that many politicians pay a visit to Haiti to ensure success at the polls.

Many Bahamian Obeah men and women were apprenticed to older wise men or women, and some learned the art from their parents; or they were born with their special gifts recognized at an early age. Some received their power in adulthood during a vision or while in a trance. The more professional of these Obeah practitioners have studied in Haiti, Jamaica or Harlem, New York.

Pa Beah, Uncle Boy

The claims of Obeah practitioners are legion, and people profiting from these ministrations often attest to the "powers" of these people. Two Obeah men, now deceased, were greatly renowned. Zaccharias Adderley had the repu-

tation for being a very powerful Obeah man. He was affectionately known as "Pa Beah," ("Beah" naturally being a derivative of Obeah) and was the "king" of Obeah on New Providence Island.

He lived in Fox Hill, was a farmer and started practicing Obeah in his spare time as a hobby. He once told someone, "If people are stupid to gimme money, I ain't too stupid to take it."

According to legend, Pa Beah could fix his field so that if anyone went in to steal his cassava, they wouldn't be able to find their way out of the field until he arrived to catch them. One day, someone foolishly stole his groceries

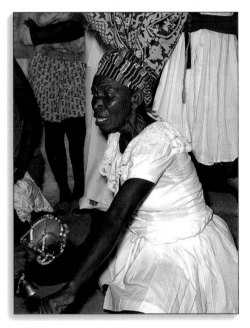

and a friend said to him, "My Lord, how yer ginna manage this week fer food?"

"Don't worry yer head 'bout me, yer betta worry 'bout the fella who take ma food. He'll soon bring ma food back or else!"

Pa Beah then took a doll, measured it against a candle and cut the candle to the length of the doll and stuck pins in the doll and the candle, the same distance apart in each. All the time he was doing this, he was calling the names of known pilferers in the area. He then lit the candle and said: "When the candle burns down to the first pin, the thief will have a bad, bad pain." That evening, Pa Beah's stolen groceries were put back on his doorstep.

LEFT: Obeah can be used to protect or persecute.
RIGHT: some people believe that Haitian voodoo is more powerful than Bahamian Obeah.

"Uncle Boy" was the reputed "king" of Obeah on Cat Island. The nephew of Uncle Boy lives in Nassau and has told stories that have been authenticated by people who lived on Cat Island, including a religious leader who knew Uncle Boy.

Uncle Boy had a coconut farm that was the pride of Cat Island. He worked hard, was a shy retiring man, and lived in the middle of his farm. He had few visitors and very few friends. He was well read, and had quite a library. It appears that someone was constantly stealing Uncle Boy's prime coconuts. Fed up, he posted the following notice:

"To whom it may concern: Whoever been in my white land and poached my coconuts for the purpose of shipping, come to see me immediately. You could be carried down and would be carried down if you don't come see me. In the future, be more careful!"

No one turned up in answer to Uncle Boy's notice. A short time afterwards, a man in the village started to swell up. No amount of medication or treatment could help him and he soon died. It was learned later that this man stole Uncle Boy's coconuts.

Obeah options

Other Obeah practitioners use primarily bush medicine and white magic. One such practitioner was a 75-year-old Nassau woman. Her father, born in Cat Island, was a well-known herbalist. She learned from him at an early age to distinguish between different "bushes and barks" and the effect they had on people.

This lady lived in an unpretentious house in the heart of the "Over-the-Hill" district. There a little shop adjoined her home and was stocked with rice, grits, flour, canned goods, jars of Mortimer brand candies, bubble gum, chicklets and the proverbial kerosene oil dispenser. A small refrigerator stored cold sodas, malt tonics and other bottles of her own "tonics" and "medicine." Behind her counter were about three rows of "sets" – photographs, articles of clothing and other memorabilia belonging to her clients, clients' relations or enemies on whom a "fix" was to be directed.

She attributed her power to God and used white magic exclusively. She said that she never utilized her "gift" to harm anybody, and would remove the harm from a client if they had an "evil fix." Although she was a known

Obeah woman, she claimed that it was not really Obeah, but rather the power that God gave her. She warned others not to "fool around" with "calling the Spirit!"

"Even though I can do it," she explained, "dat's very dangerous, and it must be done with someone who knows what they're doing, 'cause it can ruin you for life. Don' mess wid dat at all – dat's de devil and evil forces – de devil is powerful too – don't mess wid dat!" So the Obeah practices described below come with that warning.

Fixing

Fixing a person is the most common Obeah practice in the Bahamas. It entails placing a spell, a "set" or a "hagging," depending on whether the object of the spell is an individual, property or object. Being fixed must be distinguished from a curse directed through use of the Bible. Also, "putting mouth on ya" is a type of curse, but does not necessarily have to originate from any Biblical implication. There are subtle differences between a fix and a curse. A fix can be "cleared" or "cured" by an Obeah practitioner or even a medical doctor. But with a curse, only the individual who gave the curse can clear it. Unfortunately, if the one who gives the curse dies, then no one can remove it.

You can be fixed either by black magic or white magic. In black magic, not only is the Devil used, but all the "demons" and "imps" can be called upon, or those in the Bible who were against God or died as a result of defying God. *Seven Steps to Power, Black Guard, Seven Keys to Power*, and *Master Key* are the principal books used in Bahamian black magic.

White magic entails using the name of Jesus, the Bible, prayer, objects (e.g. handkerchiefs, scarves, underclothing) and religious symbols. The psalms are particularly valuable. "I gon read the Psalms to you" or "God don't like ugly" are common Bahamian threats.

White magic is evidently more powerful than black magic. For example, a combination of a fix and a curse, put on by black magic, can be cleared or cured by a white magic practitioner. If, however, an individual who is cursed by white magic goes to the curser and asks for forgiveness, then the curse will revert to the person who made the curse.

White magic can be used to cure alcoholism by paying the Obeah person money; the Obeah person will read Psalms 109 and 110 and place the money on the psalms in the Bible, then close the Bible on the money (no coins, however). The Obeah person prays that the spirit of drunkenness will be taken away, and the patient will be "cleared" of their drink problem.

Calling the spirit

Necromancy, the art of "calling the dead," is universal and goes back to earliest antiquity. "Calling the spirit" is a ritualistic Obeah practice used to obtain knowledge to be used either for good or evil. Belief in the spirit world and ancestor worship are strong components of

Bahamian *sperrids* engage in all kinds of mischief – haunting houses, hagging people, influencing human habits (good or evil), or simply scaring the hell out of someone.

Bahamian *sperrids* wander around "willy nilly," but only the Obeah practitioner can "call," "control" and utilize the *sperrids* for good or evil deeds. Bahamian believers claim that to protect oneself from a *sperrid*, all you have to say is "Ten, Ten the Bible Ten." To actually see a *sperrid*, remove some *bibby* (a local name for mucus) from a dog's eye and put it in your eyes, and you will have the gift of seeing *sperrids*. Horses see *sperrids*, too, so their *bibby* will help you also.

ABOVE: snake or witch?

African belief, and, although there is no evidence in Bahamian literature to suggest that enslaved Bahamians practiced ancestral cult worship, the belief in ghosts or spirits was, and still is, widespread among many people.

The common word in the Bahamas for any form of ghost or spirit is *sperrid. Sperrids* may be found anywhere but, according to local tradition, they like to reside in the very large silk cotton trees that abound in the Bahamas. This belief probably came directly from Africa, as many African tribes venerate the cotton tree as the dwelling place of powerful spirits of the dead.

Working witch

The term "working witch" is based on the tradition that an individual can buy or hire a witch to do his bidding. Working witch is also a term for working Obeah, a term used mostly on Cat Island. Anyone could buy or hire a witch, but it was very expensive. Cat Islanders would go to South America to earn enough money. They would return home, then go to Haiti, presumably the only island where one could obtain a witch.

The most popular witches were animals like the snake, rat and rabbit. A snake witch was extremely expensive, so much so that the owner of a snake witch would sell it or will it to another person. The "snake-witch" was a short, thick snake and was always distinguishable by the ribbon tied around its neck. This snake could swim for long distances, or take a ship or plane to "fix" people in distant lands. It also had the power to go inside people – eating their insides so that eventually the "fixed" individual would have a high fever, start to have convulsions, then waste away and die.

Many pregnant women who became fixed with a snake would lose their babies, or the snake would go inside them, eat the foetus and then, nine months after, would be born in place of the baby. There are very many Obeah stories that attest to women being pregnant and

then giving birth to snakes. Many reputable people, including Bahamian midwives, would "swear on the Bible" that they have seen snakes come out of women.

Rat witches were notorious for the havoc they waged on agricultural fields and barns. Today, in the Bahamas, the old timers still threaten to "work witch on ya."

Songs and stories

Old stories, music, rhythms and Obeah stories have always been integral parts of Bahamian life. In *New World Groups: Bahamians* (1944), Dorothy Ford wrote that "the myths contributed greatly to the music and lyrics improvised for

the purpose of morale-building. Ad-libbing or 'rigging,' as the old Bahamians termed it, went on for hours at a time and supplied fun for all concerned. Morals controlled the songs of necessity: the children could not be dispatched anywhere (all members of the family were within shouting distance and facilities were close at hand) so they were in on every move that the adults made.

As children were not aware of anything implied in the songs, the composers were adept in disguising the real meaning of words, so when we sung in imitation of them, 'Mama look up in daddy's face all night long,' it never entered our guileless minds that mama and daddy were doing anything else but sitting down facing each other, talking all night. The image of adults sitting up, talking all night, was a familiar one; the other action was not."

Religious beliefs, and references to heaven, hell, *sperrids*, angels and the Devil, abound in the stories and songs of Bahamians.

In trying to understand Bahamian folklore, one must go back to the source and examine the Bahamians' ancestors who were uprooted from Africa and placed in a new world. Here, they came under Western influence through religious missionary zeal and secular education. Gradually, African names, beliefs, superstitions, foods, festivals and holidays were displaced.

Expressions of traditional culture were discouraged. The majority of domestic house slaves were Christianized and, emulating their masters, they came to look upon African cultural expression as pagan. Field slaves, a smaller group, were not tribally strong enough to find a common ground for expression. Except for the islands of Cat Island, Exuma and Andros, where the retention of African practices was strongest, the majority of Afro-Bahamians followed strongly Euro-American cultural traditions.

It is significant that, today, Bahamians are realizing the importance of the "remoteness" of the Out Islands. Both enslaved and free Africans, living in isolated pockets on these islands, maintained much of their culture. It remains today in a stronger form than on the main islands, where Western influences are more pronounced.

Robert Curry wrote in *Bahamian Lore: Folk Tales and Songs* (Paris, 1930) that "many of the Bahamian stories will be found to have a marked similarity with those of the Negroes in the southern states of America. It is indeed not always easy to distinguish the story of Bahamian origin from one which has been imported." Evidence of these stories are the Brer Bookie and Brer Rabbie stories of the animal-trickster-hero type. The "chickcharnies" of Andros Island are mysterious three-legged owl-like animals (*See page 283*). They supposedly live in the silk cotton trees and get up to all sorts of tricks and mischief.

The most important Obeah folk tale, however, is the legend of Sammy Swain, popularized by the brilliant Bahamian pianist composer Clement Bethel, who set it to music and dance.

Many spirituals told of death. "Swing low, sweet chariot, Coming forth to carry me home." Sometimes they were expressions of the feeling of God in their bodies: "Every time I feel the spirit, Moving in my heart, I will pray." More secular songs were working songs, linked to fishing, sponging, farming. There were also songs that were like the calypso songs, composed extemporaneously to cite a local event of scandal, politics, superstition, love, sex or marriage: "There's a brown girl in the ring, and she looks like a sugar in the plum..."; or "Love, love alone, cause King Edward to leave the throne"; or "Obeah don' work on me."

LEFT AND ABOVE: Christianity, a powerful influence in the Bahamas.

Spirituals

Folk songs of the Bahamas were initially religious, linked to slavery and freedom, as evidenced by spirituals. These spirituals were brought to the Bahamas by slaves accompanying their owners from US plantations. The Bahamian spiritual has added features that combine to produce what Clement Bethel described as the "rhyming spirituals." He believed that while the lyrics are traditional, the rhyming, exchange of voices and "call and answer" techniques are unique to the Bahamas.

Festivals and feasts

There were generally four annual holidays in slavery times: Christmas, Boxing Day, New Year's Day and Easter. Both master and slave participated in these Christian festivals.

After slavery was abolished, Fox Hill Day, which only those of African descent celebrated, and August Monday (Emancipation Day) were added to the people's festivals, although Fox Hill Day was not an official public holiday.

On Emancipation Day, everyone ditched work and headed for Fox Hill by whatever means. For most, this meant walking. The trip from Grant's Town, Bain Town and Conta Butta (settlements on New Providence Island) would begin early in the morning. Weeks of preparation ended in a day of celebration: dances, quadrilles, concerts and jumping-dance. The entire community went from church to church.

There was no retention of any African festivals as such in the Bahamas. No yam festival or river (or water) festivals were commemorated. The Bahamas never enjoyed such outstanding harvests of yams as to warrant the celebrating of them. Harvests of sponges, pineapples, tomatoes and conch have been sung about, and Bahamians have improvised words and music as they suited the current events.

Harvest time was celebrated as a religious festival of thanksgiving by the white population but wasn't an official public holiday. It was also incorporated into the church services of the majority black Christian denominations on a seasonal basis. This wasn't unusual, as the major black churches here were started by free American blacks who had converted to Christianity.

Junkanoo

By far, the biggest pre- and post-slavery celebration was Christmas, when Bahamians had an almost free rein to celebrate. Activities centered around Junkanoo, an African-influenced festival that persists today.

Preparations for the Junkanoo festival became a family-neighbor venture. Unlike Carnival in other West Indian countries, and in countries with a strong Lenten tradition, Bahamian Carnival – Junkanoo – is celebrated during the Christmas season with official parades on Boxing Day and New Year's Day.

The original Junkanoo – said to be a corruption of the name John Canoe (reputedly an African king) or *gens inconnu*, meaning individual with masks – is the strongest remaining African tradition *(see page 90)*.

A number of Bahamians probably come from the Yoruba tribe, and early Junkanoo garb resembles costumes worn by members of the Yoruba Egungun cult. The Yoruba, like most African tribes, worship their ancestors, a worship based on the belief that the spirit of a human being never dies.

Egungun is a secret society of masqueraders headed by a hereditary chief called "Alagba." An Egun mask usually represents the spirit of a particular person, and it is always the priest of the Ifa oracle who will decide which spirit must receive special attention. Many of these masks consist of colored cloth and leather, covering the whole body of the dancer. Some wear masks over the face, while others wear a carving on top of the head.

The original Bahamian Junkanoo dancers wore costumes of cloth or frilled paper. Another local adaptation was the use of sponges on a type of cloth netting worn over the body. Many of the "masks" were really paintings on the facial skin itself, and the depiction of the Obeah man was usually a man dressed in white with a white mask or white paint on his face, jester-like. There were also stilt dancers, street dancers, clowns and acrobatic dancers. The Junkanoo dancers were accompanied by the goombay drums (goat skin stretched over a wooden frame and heated to obtain the maximum sound), whistles and another Bahamian adaptation, the cowbell.

Junkanoo music – performed with drums, cowbells, bugles, horns, whistles and conch shells – is deeply rooted in Bahamian culture. It is played not only at Christmas and New Years, but on many occasions that call for celebration. The Junkanoo beat rang out when the Progressive Liberal Party (PLP) won the elections in 1967, at Independence in 1973, and in honor of Sidney Poitier on a return visit to the country where he grew up. Kalik beer, the Bahamas' homegrown brew, was named for the sound the cowbell makes in Junkanoo music.

Mainstream music

Since the 1920s, Junkanoo has been gradually commercialized, but what it has lost in sheer spontaneity may well be made up for by the fact that it has become perhaps the most popular Bahamian institution. Many Bahamians belong to one of the Junkanoo groups in Nassau's Boxing Day and New Year's Day parades.

Although Junkanoo is found in Jamaica and other of the smaller English-speaking Caribbean islands in some form, the Bahamas has retained Junkanoo in its most elaborate fashion – a fashion that is uniquely Bahamian. ❏

> **JUNKANOO IN JUNE**
>
> Today, Junkanoo isn't limited to Christmastime. For one week in June, revellers head for Nassau to enjoy colorful street parades and Junkanoo artists performing on stage every night at Arawak Cay.

RIGHT: drums, masks and tall hats are enduring Junkanoo motifs.

BAHAMIAN BEATS

Island music has been influenced by Africa, Europe and North America.
The result is a spectacular collection of distinctive sounds

A visitor to the Islands of the Bahamas who comes expecting to hear only reggae or salsa music is sure to be pleasantly surprised by the distinct Caribbean sounds of traditional Bahamian music. Its sources are as diverse as its 700 islands, and date back to before Columbus landed in the Americas.

The first musicians

The original inhabitants of these islands were American Indians. The Ciboney probably arrived in the 14th century, having travelled from Trinidad and Curaçao, which lie off the coast of Venezuela. By the time Columbus arrived in 1492, Lucayan Amerindians were residing on the islands.

In 1647, the Eleutherian Adventurers *(see page 29)*, a Puritan community escaping religious intolerance in Bermuda settled at Governor's Harbour on Eleuthera. Many moved on to the settlement of Charleston (later called Nassau). The Adventurers brought with them enslaved men and women, some who had worked for them at home and others imported from Africa. In their quarters, after a long hard day in the fields, the slaves would sing among themselves and to their gods *(see page 83)*.

Origins of rake and scrape

As their bondage continued, the enslaved men and women made instruments which they used to accompany their songs. A make-shift drum was created by stretching a goat skin over an empty pork barrel, which was then heated over an open fire to improve the tone. A hollowed-out bamboo log had grooves cut into it and a thin bone was scraped across the grooves, making a pleasing sound.

The drummer would beat out a rhythm, while somebody scraped the bamboo and the others would chant and dance to the sounds. Later,

PRECEDING PAGES: the Bahamas has a lively performing arts sector.
LEFT: the colors of Junkanoo.
RIGHT: playing island music, Nassau.

when metal wash tubs were invented, they too were incorporated into the band.

The wash tub instrument was created by drilling a small hole in the center, through which a long piece of chord was inserted and then knotted. The chord was tied to the top of a broom or rake handle which was placed upright against the

tub. By pulling on the stick and plucking the chord at the same time, a tone was produced. The tighter the chord was pulled, the higher the pitch of the note. A metal saw eventually replaced the bamboo scraper: a nail was raked across the teeth of the saw, producing a scraping sound. Thus rake and scrape music was born.

In the beginning

Many of the traditional island songs were rooted in the culture of the 1600s, when the fledgling Bahamas was established. At that time the black settlers were a mixture of enslaved Africans brought to the Americas to work on the plantations, and free men. They lost much of their African tribal identity over the years while on the mainland. However, some of the settlers, especially those on the Out Islands, managed to retain and nurture a rich African heritage, surrounded by the ocean and relatively isolated from outside western influences.

Music of the people

No one really knows the origins of Junkanoo, the musical tradition that evolved to become an enduring symbol of the country. Some say the name originated from the slaves who arrived in the Bahamas during the 17th century. The Africans brought with them the legend of John Canoe, a proud and fierce African tribesman. Others say the term Junkanoo comes from the phrase *gens inconnu*, translated as unknown or masked person in French *(see page 84)*. Wherever it comes from, this is undeniably the music, the art and culture of the Bahamas.

Junkanoo is traditionally celebrated at Christmas, because this was when the slaves were given time off. Celebrations also took place on January 1st, New Year's morning.

Whereas rake and scrape music had been a kind of plaintive cry for help, an expression of a terrible situation in the same way as blues music is, Junkanoo was perceived as a pagan cele-

POP GOES JUNKANOO

Bahamian people enjoy every kind of music, including reggae, disco, jazz, rap and, most of all, the local goombay music – or Junkanoo music. This is played at Junkanoo, the biggest national festival, held twice a year. The Junkanoo parade takes place the day after Christmas, on Boxing Day and again on New Year's day in Nassau and other islands. Traditional instruments such as the goombay drum (with a goat's or sheep's skin), cowbell, whistles, bicycle horns, conch shells and foghorn are now being mixed by underground musicians, who are adding to the traditional, West African-inspired rhythms with trumpets, tubas, saxophone and trombone.

It is the mix of the old and the new that has made the Baha Men the Bahamas most famous pop band. Their catchy songs have gained international appeal from their version of the soca tune *Who let the dogs out*, to *Shake it Mamma* and *You're Mine*. Isaiah Taylor, the band's founding member said "My vision was to take the instruments from our street festival, and put them together with the stage instruments like bass, drums and guitar. I wanted to blend them all together in order that people could hear the Junkanoo music throughout the world." Their music is a mesh of popular music styles: R&B, reggae and ska mixed in with percussive Junkanoo rhythms.

bration of life. The revellers wore masks, possibly to shield their faces from the eyes of snooping slave masters, and costumes. They danced and played their instruments in their compounds, in celebration of their too few annual days of relative freedom, gyrating with abandon and drumming until the next morning, sometimes collapsing from sheer exhaustion.

After the end of the American War of Independence, many slaves were freed and promptly made their way to the Bahamas. With

LOCAL RHYTHMS

Bahamians love the rush of the goat-skin drums and the blowing of brass horns. These make a visit to the Bahamian islands a musical treat, adding to the appeal of the colorful costumes worn in parades.

in categories for best costume, best music and best theme. Prizes awarded to the winners in each category can amount to thousands of dollars and so competition is fierce.

Trinidad Carnival and Mardi Gras in New Orleans have influenced modern Junkanoo, with additions to the music including trumpets and a brass section. As choreography and overall presentation has taken on more importance, so too has the prominence, positioning, and performance of female Junaknooers. This female presence is rel-

them they brought the songs heard on the plantations of the Old South.

In 1834, slavery ended in the islands, but the ingenuity and musical influence of the Africans who created Junkanoo was here to stay.

Take the African roots, add the powerful spiritual rhythms of the church, costumes and brass band music and you have all the elements of a Bahamian musical experience – Junkanoo.

In Nassau, Junkanoo festivities the participating groups can number from a few dozen to several thousand. Junkanoo groups are judged

LEFT: Junkanoo in the streets.
ABOVE: Bahamas brass band music on parade.

atively new, emerging in the late 1980s, and is now a permanent fixture. Each Junkanoo group has its own unique rhythm, which its followers can identify by sound long before the group emerges on Bay Street for the Christmas parade.

Bring on the brass bands

In 1925, the Bahamas Brass Band was formed. The founding members of the band were all God fearing men, Baptists and musicians, whose aim was to praise and glorify God by playing spirit filled music in church. The band was soon playing at weddings, leading the parade at funerals and taking their unique form of gospel music to the Out Islands.

By 1938, there were 12 musicians in the band, and today the Bahamas Brass Band has over 100 members, including a junior band who will, in time, replace the older members. The band, whose motto is "music with spirit," has played at important functions in the Bahamas and throughout the US.

A predecessor of the Bahamas Brass Band is the Royal Bahamas Police Force Band, which was established in 1893. Purveyors of the contemporary brass band sound, not only do they play military music, but they also play the music of the Bahamas, incorporating calypso and folk music.

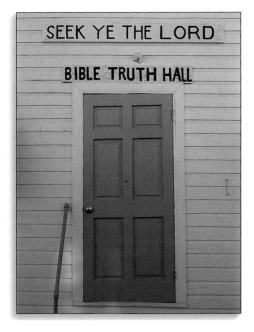

The impact of religious music

Sacred music – the music heard in churches – was influenced by music imported to the Bahamas from Europe, and also by Negro spirituals and gospel songs of the emancipated slaves from America. Bahamian anthems and spirituals were fused with rake and scrape.

Church music is traditionally solemn, but in many Bahamian churches it is entirely the opposite: if you can't sing you hum; if you can't hum you clap; if you can't clap you jump up and down and have a good time. The action referred to is most often seen in what some islanders call the "jumper churches," started by black Bahamians, early proponents of Evan-

gelical and Pentecostal denominations. When white and black churches combined, a new kind of rhythm was infused into white church music. In the Americas, variations of this may be found in Baptist and Pentecostal services.

Bahamian churchgoers have developed a unique practice known as "rushing." The practice is believed to have begun in a church one New Year's Eve, when the congregation was fundraising. A hat is placed on a table and the congregation rush – shuffle – past the table placing money in the hat, and move around church to the beat of music, singing. When their money runs out they have to sit down.

The blending of dance and music within church became so pleasurable that church members would intentionally carry bills of small denominations, and even coins, in order to "rush" for as long as possible. You can see easily how those same revellers would happily rush from the church into the outdoors on Christmas night or New Year's, for the pure enjoyment of the pulsating drums and music that would move through the streets.

Influences at home and abroad

During the Prohibition era in the US, the Bahamas experienced a tourism boom since liquor was easily obtainable on the islands. Their proximity to Florida was also a prime factor contributing to the their popularity.

In 1930, the Chocolate Dandies were formed by 14 Bahamians living in the eastern district of Nassau. They played the big band sounds of the legendary American musician, Count Basie, who lived in Freeport from 1970 until his death in 1984. The music of Duke Ellington and Louis "Satchmo" Armstrong also became part of the Dandies' repertoire.

Blake Alphonso Higgs, who came to be known as Blind Blake, was born blind on the island of Eleuthera in 1915. He was a prolific songwriter, composing songs on his guitar that focused on events and incidents occurring in the Bahamas, and also covering stories from abroad. If something happened in Nassau during the day, Blake would surely have produced a song about it by nightfall. His most famous composition, *Love Alone*, was written on December 10, 1936, the day King Edward VIII abdicated the throne of England to marry Wallace Simpson, an American divorcée. When the Duke and Duchess of Windsor later visited

Nassau in 1940, Blind Blake was asked to perform the song he had written about them. He wrote more than 100 songs; among the better-known are *John B*, *Sail* and *Gully Picking*.

Joseph Spence was a folk guitarist who became very popular during a 1960s revival of folk music. Spence was greatly influenced by the church and his songs were as jolly and as upbeat as the man himself, often written on the spur of the moment. In 1965 the folk singer Pete Seeger heard Spence and booked him for a series of concerts at the Newport Jazz Festival in the US. This led to the Bahamian securing a recording contract on Electra records. Spence died at the age of 73, but his music lives on in the hearts of folk music fans.

The Caribbean in the Bahamas

In the 1950s, music which had a distinct Caribbean flavor was introduced to the islands by Bahamian artist Franklyn Hilgrove Ellis, who was later affectionately called Count Bernadino. In 1959, he began performing his brand of Bahamian beats at Nassau's Cat and Fiddle night club. The club was run by Freddie Munnings Sr., another Nassuvian musician who was a well-known performer and recording artist in his own right.

The Count refused to be influenced by North American music, which was a powerful force, preferring, instead, to use the calypso style of the Caribbean. In his act – which endures today – Ellis sings the first few lines of a familiar calypso song and then ad-libs, making sure his rhymes fit both the music and the mood of his audience.

Meanwhile, on the Out Islands...

Nassau is not the only place that nurtured local musicians – the composers of many popular Bahamian songs heralded from the Out Islands. Exuma-born Eric Minns wrote music that had a calypso feel to it, including the Bahamian standard *Island Boy*. Timothy Gibson, a schoolteacher from Savannah Sound, on the island of Eleuthera, wrote songs containing formal, patriotic themes such as the Bahamas national

LEFT: spiritual music, found in island churches.
RIGHT: the jazz legend Count Basie, who made the Bahamas his home.

anthem, *March on Bahama Land*, which he penned just before independence in 1973.

COUNT BASIE SQUARE

Count Basie Square in Port Lucaya Grand Bahama, is named for the jazz legend, who made Freeport his adoptive home. The bandstand in the square has live local music most evenings.

Funk and folk abroad

Tony Mckay, a.k.a. the Obeah Man from Exuma, took his name from childhood folklore *(see page 77)*. He left the Bahamas at 17, when he moved to New York intending to study architecture; instead he became interested in folk music and formed his first band. His first album, *Gris Gris*, was a blend of voodoo and obeah witchcraft and mysticism,

and rhythm and blues music. Though it was hard to categorize Mckay's songs in one musical genre, it was easy to recognize the African influence in his singing and guitar playing.

Mckay was discovered in a coffee house in Greenwich Village, New York. Performing on stage he was a spectacular sight sporting long dread locks way before they were fashionable, and he usually wore gold glitter pants, ankle bells and a bright satin shirt. A throat harp accompanied his guitar. A poet and a painter, he endeared himself to the Bahamian public with songs such as *Brown Girl in the Ring*, which school children still sing today. But Mckay is most remembered for his signature tune *Exuma the Obeah Man*, which explores the mystical powers of obeah that the singer claimed infused him with special powers from his island roots.

At least two Bahamian recording artists covered Mckay's haunting melodies, but he never achieved real financial or commercial success and died penniless in the late 1990s.

Bahamian music today

Until the runaway success of the Grammy Award-winning song *Who Let the Dogs Out*, by the Baha Men, the only other Bahamian recording group who gained international recognition was a 1970s band called The Beginning of The

End. Their song *Funky Nassau* continues to be popular, particularly in film sound tracks.

Today, the Bahamas music scene is influenced by Caribbean music, such as soca, and, to a much smaller degree, reggae. Bahamian musicians often turn comparisons with American music, tongue in cheek, to their own advantage. A fine example of this is a tune called *Bahama Rock*, by enduring pop and traditional artist, Ronnie Butler.

K.B. (Kirkland Bodie) is a modern-day version of Blind Blake. Though he has no visual impairment, the Nassau recording artist uses local events as material for his songs and transforms them into music you can dance to. His

lyrics speak to the Bahamian people in much the same way that calypsonians do in their songs, which are political and social commentaries. K.B. has also helped to revive the use of rake and scrape music for a new generation of fans.

The annual Cat Island Heritage Festival, launched by the daughter of Sidney Poitier, who grew up on the island, promotes rake and scrape competitions that attract an increasing number of visitors. Over the past few years the resurgence of rake and scrape music has brought new respect for the skills required to play the unique instruments such as the saw, concertina, goat skin drum and the rake.

Phil Stubbs, known as the Storyteller, was born on Cat Island but lives and works on Grand Bahama. His albums reveal the Bahamian culture and the natural beauty of the islands through musical imagery.

Socanoo

Perhaps the most definitive contemporary representatives of Bahamian music are Visage, a 15-member band which, since the 1980s has progressed from playing high school dances to performing sell-out concerts and producing best-selling CDs. The band has created a new sound, christened socanoo, which unapologetically blends soul music and Caribbean calypso with the African-flavored drum rhythms of Junkanoo.

Music from this archipelago continues to make statements reaching far beyond its borders. The Baha Men perform at venues from Europe to Japan, and have penned a substantial portion of the music score for the 1994 movie starring Gérard Depardieu, *My Father the Hero*, filmed on Paradise Island.

While the world's music and musicians have influenced the evolution of Bahamian music styles, Bahamians have proven themselves to be innovators. Cleophas Adderley, the founder and director of the Bahamas National Youth Choir, wrote the Bahamas' first opera, which the choir performed.

But above all it is the passion and beauty of Junkanoo – its vibrant visual and musical sections, created by the sound of the goatskin drums – that remain the most distinctive element of Bahamian music. ❑

LEFT: Tony Mckay, the "Obeah Man."
RIGHT: Junkanoo, which continues to influence the Bahamian music scene.

LUXURIOUS LIFESTYLES

First pirates, then bootleggers and rumrunners brought vast wealth to the Bahamas – long regarded as a playground for the royal, the rich and the famous

The 500th anniversary of the landing of Christopher Columbus, the most famous visitor to the Bahamas, was marked on October 12, 1992. He first set foot on a tiny island to plant the banners of his sovereign. Though he could not have foreseen the future, the banner of royalty was prophetic, for these isles were later to become one of the world's foremost playgrounds for the royal, the rich and the famous.

It all began in 1919, when the 18th Amendment to the US Constitution was adopted, introducing Prohibition. In the Bahamas the decade known as the Roaring Twenties started with rumrunning and bootlegging, and a rapid influx of new wealth.

Riches and royalty

The private yachts of some of the most powerful industrial tycoons of the time crowded Nassau's harbor. They included the yachts of William K. Vanderbilt, Vincent Astor, J.P. Morgan, and E.F. Hutton, as well as the Whitneys, Armours and Mellons.

The advent of World War II brought wealthy refugees from Europe and Britain, who flocked to the sunny and peaceful isles. What stamped the Bahamas with the ultimate seal of approval and guaranteed worldwide media attention was the arrival of the Duke and Duchess of Windsor – the ex-king of England who gave up the throne to marry American divorcée, Wallis Simpson.

After the abdication, the duke and duchess lived a life of luxury at their Paris mansion and on their estate on the Riviera. When the Nazis marched into France, however, the couple fled to neutral Portugal. They became the victims of a plot hatched by German and Portuguese diplomatic officials to lure the duke into the German orbit, by kidnapping, if necessary. Prime Minister Winston Churchill learned of the plot and sent the duke as far from the war zone as possible, offering him to the post of governor of the Bahamas Islands.

Colonial splendor

The news that a man born to be king of England was coming to rule a remote outpost was greeted with great astonishment and excitement. No one could remember when royalty had ever set foot in the colony, although it was recalled that Prince Albert Victor, the second son of Queen Victoria, had once landed here.

Everyone realized that the former king would certainly draw American money to Nassau. Even as the duke and duchess were sailing toward the islands, tourists (not usually common in August) and journalists were already awaiting the royal couple.

As the great grandson of Queen Victoria, the liberator of enslaved men and women, the duke was invested with near-divine status in the eyes of many black Bahamians. The story of how he gave up his throne for love had passed into Bahamian folk legend – and into the lyrics of blind songster Blake Higgs, words that always drove the duke into fits of laughter:

It was Love, Love alone
Cause King Edward to leave the throne.
It was Love, Love alone
Cause King Edward to leave the throne
We know that Edward was good and great
But it was Love that cause him to abdicate

The duke and duchess brought not only constant media attention to themselves and their wartime home, but also a style, an elegance and a certain chic that had not been seen before in Government House.

It was Sir Harry Oakes, considered the most important man in the Bahamas at the time, who lent his house, Westbourne, to the Windsors while they were waiting for Government House to be refurbished. Oakes owned almost a third of the island and was the largest private employer. He had built an airfield, a golf course, bus lines and hotels and he loved to operate a bulldozer on his land.

PRECEDING PAGES: colonial splendor characterizes the Lyford Cay Club House.

LEFT: cuisine with panache for well-heeled guests at the Bimini Big Game Fishing Club.

It was also Sir Harry who unwittingly brought unwanted worldwide attention to the Bahamas, following his murder during a night of wild thunder and lightning on July 7, 1943. The world press tagged it "the Crime of the Century." There was an influx of American journalists and crime reporters and writers, among them the famed Erle Stanley Gardner.

The murder has remained unsolved to this day, although Oakes' son-in-law, Count Alfred Fouquereaux de Marigny, was originally charged with the crime. He was acquitted after trial but still deported as an undesirable. It was a particularly brutal murder. Sir Harry had been

Killams, Arthur Davis, Austin Levy, Rosita Forbes, Lady Oakes and Lord Beaverbrook.

Royal visitors

Although the duke was the only British royal to actually live on these isles, it has been a vacation spot for many royal families.

Queen Elizabeth II was the first reigning monarch to visit the Bahamas. A national holiday was declared when her yacht, *HMS Britannia*, dropped anchor in Bahamian waters for a three-day official visit in 1966. A highlight of her visit was the banquet served in the Government House ballroom.

beaten and burned and his body was covered with feathers from a pillow. Oakes had a house guest that night, Harold Christie; there were reports that he had been threatened. The murder and the resulting publicity caused a great deal of anxiety for the duke and duchess and may even have contributed to the duke's decision not to finish his full five-year term. He resigned in the spring of 1945, a few months before the term officially ended. He and his wife left the Bahamas on May 3.

They returned over the years, staying most winters for a few weeks. They tried to keep these trips quiet, enjoying the company of old friends such as the Vernays, the Sigrists, the

PLAYGROUND OF KINGS

The islands' exclusivity appeals to royal visitors who have helped earn the Bahamas the title "Playground of Kings". Over the years Greek and other Balkan kings have favored the Bahamas as a retreat. Bulgaria's King Simeon II honeymooned with his Queen Margarita at the Emerald Beach Hotel in 1962. King Olav V of Norway, an expert sailor, was the guest of the Robert H. Symonettes in 1981. For his 80th birthday, King Olav V was presented with a gold trophy for winning the Duke of Edinburgh Series in Nassau. Romania's King Michael and Queen Anne added a touch of royal glamor to the Hellenic Ball in 1984 at the Crown Ballroom of Paradise Towers.

Nassau has many permanent reminders of visits undertaken by the British royal family. There is a plaque at the Central Bank of The Bahamas, noting its opening dedication by Queen Elizabeth II. Another plaque commemorates the laying of the bank cornerstone by Prince Charles. Princess Anne unveiled a monument in the gardens of the former Royal Victoria Hotel. The monument was a salute to the 250th year of parliamentary democracy in the Bahamas. Princess Margaret earned herself the nickname as the "Calypso Princess" because of her dedication to music and dancing.

Nassau's largest dock was named the Prince George Wharf after a Royal Navy visit that featured a Bahamas tour by Prince George, later the Duke of Kent. He returned in 1935 for a honeymoon with his Greek bride, the Princess Marina. The honeymoon was filled with sunny days, fishing trips and social events. The royal couple also met US president Franklin D. Roosevelt, who was fishing in Bahamian waters.

Among the most famous royal visitors were Princess Diana and Prince Charles. But Princess Diana unwittingly garnered most of the publicity when a photographer with a telephoto lens caught her in a bikini. She was visibly pregnant and the photo was published in a London newspaper. Buckingham Palace was outraged and the photo was deemed an inexcusable violation of privacy. For the remainder of the royal holiday on Windermere Island, press activities were severely restricted.

Windermere Island, which is connected by bridge to Eleuthera, became a holiday mecca for Prince Charles through his late great-uncle, Earl Mountbatten of Burma. Lord Mountbatten visited Windermere Island on an annual basis and introduced the Prince of Wales to this resort. Titled visitors who have spent holiday time on Windermere Island include the Duke and Duchess of Abercorn, the Viscount and Viscountess William Astor, Lady Anne Orr-Lewis, the Marquess of Milford Haven and the Viscountess Harriet de Rosiere. Another titled fan of Bahamian holidays was the Baroness von Trapp, whose life was portrayed in Rodgers and Hammerstein's *The Sound Of Music*.

LEFT: an elegant Bahamian scene, 1802, etched by British Colonel John Irving.
RIGHT: the Duke and Duchess of Windsor, ever in the social spotlight, enjoy an evening out in Nassau.

Beyond posh

With such a strong strain of royal history in the Bahamas it is appropriate that a hotel company chose "Royal Bahamian" as the name of one of the Bahamas' most elegant hotels. Formerly the Balmoral Beach Club, this plush hotel in Nassau underwent several renovations while it belonged to the Le Meridien chain. Now the Sandals Royal Bahamian, the all-inclusive hotel reflects the physical grandeur of what was once the Bahamas' most prestigious resort hideaway.

The old Balmoral Beach Club was the creation of British developer Sir Oliver Simmonds, who began work on its construction almost

immediately following World War II. For years he had been aware that the very wealthy, very powerful world leaders, royalty, and stage, screen, opera, ballet and concert stars, were constantly searching for closed little corners of the world where they could find peace and privacy along with the best accommodations.

To further enhance the prestige of his new property, Simmonds spent a full year spreading the word that his Balmoral Beach Club was ultraexclusive, that it would operate as a private club and would be restricted to members only and their approved guests.

As a result, Simmonds found himself besieged with requests for membership and reservations from all corners of the world. The Club's guests gravitated to the club for its elegance and fanatical commitment to privacy, which went so far as to rule out records of many celebrity visits.

"The Balmoral was always one long continuing secret," said Valencia Saunders, a former Balmoral employee and later a restaurant manager at the Cable Beach Hotel. "The guests came for privacy and service and we gave them both. But you couldn't help wondering on occasion what intricacies brought a prince from Spain or a multi-millionaire from Italy to seek the seclusion of the Balmoral."

Simmonds opted for semi-retirement after 16 years of success, and the private club became a public hotel in 1967. However, it could (and frequently did) reserve the right to accept only the type of clientele to whom it had catered in the past. There were some notable exceptions. When the Beatles were being mobbed from New York to Hong Kong and could find no escape from their fame, they were accepted by the Balmoral.

The Beatles were awed by the fact that they could walk the byways of the compound, sun at the poolside, walk through the dining room and roam the beaches of Balmoral Island, seemingly unrecognized. Richard Nixon was known

NEW MONEY AT THE CAY

In Lyford Cay, an exclusive enclave of the international upper crust since the 1950s, it is easy to forget that you are in the Bahamas. Most of the people who make their homes, or second homes, here are wealthy Europeans, Americans and Canadians, from heiresses to oil barons. A 12-minute drive from Nassau, this is a place where "Sir" is an aristocratic title, not simply a polite form of address. Villas sport private beaches, circular driveways and imported household help. Social lives revolve around golf, tennis, yachting, deep-sea fishing and charity parties.

At the Lyford Cay Club, a pink mansion with stately white columns and the focal point of the resort, couples must be married if they wish to stay overnight. Public displays of affection, skimpy bathing suits and loud music or voices are not allowed. Gates, guards, a two-year waiting list, a $65,000-plus membership fee, and some $7,000 in annual dues are meant to keep out the riff-raff – or at least they used to, say some residents.

The large Polynesian-style house of fashion designer Peter Nygard, who grew up in a poor family in Finland, is surrounded by a sprawling estate that has a menagerie and many other multi-million dollar lifestyle accessories. Celebrities and royalty flock to Nygard's fabulous home, proof that life at Lyford Cay remains the same but different.

for arriving unexpectedly during his tenure as US president, often dropping in by boat.

"He knew he had perfect privacy once he got onto the property and that coming by boat he circumvented news of his arrival so that he could enjoy that privacy," remembered Tommy Thompson, who rose to maître d' during his 16 years at the Balmoral.

Other post-war developments in New Providence and some of the Out Islands served as a magnet for some of the wealthy and notable. Dr Wenner-Gren sold his Hog Island property to A&P heir Huntington Hartford, who bought up much of the remaining property from indi-

certainly the most elusive guests in recent years was the late Howard Hughes, who took over the entire ninth floor of Britannia Towers from 1970 to 1972.

Highly exclusive

Lyford Cay, actually a peninsula on New Providence, is another Bahamian haven for international socialites, royalty, titled people, and financiers. The club was founded in the 1950s by multimillionaire Canadian developer E.P. Taylor. He set out to create a top-notch club resort which operates more like a community. Behind the pink walls and guarded gates is a lush 1,200-

vidual owners. Hog Island was renamed Paradise Island and Hartford embarked on an extensive development program designed to attract the jet set. Dr Wenner-Gren's guesthouse by the shore of the man-made Paradise Lake, was converted into the now famous Cafe Martinique, while the Ocean Club, which used to be Dr Wenner-Gren's winter home, became the center of a luxury resort.

The late Shah of Iran stayed at the Ocean Club while he was in residence on Paradise Island. One of the island's most famous and

acre (500-hectare) residential resort. It is geared toward golf and tennis, yachting and deep sea fishing. More than 225 private houses are set on winding sea canals, along white-sand beaches and around an 18-hole golf course.

There is a diverse mix of nationalities here. One thing that has remained constant is the privacy and security the club continues to offer. "It is the only private place left in the world today," declared Baroness Meriel de Posson, a long-time Lyford member who returned year after year from London. The club maintains its own fire and security staff once headed by Arthur Hailey (author of *Airport* and *Hotel*), a permanent resident of Lyford Cay.

LEFT: wealthy yachties sail to the Bahamas.
ABOVE: poolside posh at the Lyford Cay Club.

Other residents include the Greek shipping magnate Stavros Niarchos, who usually has his 380-ft (116-meter) yacht brought to the Bahamas as an annexe to Villa Niarchos. Other residents include Sean Connery, Princess Annmarie von Bismarck, Sir Harold Christie, Wendy Vanderbilt Lehman, Count and Countess de Rovenel, Lord Martonmere, a former governor of Bermuda, and the Canadian actress Rosanna Seaborn, whose house includes Roman baths.

Today, a new crowd is slipping in – still multi-millionaires but, unlike some of the old guard, whose money stretches back genera-

tions, many of the more recent arrivals have earned their millions themselves. With this new money have come new values, new lifestyles and new headaches for more than a few long-time residents.

In a community where 6,500-sq.-ft (604-sq.-meter) European-style villas are the norm, newcomers have built larger – and more ostentatious – homes. Take the 150,000-sq.-foot (13,935-sq.-meter) Polynesian-style house of Finnish designer Peter Nygard. His vast compound has hundreds of roaming peacocks, cockatoos and parrots; a lagoon that meanders through the house; a huge dining table that turns into a dance floor, and young women who

wiggle while Nygard sings on karaoke nights. Yet, if past visits from Prince Andrew and Sarah Ferguson, Michael Jackson, Robert DeNiro and George and Barbara Bush are any indication, at least some people approve of Lyford Cay's new look.

Not far from Lyford Cay is a waterfront mansion called Capricorn, believed to be owned by singer Julio Iglesias. It was once the home of Sir Francis Peek and was where United States president Lyndon Johnson's daughter, Lucy, spent her honeymoon.

Out Island hideaways

Eleuthera is another popular gathering spot for the wealthy and powerful. The Windermere Island Club continues to be favored by royalty and financiers. The Pink Sands Resort, on Harbour Island, is the luxury getaway for high profile guests, such as actress Susan Sarandon and Microsoft founder Bill Gates.

The Bimini Islands are still known as the "Big Game Fishing Capital of the World." They first gained attention in the 1930s with the visits of novelist and big game fisherman Ernest Hemingway, as well as Howard Hughes and Zane Grey. Hemingway headquartered in Lady Helen Duncombe's Compleat Angler Hotel *(see page 220)*, and was the first person in memory to land a bluefin tuna on rod and reel. The hotel's popular bar has on show a priceless collection of Hemingway memorabilia.

Hemingway's property on Bimini was given to him by Mike Lerner, the philanthropist who shared Hemingway's passion for big-game fishing and hunting. Lerner's elegant home, "The Anchorage", is now the hotel and restaurant of Bimini Blue Water Limited's complex *(see page 224)*. One of the cottages is famous as Marlin Cottage, Hemingway's hideaway.

Tracking 007

Ian Fleming liked the Bahamas so much that he set some of his most glamorous James Bond novels here, allowing 007 to amuse himself playing baccarat in the gambling rooms of Nassau's casinos.

The settting for *Dr No*, the first Bond film, was inspired by Fleming's visit to Inagua. He found this Bahamian isle as strange as it is beautiful. He realized that this island, with its lake "only a couple of feet deep and the color of a corpse," would make a fitting home for Dr No.

Besides Sean Connery, the other star of *Thunderball* was the Bahamas itself, and the screenplay was designed to take full advantage of the islands' natural assets. This film revealed to the world the Bahamas' fabulous underwater world. Bond (Sean Connery) and Domino (Claudine Auger) meet underwater among coral gardens and brilliantly-colored tropical fish, swimming to a perfect beach where tall palms grow from a crescent of sugary sand.

A TRIBUTE TO BOND

The James Bond Suite at the British Colonial Hilton in Nassau pays tribute to the film legend: walls adorned with movie posters, and a video library containing the entire collection of 007 films.

At the time that *Thunderball* was made, in 1965, Paradise Island was still called Hog Island. There were only a handful of estates in those days, and one of its biggest attractions was the glittering Cafe Martinique.

Filmmakers promised a hefty contribution to a favored charity and convinced the local gentry to allow themselves to be filmed enjoying their favorite haunt with their customary refreshments – a bucket of Beluga caviar and several cases of Dom Perignon. The result was a splendid affair that was captured on film as Nassau's finest citizens stepped from their motor launches dressed in black tie and sipped champagne in the tropical night.

Although Connery moved from island to island in *Never Say Never Again*, the Bahamas once again figure in this film as Bond travels to Nassau, walking through the famous straw market and along a street lined with colonial buildings. Later, Bond stands at an outdoor bar over the water as an ocean liner steams toward the Nassau dock. Clearly, James Bond had become one of the Bahamas' most visible and elegant visitors.

Island kingdoms

In a nation that numbers at least 700 islands, there are enough isles for wealthy Bahamians to set up their own island kingdoms. For some, the islands are a weekend refuge from the bustle of Nassau. For others, the islands are their winter or year-round home.

"Most people who own their own islands are very wealthy people who look to the island as their own little kingdom," explained a Bahamian whose family owns their own island. "The island idea makes it possible for someone to set up everything as he wants it. The police hardly ever appear and to a limited degree one is the law on his island.

"The trip down to the island is somewhat like Fantasy Island. We fly down on an old seaplane from Nassau and when we arrive we are met by the caretaker and taken up to the main house. As soon as you step on the island

there is a feeling of incredible peace. The sounds are the sounds of waves, sea gulls and other birds. There are no intrusions. You just don't have to have anything on the island you don't want. It is really a rare privilege to be on the island and know that it is yours."

Some of the private islands aren't developed at all and the owners use them as private campgrounds. Others are elaborately developed with a number of houses, guesthouses and boat houses. Owners use their isles as a base to enjoy the beaches and remote fishing and diving spots. For those who are seeking the ultimate in privacy a personal island offers the perfect solution. ❑

LEFT: English teatime on the terrace, still the custom at the Windermere Club on Eleuthera.
RIGHT: a hammock in the shade of palm trees – all you need on a remote island retreat.

UNDERWATER BAHAMAS

Divers and snorkelers of all abilities can discover a spectacular world offshore,
from shipwrecks to banks of coral, blue holes and brilliantly colored marine life

Most of us will never walk on the moon or take a flight through space. But almost anyone can experience the indescribable feeling of floating "weightless" beneath the sea amid a panorama of remarkable beauty. Scuba diving is booming, and even greater numbers enjoy snorkeling, which requires only a mask, snorkel and fins. With at least 100,000 sq. miles (259,000 sq. km) of crystal-clear seas, the Bahamas is a diver's paradise.

Although sport diving in the Bahamas has flourished only in the past 30 years, the wonders under these seas were known back in the mid-1800s. John B. Green, "the celebrated submarine diver" as he called himself, took a break from his usual treasure diving in the Great Lakes to look for treasure in Bahamian waters. He discovered the lost wreck he had been hired to find, but wasn't able to bring up the entombed silver because it had become so encrusted with coral. Green did find treasures of another kind, however.

"On this bank of coral is presented to the diver one of the most beautiful and sublime scenes the eye ever beheld. The water varies from 10 to 100 ft (3 to 30 meters) in depth, and is so clear that the diver can see from 200 to 300 ft (61 to 91 meters), when submerged with little obstruction to the sight," he wrote. He described the sharks, colorful fish and corals that grow in profusion in these waters. Green was clearly in awe as he swam among these fascinating creatures.

Natural wonders

Floating slowly over one of the isles' many shipwrecks, a diver enters another world of natural wonder. Large Nassau groupers approach divers looking for handouts. Disappointed at not being fed, they back off a little but still tag

along like friendly puppies or curious cats trying to be affectionate without getting in the way. Brilliant-hued parrot fish feed head down, crunching hard coral with their beak-like teeth. They are sand-makers: they graze on the stony surface of the coral, spitting out bits of hard exterior skeleton and devouring the algae grow-

ing there. This is a quiet world, and the parrot fish's crunching can be heard by divers a few feet away.

A lifetime of diving would not be long enough to explore the underwater world of the Bahamas. These isles offer ideal conditions for new divers, with many certified instructors and safe, calm seas. There are an amazing number of sites and experiences to fascinate even the most experienced diver; shallow reef diving, wall dives, shark diving, blue holes, canyons and more.

These islands also feature one of the world's finest fleets of live-aboard dive boats, offering more dives per day and better access to remote reefs than land-based diving.

PRECEDING PAGES: coral branches.
LEFT: the solitude and mystery of exploring the Bahamas' many underwater wonders.
RIGHT: a diving instructor prepares a student to take the plunge.

Ships claimed by the sea

Wrecks liberally sprinkled throughout the islands give mute testimony to the extensive – and potentially dangerous – coral reef system that surrounds them. The history of the Bahamas is written in the wrecks.

There is something magnetic and surreal about a shipwreck, even an oft-visited one. Some wrecks date from the two centuries when the islands were a refuge for pirates. Rumors of hidden treasure abound in the southern Baha-

> **BLUE HOLES**
>
> The Bahamas has one of the world's largest number of blue holes, second only to Mexico. The holes are part of vast underwater caves systems that developed during the Ice Age.

Greek mythology attributed corals to the seeds of seaweeds petrified by Medusa, whose hideous face turned all who saw her to stone. Early naturalists assumed corals were some sort of marine shrub. It was not until 1726 that French naturalist Jean André Peyssonnel showed that a reef was made up not of plants but groups of tiny animals. Though they don't roam for food, corals are efficient predators and reef builders. It takes all kinds of coral to make a reef: star coral in mounds, elkhorn and staghorn

mas. Filmmakers have flocked to Nassau on New Providence Island to shoot a string of James Bond movies: *Thunderball*, *Dr. No* and *Never Say Never (see page 104–5)*. Parts of *Splash!*, *Wet Gold* and *Cocoon* were filmed here as well.

Coral cathedrals

Coral reefs are enchanting and magical places, and the Bahamas abound in these special gifts of nature. To dive on a coral reef is to dream. Drift, soar, glide through sprawling cities. Domes of brain coral closely resemble their namesake. Staghorn corals forest the reef with their stony trunks and branches.

coral with spreading branches – the kind of variety that can be seen in Bahamian waters.

Coral reefs are created by polyp colonies which build external skeletons of calcium carbonate. The calcium waste is deposited over countless generations to build a solid reef covered by a thin veil of living polyps, which continue the process. Some coral heads are so huge that divers can swim inside the cavernous structure. It is easy to feel dwarfed by these dark and awesome mini caverns, but also uplifted by the cascades of light that stream in.

Elusive black coral that has become as rare as jewels elsewhere is prolific on some of these reefs. Vivid sponges grow in patches of bright orange, deep rust and fluorescent yellow. Tiny feather dusters – the gills of burrowing worms – sprout from brain corals, retreating at the slightest motion.

Each coral reef is an entire community. Many reef dwellers are territorial, and divers can usually count on seeing the same curious angelfish on each visit to a particular reef. Look carefully under a ledge and there will be a moray eel, under another ledge a spiny lobster. The reef is a fascinating mosaic of colors, forms, shapes and constant motion. It is also one of the most complex and delicately balanced communities anywhere, and hence easily damaged.

groan, click, vibrate. Lobsters and sea urchins march boldly across the seabed. Corals open their polyps for feeding. Some fish do sleep, allowing a diver to approach closely, and even pet them as they hang motionless under coral ledges. Other fish sleep hidden in packets of their own mucus, which prevents their scent from attracting predators.

Run your hands through the water and you will see the bioluminescene, the phosphorescent streaks and sparks that light up the sea.

The climate for diving varies according to the seasons – anytime is great but summer is best of all. In the winter, the air temperature

Night dives

The Bahamas are an ideal spot for an introduction to the fantastic and surreal world of the reef at night. Colors disappear or become transformed one by one as increasing depth steals light of varying wavelengths. Red is transformed first; at 30 ft (9 meters), a cut finger oozes green blood.

Most coral polyps are nocturnal, withdrawing deep within their skeletons by day. But at night, the reef is alive – and much noisier. Fish grunt,

LEFT: gliding through coral gardens.
ABOVE: a grouper, famous for its phlegmatic nature, poses with three divers.

ranges from 68°F to 78°F (20–25°C) while the water temperature ranges from 70°F to 76°F (21–24°C), – making a good quality wetsuit essential.

Summer is the most spectacular season, with air temperatures ranging from 76°F to 88°F (24–31°C) moderated by cooling ocean breezes. The water can warm up to the high 80°s F (30–31°C) and the seas are usually calm and glassy. Underwater visibility can extend to as much as 200 ft (60 meters).

Several dive operators in the islands feature both windward and leeward dive sites; even if winds are up divers can still experience some fine diving.

Photogenic wrecks

Despite its population and development, New Providence Island has some surprisingly fine diving and is one of the best-kept diving secrets in Bahamas. On the north side of the island, close to Nassau, there are shallow reefs and several outstanding wrecks: the *Mahoney,* the *Alcora* and the *LCT.* On the south side is Clifton Wall, a dramatic wall near a dozen dive sites clustered within a mile of each other.

The wreck of the vessel, *Tears of Allah*, formed a perfect backdrop for the James Bond film *Never Say Never Again*. The 110-ft (34-meter) freighter, which was seized as a mari-

the northern Exumas. The reef has numerous brain and star coral heads. Since it is shallow – no deeper than 25 ft (8 meters) – and since the tops of the coral heads come to within 10 ft (3 meters) of the surface, this is an excellent snorkeling area as well.

Another wreck, the *Alcora*, is a 130-ft (40-meter) ship, which was confiscated by the Bahamas government and turned over to diving operators. This is a deep dive, 80 ft (25 meters) to the deck. The boat sits upright on a sand bottom, surrounded by low corals. The water is murky at this depth and a light is needed to penetrate the engine room.

juana runner by the Bahamas government, was sunk here by the film crew. It is one of the most photogenic wrecks in the Bahamas, if not the entire Caribbean.

Just a few dozen yards away are the remains of the *Vulcan Bomber*, the airplane prop created for the feature film *Thunderball*. The frame is carpeted with gorgonians, with large basket stars (basket-like starfish) clinging to them. Plant-like seafans and seawhips form vast underwater coral gardens, their elaborately branched colonies swaying and bending with the motion of the sea.

The speargun sequence of *Thunderball* was filmed on Thunderball Reef, off Staniel Cay in

Around the northern islands

The Abacos face the open Atlantic on one side and the Little Bahamas Bank on the other. At the northern tip of this chain is Walker's Cay, a private, 100-acre (40-hectare), single-resort island. Just off Walker Cay's eastern shore, a line of coral heads loom upward from 70 ft (21 meters) to just below the surface. Huge 300-lb (135-kg) jewfish roam under ledges here. Spacious corridors domed by high-vaulted ceilings wind endlessly inside the coral formations, and there are hammerhead sharks, perhaps 12 ft (3 meters) long. Fortunately, human divers are of little interest; sharks are much maligned – they rarely molest humans without provocation.

Just off Treasure Cay, on Great Abaco, approximately 30 miles (48 km) north of Marsh Harbour, fine sites include the wreck of the *San Jacinto*, a 140-ft (42-meter) Union gunboat that ran aground in 1865 while in pursuit of a Confederate gunrunner.

Near Marsh Harbour the Abacos Train Wreck lies in only 15 to 20 ft (4½ to 6 meters) of water. This wreck consists of two mostly intact locomotives on their sides, huge wheels and other wreckage. The locomotives were being shipped on a barge that ran aground. It is mostly rubble, but 12 cannons are still visible.

Grand Bahama, the country's second largest

sunk as an artificial reef. It is 110 ft (33 meters) deep, close to the edge of the Grand Bahamas Ledge drop-off. The wreck hangs along the edge of a 2,000-ft (600-meter) precipice, which provides for exciting dives.

Into the abyss

The colossal canyon called the Tongue of the Ocean lies just off Andros' eastern shore. It wasn't until 25 years ago that man first viewed this incredible natural wonder, where a vertical drop-off borders a broad, steep-sided ocean bowl. At a drop-off named Over the Wall, the projecting ledge juts out at 165 ft (50 meters),

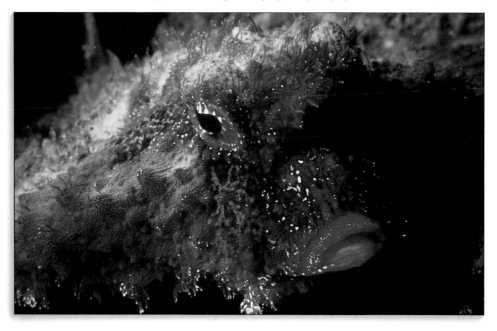

resort community, is home to the 20-year-old UNEXSO (Underwater Explorer's Society), a highly rated scuba facility with superior instruction facilities. There is an 18-ft (5½-meter) deep training tank for resort courses and scuba instruction, modern rental gear, classroom space and instructors who offer classes in the basics as well as specialities. Theo's Wreck is a 230-ft (69-meter) steel cargo ship deliberately

FAR LEFT: a juvenile angel fish.
LEFT: a spotted moray eel.
ABOVE: the bat fish, is a highly camouflaged creature which could blend in anywhere if it weren't for her stunning red lips.

where delicate black coral forests reach out in these deep blue depths. The stone ledge drops for 6,000 ft (1,800 meters) into an inky black abyss. Divers seem so very small and insignificant hanging suspended in mid-water and looking down into the drop-off.

Andros has the most untouched, virgin diving. A magnificent 142-ft (43-meter) wide barrier reef stretches right along the length of the island. Sites include the wreck of the *Potomac*, run aground in 1952 and now split into two sections 200 yards (182 meters) apart, with both sections exposed at low tide. The Barge Wreck, a sunken World War II navy landing craft, sits upright in 70 ft (21 meters) of water.

At Bimini, a mere 60 miles (100 km) east of Miami, underwater visibility often reaches 200 ft (60 meters). Along a wall beginning at 120 ft (36 meters), a current of about five knots provides an exciting drift dive amid spectacular scenery, including giant tube and basket sponges, black coral, school of giant tuna and amberjack, eagle rays and huge groupers.

Another favorite Bimini dive site is the *Sapona*, a 300-ft (90-meter) cement-hulled ship that ran aground in the shallows during a hurricane. It sits upright in only 15 ft (4.5 meters) of water, making an excellent snorkeling site. It is home to an amazing number of fish, including

pufferfish, grunt and snapper, stingrays and sergeant fish.

At the northern end of the Eleuthera cluster, smaller islands include Spanish Wells and Harbour Island. High on the Spanish Wells dive itinerary is another train wreck – one of the strangest in the Bahamas. This stolen train was being transported by the Confederates during the Civil War to be sold to Cuba. Now mostly wheels and axles, it is also a feeding station where hand-fed fish pose happily for photos.

Fantastic flight

The Current Cut rates as the wildest scuba experience in the Bahamas. The cut is a narrow pass between the tip of North Eleuthera and nearby Current Island. At peak tide the water rushes through at an estimated seven to 10 knots. Seven knots does not sound like much, but the drift feels like a sky dive or roller coaster ride. Extending their arms for wings, divers soar and glide. Furthermore, divers feel as though they are in a giant aquarium, since more fish can be seen here in 10 minutes than on a dozen wall dives.

The Freighter Wreck is another special dive near Eleuthera. The Lebanese ship *Arimora* wrecked in 1971, is a 260-ft (78-meter) steel freighter sitting upright on a coral bar with three quarters of the hull above water. The wreck is home to a remarkable array of macrolife which includes shrimp, anemones, arrowcrabs, sea urchins and crabs, as well as schooling angelfish, nurse sharks and giant jewfish.

In the Exumas, a number of ocean blue holes are regularly dived from operations in George Town, the largest settlement. Angelfish Blue

---

SHARK DIVING

With its abundance and variety of marine life, the Bahamas is a magnet for divers and underwater photographers who flock to the islands all year round. But if discovering brightly-hued coral gardens and reef fish seems a little tame, then communing with sharks may be for you.

Definitely not an activity for the faint hearted, a shark diving or shark feeding excursion will get the adrenalin pumping. Make no mistake sharks can be dangerous and should be treated with respect; they are predadtory fish eaters and not usually human flesh eaters. However, to get up close and personal with the sharks most dive operators will require participants to sign a release form.

Popular sites for an encounter with docile nurse sharks and the more aggressive varieties include the waters off Grand Bahama, Shark Reef off Long Island, New Providence and Abaco.

In Grand Bahama, at Port Lucaya dock, UNEXSO (Underwater Explorers Society; tel: 373-1244) organizes dives and feeding trips. Highly-trained and brave – some might say foolhardy – guides don special wet suits and protective clothing, which resembles chainmail, before entering the water to feed the sharks. The chainmail protects the divers from enthusiastic, hungry creatures who may, literally, try to bite the hand that feeds them.

Hole takes its name from the many friendly angelfish found near the opening. Mystery Cave opens on to a huge horizontal tunnel over 400 ft (120 meters) long beneath Stocking Island.

Feeding the sharks

Long Island has one of the Bahamas' more unusual dive sites: the famous shark reef off the Stella Maris Resort, where divers have the rare opportunity to watch sharks feeding in a natural setting. Sharks have been overrated as vicious creatures of the deep, but still an element of danger cannot be discounted. Visions of *Jaws* dance through the head. Will they

Marine marvels

Rum Cay, off Long Island, has a fine dive resort and a number of top sites, including vertical walls, shallow reefs, coral caves and pinnacles, as well as more fish feeding experiences. Grand Canyon is one of several feeding stations, and as soon as the divers enter the water, groupers eagerly flock around looking for hand-outs. Jewfish Wall, with its vibrant orange basket sponges and purple tube sponges, is one of several extraordinary well dives.

It would take months to explore the hundreds of dive sites off the island of San Salvador, of which 60 are marked and named. The reefs here

come? Where will they come from? How many? Will the whole scene be too fast and nerve-wrecking to photograph?

Down on the reef everything is calm and quiet. After the divers settle down, divemasters throw a bucketful of fish into the water and the sharks rush in for the kill, hitting and severing the bait. Sharks snatch falling pieces of bait in mid-water. The feeding ends, and after a few more passes the sharks disappear from where they came – into the depths of the sea.

LEFT: diving with dolphins.
ABOVE: there is an element of danger when diving with sharks.

are some of the least visited in the Bahamas and teem with life: flamingo tongues (with shells the size of a thumbnail), shrimps, hermit crabs, Christmas tree worms and seahorses. Larger fish use sections of the reef as cleaning stations. You can see then settle in the coral and wait patiently while tiny cleaner fish go to work on their parasites. The large groupers can be surprisingly tame and often don't mind you giving them a friendly chuck under the chin.

Christopher Columbus first made landfall in the New World on tiny San Salvador, and divers are still discovering offshore wonders there and throughout the rest of the Bahamas' warm, shallow waters. ❏

HOOKED ON FISHING

Sport fishing in the Bahamas won't disappoint – conch, grouper, bonefish,
billfish and marlin abound – but beware the barracuda and the sharks

The sign on any closed shop door that says "Gone Fishing" could well have been invented in the Bahamas. Fishing, in its many and varied forms, is a national pastime among the locals.

The surrounding seas and their incredible bounty have always played a significant role in the life of Bahamians. So much so that in 1670, when Charles II of England granted the Bahamas to the Lord Proprietors, the document was written to include, "those islands lying in the degrees of twenty and two, to twenty and seven north latitude ... with the fishing of all sorts of fish, whales, sturgeons, and all other royal fishes in the sea, bays, inlets, and rivers within the p'misses, and the fish therein taken, together with the royalty of the sea upon the coasts with in the limit aforesaid."

For the next 300 years, and beyond, Bahamian history takes on the appearance of a roller-coaster ride, with times of great prosperity followed by slumps of almost total despair. Pirates, cotton plantations, wrecking, gun-running, sisal, sponging, rum-running and tourism have brought these islands prosperous times. But the people always kept their hand in fishing. Commercial fishing has seldom been an outstandingly successful business in the Bahamas. Nevertheless, certain historical highlights are worthy of mention.

Sponges and conch

Perhaps the only time that fishing has been the number-one industry of the Bahamas was during a relatively short period beginning from the end of the 19th century up to 1940. These were the days of sponge fishing.

In his 1902 Annual Report to the British Colonial Office, Royal Governor G.T. Carter wrote that 1,319,270 lbs (597,629 kg) of sponges valued at £97,548 sterling were export-

ed from the colony. This represented 48 percent of total exports and employed 265 schooners, 322 sloops and 2,808 open boats. In all, 6,200 men, women and boys were employed in the industry, at a time when the entire population of the Bahamas amounted to just slightly over 50,000.

Unfortunately, sponge fishing came to an abrupt halt in 1940 when a blight destroyed almost all of the sponges. Attempts to revive the industry in the 1950s were unsuccessful, especially with the introduction of cheaper synthetic sponges. A more recent attempt has proved mildly successful but involves the sale of sponges to tourists as souvenirs, and for export to distributors in North America.

Today's commercial fishermen catch scale fish all year round, mainly to supply domestic needs – a task which should not be underestimated, because each year the Bahamas receives visitors equal to more than 10 times its own population.

LEFT: Bahamian sponge fishing from Frank Leslie's Illustrated Newspaper of New York.
RIGHT: a Bahamian boat captain must be able to "read" the water's depth by its color.

Many of the smaller fishing vessels, especially the traditional Bahamian workboat sloops, actively engage in "conching." Famous for its large and beautiful pink shell, the conch has long been a staple part of the local diet. Its versatility can be illustrated by naming only the most popular ways in which it is eaten: raw, in a "salad" or "scorched," cooked in fritters, in chowder, "cracked," in burgers, soused, as conch 'n rice, stewed, steamed, etc. Despite its popularity, it has never quite made it to the grade of *haute cuisine*, although one renowned French chef is said to be working hard to perfect a recipe for "Conch á l'orange."

During the spiny lobster season, August to March, many fishermen switch to this more lucrative trade, supplying both local and export markets. In 1984 the Bahamas exported 2.57 million lbs (1.16 million kg) of lobster, known locally as "crawfish," valued at nearly $17 million. Sixteen years later spiny lobster exports amounted to almost $60 million.

Oddly enough, it is only since World War II that the Bahamians have come to realize the value of crawfish. Previously, they had, been considered well nigh unfit for human consumption and were used primarily as bait for catching other fish. Now they have risen to the rarified status of a gourmet's delight. They cost a fortune, and you can rarely find them when you want one.

Although some of the more organized fishing communities, notably Spanish Wells in North Eleuthera, do very well for themselves, the fishing industry as a whole contributes little to the country's overall export figures. Nevertheless, its local contribution remains highly significant, both in supplying local needs, and in foreign exchange savings.

Fishing for sport

By outlining the historical background to fishing in the Bahamas, it is easy to understand the deep-rooted love today's Bahamian has for recreational fishing. There are many reasons why Bahamians are so happy to venture forth at the slightest excuse – spear, fishing lines and rods in hand. Obviously the beautiful seas, sunny weather and abundant fish are key factors, but mostly it is geography that is the deciding factor. In this nation of long narrow islands, virtually the entire population lives within three miles of the sea – fishing is really on everyone's doorstep.

Handline, or "bottom," fishing may seem an odd choice with which to begin describing Bahamian recreational fishing. Most tourists would tend to think first of "deep sea" or possibly "spear" fishing. But the choice is perfectly logical since it is the only native form of recreational fishing with historical roots in the islands. Other types of recreational fishing described below are modern-day introductions relying on motor boats, diving gear and other technical equipment.

Handline fishing grew from the simple necessity of catching fish for sustenance. It continues to exist as such, particularly in the less populated and more remote Out Islands. To some extent this explains some of its less sporting characteristics, such as the use of 40-lb (18-kg) test line for catching 5-lb (2-kg) fish! It is also the least expensive method of fishing – all you need is a hook, line, sinker and bait.

Although handline fishing can be done from the rocks or off dock, the more serious fisherman will often take to his boat. This is usually small with a minimum of rigging, enabling the fisherman to cast his line freely and to "work" the 360 degrees around the boat without obstruction. Having a Bimini top, three-radio antennae, a flagpole and a girlfriend between you and the 25 lb (11 kg) hogfish on the other line is a decidedly unhealthy situation. If one doesn't lose the fish, then perhaps the girlfriend.

The required tackle is simple. The line should be as heavy as possible. Light lines tend to cut the hands, are more difficult to grasp and are more likely to get knotted. There should be two or three sizes of hooks, ranging from smallish to medium and large-medium. Sinkers are usually nuts, bolts or lead (often made from cutting up old car batteries). Bait, of course, is also needed, the most popular being conch and hermit crab.

Finding the perfect spot

With a sunny day, boat, tackle, bait and a rising tide (the best time for fishing), it's time to find a "drop" – someplace where there are fish. This is usually learned from experience, aided by a glass-bottomed bucket that enables the fisherman to check a prospective site. Often this will be near a small head of coral or in a rocky channel. Once a good location is found, the boat is anchored so as to "tail off" into a position from which lines can be cast in or near the targeted site.

In order to get the fish into a receptive mood, the area is usually "baited up" by throwing bits of conch and crab shells, plus sand mixed with conch "slop" (the slimy guts of the conch), into the water around the boat.

The fisherman then unravels 50 to 100 ft (15 to 30 meters) of line, depending on the depth of the water. The hook is baited with conch or crab, then cast towards the "baited up" site. The line is run out until the sinker hits bottom. At this point slack must quickly be taken up or the bait will be stripped away. The line is then held waiting for a "pick," a nibble. If the fisherman recognises the sharp pick of a turbot (queen triggerfish) or "porgy," he has to be prepared to strike quickly. If it is the slow pull of the Nassau grouper or hogfish he must let the line run out before striking.

Once he strikes and hooks a fish he has to pull it quickly, but steadily, to the boat. If any slack is

> **CONCH POWER**
>
> Conch has a reputation as an aphrodisiac, which perhaps accounts for the Bahamian population growth – the second highest in the Western world, until the advent of local television.

on the line he will probably lose the fish. If he takes too long, chances are a lurking barracuda will "hit" the line, leaving the fisherman with a mangled fish head and hands injured by the line ripping through them.

Fortunately for the beginner, there are so many fish in Bahamian waters that even the least proficient fisherman will usually catch something. It is a fact of life, however, that the best eating fish – grouper, hogfish amd mutton snapper – are the most difficult to catch.

Spearfishing

In contrast to handline fishing, spearfishing is one of the introduced forms of recreational fishing. Its rapidly increasing popularity comes from several special factors.

First, it is the only type of recreational fishing that requires physically entering the space of the underwater prey. Second, since scuba gear is not allowed, under Bahamian law, to be used in the "capture of any fish or marine product," the spearfisher needs to be both physically fit and an accomplished swimmer.

Spearfishing allows selecting the type and size of the prey, limited only by one's ability to dive deep, pursue and shoot straight.

LEFT: a fisherman cleans his catch, parrotfish.
RIGHT: the gear needed for bill fishing is complex, but handline fishing requires only a hook, line and sinker.

Lastly, spearfishing involves certain dangers which, although acceptable to the prudent diver, nonetheless produce moments of great excitement, such as a sudden meeting with an agitated 14-ft (4-meter) hammerhead shark. These moments are accompanied by an overwhelming desire to walk on water. Fortunately, they are mercifully rare and most dangers take the form of a curious barracuda, the more docile nurse shark, moray eels, hidden sting rays, fire corals and jelly fish – not that any of these should be taken lightly.

Spearfishing equipment consists of flippers, a mask, a snorkel and a "Hawaiian Sling." The

sling is the only type of spear allowed by law: a 6- or 7-inch (15 to 18 cm) cylinder of wood with a hole down the middle, onto one end of which is bound a loop of rubber surgical tubing. The spear is between 5 and 6 ft long (1.5–2 meters) and usually made of spring steel so that it won't become bent out of shape (a crooked spear doesn't travel in a straight line). To fire it the spear is fitted through a hole in the wood and the tip inserted into a special fitting in the middle of the loop of surgical tubing. It is then pulled back, aimed and released rather like a crude form of bow and arrow.

Unlike the more sophisticated spear gun, the spear of the Hawaiian Sling is unattached and relies on its weight or a good "brain" shot, to bring down its prey.

The effective range of a spear fired in this manner is about 15 ft (4.5 meters), although longer shots are possible. Usually the spearfisherman will try to get within 5 to 10 ft (1 to 3 meters) of his target. For crawfish, the tip of the spear is often only 2 or 3 ft (less than 1 meter) away when fired.

An accomplished spearfisherman can usually free dive to a depth of 35 to 45 ft (10–13 meters). One's ability to stalk prey effectively also depends on how long one can hold one's breath and one's ability to dive and swim under water with a minimum of exertion, thus conserving oxygen.

Most spearfishing is done on reefs or around heads of coral, where the fish hide. Spotting suitable prey is something of an acquired technique amid all the distractions of fabulous sea fans, corals, refracted light and hidden shadows. The spearfisherman has to know where he should be looking, which will often involve a series of tiring dives as he gets down to look under ledges or into holes. In hunting for crawfish he may only glimpse a few inches of the tip of their whips (antennae) poking from under a rock.

Moving in for the kill

When shooting a fish, the best spot to aim for is the brain, a little way up and behind its eye. The advantages of a "brain shot" are considerable. First, it kills the fish outright so you don't have to chase it all over the place and maybe, if it's a larger fish, lose your rather expensive spear. Second, it doesn't have the opportunity to shake out the spear and escape. Third, it doesn't give out distress signals in thrashing about while trying to get away, thus attracting unwelcome visitors like sharks, and also, there is likely to be less blood in the water.

Last, but certainly not least, a spear hole in the head does not spoil the meat on the body of the fish which, after all, is the ultimate reason for going spearfishing in the first place.

Safety is an extremely important aspect of spearfishing but, as with most things, the rules are simple and based on common sense. No one, however experienced, should dive alone. One should always have a boat close by – preferably within 30 to 40 ft (10 meters) – and, furthermore, it should be operated by someone who knows what he or she is doing. Always keep a lookout for large sharks or barracuda and leave the area if any are spotted. Never stick your hand or head into blind holes or caves and, when you do spear something, get it out of the water with as little fuss and as quickly as possible.

Inshore trolling

"Trolling" is any form of fishing where a line is towed behind a boat. However, its form varies, depending on location, size of boat, bait and

CAMERA OR SPEAR?

If the idea of spearing marine life in the brain is as unappealing as a lurking barracuda and fish guts, then join a growing number of people who enjoy the sea by substituting a camera for a spear.

putting out a few lines on the trip home from the beach or going out for a couple of hours before sunset for a few beers, a cool breeze and, just maybe, a fish or two.

Usually the inshore trollers' boat will be small, highly maneuverable and of shallow draft. A captain with a good knowledge of the area and the ability to "read water" (know how deep it is by its color) is also useful.

The most common tackle consists of a spinning rod, light line (8 to 12 pound test) and an

equipment; it is, perhaps, best described under three separate headings: inshore trolling, deep sea trolling and bill fishing.

Referred to by some locals as "strollin'," inshore trolling is done in shallow water, either close up against a rocky shoreline at high tide, or in amongst shallow coral heads and reef. Although some people are capable of getting carried away with anything, inshore trolling tends to be treated by most as a somewhat lighthearted venture. Very often it will involve

LEFT: the chances of meeting an aggressive shark while fishing are few and far between.
ABOVE: fishing with a few friends and a few beers.

assortment of feathers, spoons and lures. This writer's personal favorite is a small yellow feather readily taken by jack, mackerel, yellowtail snapper and gray snapper. Some fishermen swear by red and white striped feathers, or "jellie-bellies," silver spoons, and a host of other lures, silver spoons reputedly being excellent lure for catching barracuda.

Stalking big game

As opposed to the inshore variety, deep sea trolling and bill fishing require a larger boat, fully fledged deep-sea fishing rods and tackle, and a fighting chair.

For deep sea fishing, one heads out over the

reef where the fish are bigger, if somewhat scarcer. The color of the water changes from various shades of turquoise to a deep cobalt blue, and the surrounding islands recede to sit low on the horizon. Attention becomes focused on the boat as it picks up the motion of the waves. Diesel fumes creep over the stern as the lines are baited: a deep wire line with lure and fish bait, and three shallow with an assortment of feathers, lures, jigs and ballyhoo.

One might begin by trolling along the out-

FISHING COMPETITIONS

The Bahamas has many fishing tournaments throughout the year; April to June are the busiest months. The Biminis, Abacos, Eluethera and the Berry Islands are the most popular locations.

feather and fish bait substituted. Success is instant and on the first pass three lines get strikes. The back of the boat is full of people shouting encouragement, pulling in lines, gaffing fish, rebaiting lines, letting them out and pulling them in again. Twenty minutes and probably at least 12 fish later, contact with the school of dolphin fish is lost. The lines go suddenly quiet and lunch is served to the weary fishermen by the crew: a welcome respite for aching muscles.

side of a reef, hoping that a large grouper will take the deep line, or for a kingfish, mackerel, wahoo or large jack or one of the others. Nothing happens and the anticipation wanes... The hat slips over the eyes and all relax comfortably in their chairs, soaking up the warm Bahamian sunshine.

An hour later the captain spots a line of seaweed and alters course to check it out for dolphin. The dolphin fish (not the mammal) is known for its speed, tremendous fight and the brilliant colors which it assumes in the act of dying – it is also regarded by many people to be the best big game fish to eat.

The deep wire line is reeled in and a shallow

The one that got away

After lunch the trolling continues with an occasional strike, checking bait, a couple of fish landed: a small bonito and a barracuda. By mid afternoon everyone is tired but happy and thoughts are of getting back to a warm shower and cool drink. Someone notices the captain studying something through his binoculars – a flock of birds wheeling and diving over an agitated sea – tuna! The boat turns, lines are reeled in, and heavy gear is substituted.

Approaching, the sight is almost frightening as enormous bluefin tuna engage in a feeding frenzy on the surface of water, which literally seems to boil. The captain increases speed and passes ahead of the school – nothing. He turns and heads back. Suddenly a ratchet screams; the rod is bent double. The engines are throttled back. The fisherman jumps into the fighting chair as a shoulder harness is strapped on. The boat is dead in the water but the line continues to scream out; it starts to smoke and someone pours water over it; a pause and the rod is jammed into the fighting chair holder, hands grabbing ahold.

The line screams again and mercifully someone clicks off the ratchet. Almost a half of a mile of line is out before the fish stops. Pull, crank, pull, crank – slowly the fish is coming the fish; it's huge, at least 400 lbs (200 kg). Pull, crank; again the line screams and then… slack. The big one gets away… this time.

Big bills

Bill fishing in the Bahamas involves the pursuit of blue and white marlin, sailfish and swordfish. There are numerous similarities with deep sea fishing and, in fact, both are often carried on simultaneously. The main difference between Bahamas billfish and other deep game sea fish, apart from the obvious fact that one has a "bill" and the other does not, is in the way the fish catch their prey.

in. The line scorches out again; ten minutes' work is lost in a few seconds. Back, fighting the fish; forward, reeling frantically for every inch of line.

After twenty more minutes every muscle aches, legs are shaking, but the big fish is within 50 ft (15 meters); it takes one look at the boat and the line screams out again; this time it goes deep. Pull, crank in line, pull, crank. An hour after the strike, success is near. People on the flybridge can see the shadow of

Most large fish simply pursue their prospective dinner, open their mouths and "chomp". Various methods such as driving schools of small fish up to the surface where they are more easily trapped, the ripping attack of barracuda or the gaping mouthed pounce of grouper, are used; but the result is the same.

To be sure, billfish are also known to employ this form of direct attack (known locally as "committing suicide"). However, their usual technique is somewhat more refined and involves swimming up alongside their unwitting target and then hitting it sharply with their bill. This either stuns or kills their prey outright, which is then swallowed. The time lapse

---

LEFT: the king of the Gulf Stream billfish, a blue marlin, puts up a vain, but valiant fight off Walker's Cay.
ABOVE: blue marlin are mostly caught in June and July.

between the "hit" and "swallow" is approximately five to 15 seconds.

If billfish hit a bait being trolled behind a boat and it did not stop as expected, they may try to hit it again a few times but, eventually, will probably disappear in a fit of pique, much to the chagrin of the fisherman who will undoubtedly have witnessed the whole episode, have jumped into the fighting chair, had his shoulder harness strapped on, braced his feet on the transom and be clutching his rod in contemplation of how his name will look in the next edition of *The Guiness Book of Records*.

Therefore, to create the correct sequence of

"outrigger." The outrigger is then swung out at an angle of about 45 degrees from the side of the boat (this keeps the bait in clear water outside the wake). Finally the fishing reel gear is put into neutral with the ratchet on; everything is set. The line is now firmly rigged so that it goes back, up and out from the tip of the rod to the clothespeg secured at the end of the outrigger, and then trails off, slightly to one side, behind the boat.

Snagging a billfish

Once the fishermen are prepared and the boat set up, in theory, it works as follows: first the bill fish sees the bait and comes up to take a

events, bill fishermen have devised an ingenious, if simple, rig, which allows the bait to act in a manner acceptable to the fish.

First the line is baited up, using various types of fish bait; ballyhoo, small dolphin and mullet are among the favorites. This is let out behind the boat to a distance the fisherman feels is best (usually not as far as with other rigs). The drag is then set and tested. The bait should be running just below the surface of the water, occasionally breaking up to the top.

The line coming from the tip of the rod is clipped into a glorified sort of clothespeg which is hoisted, rather like a flag, some 25 to 35 ft (10 meters) up a thin antenna-like pole called an

look. From his position on the raised flying bridge the captain should spot what's happening and shout down a warning to the fishermen, "bill fish!"

Meanwhile, if the fish is satisfied with the bait he hits it with his bill. The jolt causes the line to snap out of the clothespeg at the end of the outrigger, usually like a pistol shot. This causes slack in the line which, in turn, causes the bait to stop dead in the water. Simultaneously the captain drops back on the throttles.

By now, line is running slowly off the fishing reel, the ratchet buzzing gently. The rod is taken quickly from the gunwale holder and placed in the fighting chair holder. The fisherman grasps the rod and braces his feet against the transom. On a count of 10 from the snap of the outrigger, the captain throttles up and simultaneously the brake (drag) is thrown on the fishing reel. This maneuver is designed to "set" the hook and is followed by one or two things; either some agricultural phrases to the effect that the fish didn't take the bait or, an explosive scream as up to half a ton of angry, untamed muscle rips hundreds of yards of line off your fishing reel in a matter of seconds. The fight is on.

SEA-FISHING CAPITAL

Ernest Hemingway, an avid deep-sea fisherman, based the book *Islands in the Stream* on his experiences on Bimini, often regarded as the Bahamas deep-sea fishing capital.

mounted by a taxidermist as a trophy, or if he intends for it to be eaten, then fair enough. Otherwise, whenever possible, all catches should be tagged and released.

The bonefish

The bonefish (in Latin, *abula vulpes*, or gray fox) has been described many times in many ways but never better than by one seasoned and widely experienced fisherman who said (with deep emotion), "He is the gamest fish of any size or type, in either fresh

Bill fishing is one of the most exciting and glamorous types of fishing, but it creates an all too common scene: in the late afternoon a "sports" fishing boat comes in, full of people laughing, bragging and drinking. They tie up to the fish dock and begin unloading half a dozen bill fish. These are hoisted up with ropes around their tails and hung from a metal cross bar. Pictures are taken of the fishermen and their catch. Someone says, "let's go to the bar," and off they go leaving the fish behind.

If a sports fisherman wishes to have a fish

LEFT: the marine life is rich.
ABOVE: fishing in the shallow, clear waters off Andros.

or salt water, that any angler could ever hope to catch." And, by all accounts, there are more bonefish in the Bahamas than anywhere else in the world.

To be sure, the world record is temporarily held by Brian W. Batchelor who caught a 19-pounder in Zululand, South Africa. However, Bahamian commercial fishermen quite frequently net specimens in excess of this weight and it is surely only a matter of time before one is brought in on rod and reel.

The bonefish's feeding habits are such that they move in schools onto shallow sandbanks with a rising tide, and off again as the tide goes down. In all fairness to prospective bonefishermen, this is one of only two predictable things which this fish does; the other being that, once hooked, it will give you, ounce for ounce, the toughest fight of any fish you have ever had the privilege to have on the other end of your line.

Bonefishing comprises two quite distinct elements. First of all, it is necessary to find ("stalk") the fish and, since his likely whereabouts tend to vary enormously, depending on tide, wind direction, water temperature and weather, you will almost certainly

THE GRAY FOX

The bonefish, also known as the gray fox is difficult to catch and rarely eaten, because as it's name suggests it is full of fine bones. There is good bonefishing off the Exumas and Grand Bahama.

in the entire school taking off like scalded cats. The technique employed is more one of ambush, where you locate the fish, work out in which direction they are moving, and try to cast some 20 to 30 ft (6 to 10 meters) ahead of them.

Bonefishing is usually done in very shallow water (9 to 30 inches or 23 to 76 cm), either wading or operating from a flat-bottomed, shallow draft skiff. Because the water is so shallow it is often easy to spot the bottom being stirred up as the fish rummage

need to employ a local guide. Several Bahamian fishing guides have earned enviable reputations over the years. This sport is more tricky than it looks and the fish, too, are smarter than they look.

The bonefish spook easily and any sound, such as something banging in a boat or someone splashing through the water, will likely set them off like a flock of birds. They also have very keen eyesight and have even been known to take off because of the shadow of a bird passing overhead. Almost instinctively, many fishermen will crouch as the fish get close. It is, therefore, virtually impossible to cast your line amongst them as the splash will probably result

through the sand and mud for small crabs and other crustaceans. Alternatively, in extremely shallow water one will often see their caudal (tail) fins breaking the surface ("tailing") as they angle down to feed with their "bottoms in the air."

Catching the wily fox

It is a fact that bonefish are harder to catch in very shallow water than in water which is a couple of feet deep.

Wet fly fishing is occasionally employed when going after bonefish or, more often, a weighted jig with feather. But the most usual tackle is a spinning rod with as much line as it will carry of between four to 10 pound test. The common bait is crab, but also popular are small squid, shrimp, crawfish and conch.

Once you have cast your line it is a matter of waiting patiently as the fish work back and forth across the bottom, toward your bait, you hope. Once there, the fisherman has to play by instinct. A tweak on the line; has the fish taken the bait, or is he sitting there watching it to see if you give the game away by striking too soon? Sometimes he'll pick up the bait and swim straight towards you, chewing it off before you can reel in the slack. If you do manage to strike and hook your fish, the result is explosive. The first run is lightning fast and long.

More often the first run will take 300 to 500 ft (100 to 150 meters) of line, followed by the frantic reeling of the fisherman before the second run which, although usually shorter than the first, will probably result in an additional net loss of line. There then follows a series of frantic reelings, and powerful runs as fisherman and fish fight to gain the upper hand. But the gray fox has only just begun; if he spots anything in the water that he can wrap the line around, he will make a bee line for it. Mangrove roots, a solitary sea fan (the only one within a mile), a channel marker pole, even the propeller of your boat; if he reaches his objective you can kiss him goodbye.

If the fisherman survives all this and brings the fish to within 100 ft (30 meters) or so, its frantic tactic will usually involve running rapid circles back and forth with short bursts aimed at trying to pass under the boat. The scene can be quite interesting as the fisherman pirouettes around with everybody ducking frantically to avoid the slashing line.

Unorthodox techniques

Fishermen will go to great lengths to snag a fish, such as spearfishing by being towed on a rope behind a boat (this is widely practiced), handline fishing for bonefish, or running hooked fish down in the mangroves (not widely practiced).

It has been said that out of 10 bites a good average would be to hook three and land one, but once that "one" is in the net, the triumphant

fisherman can only sit back and reflect in respectful wonder at the tremendous battle which this little fish has just given him.

Sharkfishing and more

Of course there are many less popular types of fishing in the Bahamas. Specialized areas of the sport such as sharkfishing, fishing the "drop off," spinning, night fishing or the use of down-riggers as in swordfishing, would all need lengthy and, in some cases, highly technical descriptions. However, with the possible exception of swordfishing, the visitor is not likely to come across these types of fishing.

Doubtless many local fishermen will find fault in the foregoing descriptions of fishing techniques, tackle, bait, etc. This is to be expected. Bahamian sportsfishing is approached in a highly individualistic manner; virtually every Bahamian fisherman has his own bag of tricks, knows more than any other Bahamian fisherman and, even if you ask politely, he "ain't gonna tell he secrets to no one, no suh."

Perhaps the most important thing about sportsfishing in the Bahamas is that there are plenty of fish in the waters around the islands, they come in a variety of shapes and sizes, and they bite. ❏

LEFT: the legendary Bonefish Foley, in West End, Grand Bahama.
RIGHT: bonefishing is reserved for foreign visitors.

PLACES

A detailed guide to the entire Bahamas islands, with principal
sites clearly cross-referenced by number to the maps

Around these 700 islands, tiny cays and nameless rocks, the many-shaded sea sometimes seems to rise around the land like a billowing quilt. The sea has been a source of isolation, of sustenance in hard times, and a bearer of fortune to the Bahamas, and for many visitors the sea is the siren that calls them here – to sail, to swim, to dive among coral-encrusted wrecks. Spanish explorers called the sea here *bajamar*, or shallow sea, yet to know this sea is to know only the approach to the Bahamas, the beginning.

On Inagua, flamingoes posture and preen unseen. On Cat Island, at the end of an overgrown road, an old plantation lies in ruins, covered with vines. These are islands of secrets, and of brash realities of tangled gardens and manicured lawns, of satellite dishes and weathered sloops.

On the streets of Freeport, in the high-rise resorts, and with Bimini just a 30-minute flight from Miami, the Bahamas might seem like an offshoot of America. But a step beyond the well-known destinations can take you worlds away, to a land of unexpected colors and characters – the flamingo red blooms of a poinciana tree against a bright yellow house, *warri* players on a shady porch, a young woman in a dark business suit hurrying down a narrow road to work.

Although the distances between the islands aren't large, travel between the less populous ones must often be leisurely – on hit-and-miss scheduled flights or by boat. It is at this gentle pace that they are best enjoyed. A seaplane rumbles, roars and take off; the tide laps against a dock; a diver's splash breaks the skin of the water; sailboats return home to the harbor in the last of the light. From the mud-flats of Andros to the fish-laden waters off the Berry Islands, it is a country to be felt, seen and heard, and – in some quiet moment between high tide and the turning back out to sea – discovered.

Organizing the islands

The following chapters have been divided into three sections: New Providence Island, Grand Bahama Island, and the Out Islands.

Though small in size, **New Providence Island** is the hub of the Bahamas and the site of the capital, Nassau. Easy to reach, with many large hotels and other facilities, New Providence attracts more visitors than any other Bahamian island, followed by **Grand Bahama Island** and its city, Freeport. The rest of the islands – the **Out Islands** – are like the family jewels of the Bahamas, each one unique. Insight Guides has covered the major Out Islands and a number of those that remain virtually "undiscovered". ❏

PRECEDING PAGES: Nassau Harbour; a quiet street on Green Turtle Cay; Sunday best in George Town, Exuma.
LEFT: a view from the Nassau water tower.

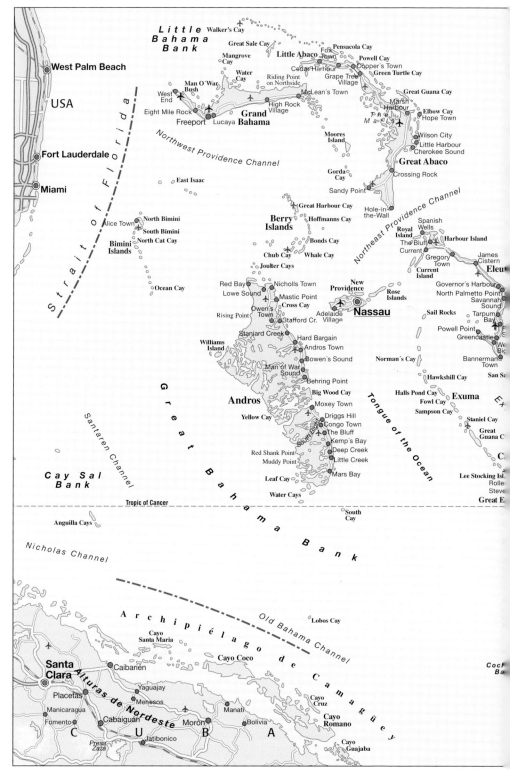

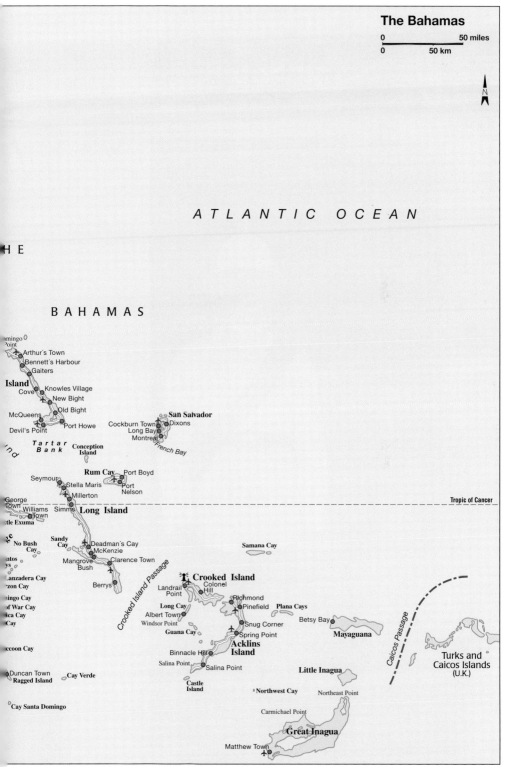

The Bahamas

| 0 | | 50 miles |
| 0 | 50 km | |

N

ATLANTIC OCEAN

HE

BAHAMAS

amingo
Point
Arthur's Town
Bennett's Harbour
Gaiters
Island
Cove Knowles Village
New Bight
McQueens Old Bight
Devil's Point Port Howe
San Salvador
Cockburn Town Dixons
Long Bay
Montreal
French Bay
Tartar Bank Conception Island

nd

Rum Cay Port Boyd
Seymour
Stella Maris Port Nelson
Millerton
George Town
Williams Simms **Long Island**
Town
tle Exuma

Tropic of Cancer

ge
No Bush Cay
Sandy Cay
Deadman's Cay
McKenzie
Samana Cay
atos
ys
anzadera Cay Mangrove Bush Clarence Town
zon Cay
ingo Cay Berrys
f War Cay
ica Cay
Cay
Crooked Island Passage
Crooked Island
Landrail Point
Colonel Hill
Richmond
Pinefield
Plana Cays
Long Cay
Albert Town
Windsor Point
Snug Corner
Betsy Bay
Mayaguana
ccoon Cay
Guana Cay
Spring Point
Binnacle Hill **Acklins Island**
Salina Point
Salina Point
Little Inagua
Duncan Town Cay Verde
Ragged Island
Castle Island
Northwest Cay
Northeast Point
Cay Santa Domingo
Carmichael Point
Caicos Passage
Turks and Caicos Islands
(U.K.)
Great Inagua
Matthew Town

NEW PROVIDENCE ISLAND

*Life is fast in the tightly packed national capital, but
Nassau's outskirts offer a more leisurely pace*

For centuries New Providence Island has been the hub of the Bahamas, where "everyone" went, "everything" happened – the center of it all. Reclining seductively on the northern end of New Providence Island, Nassau is the island's Victorian mistress, idyllic paradise, financial center and worldly capital – a coquette with many masks.

Located on a large, sheltered harbor, Nassau has swung many times from boom town to backwater and back again. But she has always been an enticing lure for both Bahamians and foreigners seeking easy riches or just an honest day's work.

Young people from the Out Islands have traditionally come to Nassau to "make it" when employment prospects on their own islands are non-existent or grim, and to be born on New Providence Island implies an automatic sophistication. (You might hear an old-timer boast, "I don't know those other islands. I'm a Nassau boy.")

Magnetic is the appeal of diamond watches, pearls and seductive perfumes in the windows of the Bay Street shops. Nassau is an enticing figure, half dressed in old, half in new, where cool verandahs, limestone walls and jalousies cracked open to catch the afternoon breeze compete for space with traffic circles and offices.

If the sights and sounds of Nassau grow too heady, or too tiring, just a short drive will take you away from it all – to the rest of New Providence Island. From the old settlements of Adelaide and Fox Hill, to the posh seclusion of Lyford Cay and Mount Pleasant, you will find another fascinating world. Old money, new money, foreign money and money eked out to "get by" combine to give New Providence a generous helping of Bahamian tradition, improvisation and pizzazz.

Then, there are the warm days and bright nights of Paradise Island. She is an upstart can-can girl compared to elegant Nassau – and attracts more tourists than any other island in the Bahamas. East of Miami, west of the French Riviera, her grand hotel towers dominate the skyline, and the casino is the natural habitat of sheiks, financial wizards, grandmothers and bikini-clad beauties.

So, let the chapter on Nassau be your guide to a fascinating walk about the old town – the government buildings, bustling Bay Street, dozens of historic homes. The New Providence chapter will introduce you to the island beyond – ancient forts, old African settlements, quiet beaches, elegant homes. And when you're through, the twin bridges over the harbor will take you to Paradise Island. There, you can discover the intriguing story of the men and dreams who made this tiny island across Nassau Harbour what it is today. ❏

LEFT: a Nassau policeman stands guard.

NASSAU

Combining old-world architecture with stylish modernity, the national capital is a hive of activity by day. Visitors can shop in upscale stores, or explore local crafts, museums and historical relics

For many people the city of Nassau *is* the Bahamas. Located on the island of New Providence, since early times it has been the commercial hub of the archipelago. Once a quiet, sleepy sort of place, Nassau is now a rapidly expanding city, where the pace is sometimes hectic and traffic often crowds the narrow streets.

Downtown Nassau retains much of its colonial architectural heritage and charm. While downtown Nassau developed into an attractive colonial town with the major commercial outlets and the white elite, Grant's Town – or "Over-the-Hill" – had much more humble buildings. Its settlers lacked the necessary capital to develop it properly and it grew without supervision. Today the streets of Grant's Town are seething with life. Small wooden ramshackle shops abound, though concrete buildings are becoming common.

Originally known as Charlestown, the city was renamed in honor of the prince of Orange-Nassau, later William III of England. At the time, Nassau comprised about 160 houses, one church and two public houses. The buildings, constructed mainly of wood with thatched roofs of palmetto leaves, huddled around the large, sheltered harbor that was to make Nassau both the most suitable place for the seat of government and a haven for pirates and privateers.

After about 1670, privateers and pirates used Nassau increasingly as a base from which to plunder and destroy French and Spanish ships. The town suffered from **PRECEDING PAGES:** view over Nassau.

Map on page 144

several attacks of retaliation by the Spanish and French in the early 18th century, and the attack on the town in 1703 by a combined Spanish and French fleet frightened most of the inhabitants away. Those people who remained "lived scatteringly in little huts, ready upon any assaults to secure themselves in the woods," wrote a contemporary observer who visited Nassau in the early 1700s.

Rogers rebuilds

Woodes Rogers, the first Royal Governor of the Bahamas (1718–21 and 1729–32), arrived in Nassau to find the town in a dilapidated state and immediately set every available man, including pirates, to work to clean and rebuild Nassau "so that it began to have the appearance of a civilised place." When, during Rogers' second term of office, the House of Assembly convened for the first time, the 12 acts passed included one with the aim to "lay out the town of Nassau."

Further expansion occurred in the

1740s, when Fort Nassau was extensively renovated and Fort Montagu built. During William Shirley's governorship (1758–68), Nassau was expanded and developed. He initiated a new survey of the town and reclaimed much of the mosquito-breeding swampland, so that the town could expand eastward. Among the many streets, lanes and paths laid out then was Shirley Street, which still honors the name of the governor who created it.

During his brother Thomas Shirley's governorship, the town faced bankruptcy and poverty. In 1783 a man named Schoepe, a German traveler in the Bahamas, described Nassau as having one tolerably regular street which ran next to the water.

Perhaps the greatest impact on the architecture of the town, until the building boom of the 1860s, was made by the Loyalists. Fleeing from the newly independent United States of America, those colonists loyal to King George III soon transformed the shabby little port "into a town as well as

LEFT AND BELOW: the town and port of Nassau, as drawn for the *Illustrated London News.*

any… and one which promised to become distinguished for its beauty." In four years the Loyalists and their slaves more than doubled the population of the Bahamas, and they brought with them the architectural style of the southern United States.

Prompted by the sudden flow of money brought by the American Civil War, construction in the town accelerated in the mid-19th century, when Nassau became the headquarters for the colorful blockade runners *(see page 146)*. In the late 19th century, the town relied on the development of local industries, especially sponge, pineapple and sisal, but her spirits rose again – stimulated by profits from the transshipment of liquor (otherwise known as bootlegging) to the United States during Prohibition (1919–33).

By the early 1950s, tourism was established as the Bahamas' main industry. Parallel with the phenomenal growth of the tourist industry came Nassau's entry into the international banking and business arena as tax haven and resort hideaway.

The old town

Perhaps the most interesting streets and buildings in the city are in the old town district, in 1788 bordered on the east by East Street, the west by West Street, the north by Bay Street, and the south by West Hill and East Hill streets.

If this seems complicated, remember that **Bay Street**, or the Strand as it was called, was the oldest street and bounded the town along the harbor. It is still the main street through Nassau. Facing Bay Street, in the center of the old city between what is now Bank Lane and Parliament Street, are the **Public Buildings Ⓐ**.

Built between 1805 and 1813, the three buildings originally housed the Post Office, Legislative Council and Court Room (center building), the Colonial Secretary's Office and Treasury (eastern building), and the House of Assembly, Surveyor General's Office and Provost Marshal's Office (western). They then overlooked the harbor, and the sea came right up to Bay Street immediately in front

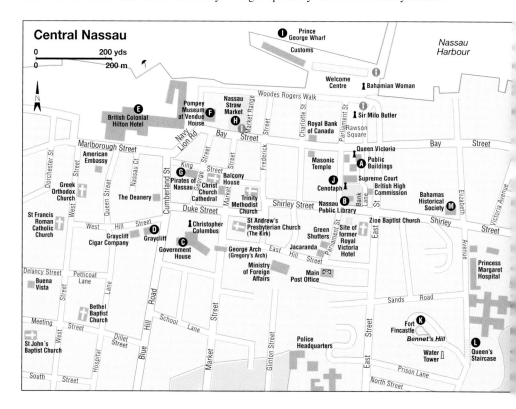

Central Nassau

Map on page 144

of them. Loyalist influence is evident here, for the Public Buildings were based on Governor Tyron's Palace in New Bern, an early capital of North Carolina.

The middle structure now houses the Senate Chamber, the Supreme Court and the Government Publication Office. The eastern building contains an office of the Ministry of Tourism while the western building still houses the House of Assembly. It was from an upstairs window of this latter building that the then opposition leader Lynden Pindling, later a long-serving prime minister, threw the mace out in protest at the Government Boundaries of the Constituencies. As he walked over to the Speaker's table and took the mace up, he said, "This mace is the symbol of authority of this House and the authority belongs to the people, and the people are outside." He then hurled it through the window. This day in 1965 was destined to go down in political history as "Black Tuesday."

Immediately south of the Public Buildings is the more modern **Supreme Court** building, which is adjacent to the unusually shaped **Nassau Public Library** Ⓑ. Built as a prison, between 1798 and 1800, it was converted to house Nassau Public Library in 1873. Since then its exterior has been renovated and repainted. Inside this quaint building can be found one of the best collections of books on Bahamiana. It also houses a collection of prints, maps and old photographs, which have been restored. There is a fine newspaper collection, and a stamp collection, too. The library contains a small collection of Arawak artifacts, which includes a Lucayan skull, stone celts and a stone *duho* (an Amerindian ceremonial stool).

Smugglers, spies, royalty

Just across Shirley Street from the library are the grounds of the former **Royal Victoria Hotel**, which was constructed between 1859 and 1861 to accommodate winter visitors. The remains of the main building can be best seen from East Hill Street and East Street.

BELOW: a straw vendor near the waterfront.

Horace Greely called the Royal Victoria "the largest and most commodious hotel ever built in the tropics," and the three-story structure with its lofty encircling verandahs lived up to the praise. Floor-to-ceiling windows assured natural air conditioning for the luxurious bedrooms. It had separate gentlemen's and ladies' parlors, a hair-dressing salon, billiard room, bar, botanical garden and a dining room in which servants outnumbered the guests. The centerpiece of the botanical garden was a kapok tree so enormous a bandstand reached by a flight of stairs was erected in its branches.

With the American Civil War, the Royal Victoria overnight became a hive of activity for buyers of cotton, dealers in munitions, Confederate officers, Yankee spies and newspaper correspondents. According to legend, the man who inspired the character Rhett Butler of *Gone With The Wind* frequented the hotel bar and lounges. Blockade-runners lived there like sultans, and at the hotel's Blockade Runners' Ball,

300 guests consumed 350 magnums of champagne. Later, the Royal Victoria was used for more sedate social gatherings. The hotel hung on tenaciously through the Depression, but the century-old hostelry could not keep up with the demands of post-war tourists, and closed in 1971.

Historical houses

South on Parliament Street, one passes the **Green Shutters**, a lively and popular restaurant, with a pub-like atmosphere. The actual structure is believed to date back to 1865. Next door, on the southwest corner of Parliament Street, is **Jacaranda**, built in the 1840s with a low pitched shingled roof, wide latticed verandahs, and the south side covered with the traditional jalousies.

Opposite Jacaranda is the **Post Office Building**, which houses various government ministries. Just west of the Post Office is **East Hill**, another 19th-century mansion. Built between 1840 and 1860 on a 5½-acre (2-hectare) site, East Hill is built in the Georgian colonial style of handcut

LEFT: a peaceful moment befo[re] lunchtime, at Graycliff.
BELOW: Columbus poised before Government House.

Map on page 144

limestone blocks. Behind the house is the original stone kitchen with two ancient fireplaces, an open hearth and dome-shaped ovens. The residence served as a club and restaurant for many years, but in 1968 was renovated to house offices.

To the west of Jacaranda is **Glenwood**, one of the oldest houses in Nassau. Its expansive grounds contain the grave of a former chief justice, Thomas Walker, a friend of Woodes Rogers. Opposite this property is **St Andrew's Court**, formerly called Bank House. This fine old home contains law offices, but it was once owned and occupied by Alfred E. Mosely, editor of the *Nassau Guardian* from 1887 to 1904.

Continuing west, you pass the clean, white, fresh-looking **St Andrew's Presbyterian Church** (The Kirk), built in 1810, but added on to over the years. In 1864 the sanctuary was enlarged and the modern transept, portico and bell tower were built, and extensive renovations were made in the early 1950s.

Leaving the Kirk you pass over

Gregory Arch, named after John Gregory, Governor of the Bahamas 1849 to 1854. On top of the hill known as Mount Fitzwilliam is **Government House** Ⓒ, the official residence of the Governor-General, the Queen's representative in the Bahamas. Commanding an extensive view of the island, it is a pink and white neo-Classical mansion built in 1801. On the front steps you pass a statue of Christopher Columbus, modeled in London.

The Columbus statue was brought to the Bahamas by Sir James Carmichael Smyth. He became governor of the Bahamas in 1829, working diligently during his governorship to ameliorate slave conditions and to abolish corporal punishment for enslaved females. He met with fierce opposition in the House of Assembly, which he was forced to dissolve twice. Ironically, more cases of cruelty were evident under his administration than at any other time.

Immediately across the road from Government House's western gate, on picturesque West Hill Street, is **Graycliff** Ⓓ,

LOW: "the k", St drew's esbyterian urch.

partly hidden behind a high, handcut limestone block wall. This elegant house is one of the leading restaurants in Nassau. The graceful main doorway is supported by pillars; the house has an airy porch at the front and back, the rails and lattice work showing considerable craftsmanship. The upper floors have several tastefully decorated suites furnished with antiques. It is believed that the house, which was once French's Hotel, housed the West Indian Garrison, which protected the city in the 18th and 19th centuries.

Leaving Graycliff you immediately pass a plaque set in the "cliff" claiming that the oldest church in Nassau was on this site. Continuing west along West Hill Street, you pass several interesting old houses. These buildings, still part of the Graycliff property, house the **Graycliff Cigar Company** (tel: 322 2796), which features the **Humídor Restaurant**, an elegant bistro. The Bahamas cigar was catapulted to international status when aficionados named it second only to the Cuban cigar,

for the quality of its production. On one of the daily tours of the cigar factory, visitors can watch Bahamian and Cuban cigar masters at work, blending fragrant leaves from Indonesia, Cameroon, Brazil, Nicaragua and Honduras into cigars that are sold on the premises.

Outstanding architecture

Further along, at the junction of West Hill and West streets, is **St Francis Roman Catholic Church**. Built between 1885 and 1886, it was the first Catholic church in the Bahamas.

Turning north on West Street and descending the hill, there are some fine old buildings and the **Greek Orthodox Church**, built in the 1930s to accommodate the small Greek community which, until the late 1930s, was mainly employed in the sponge industry.

Turning east on Marlborough Street, one passes quaint **Queen Street**, which still has an air of the past. No. 16 Queen Street is said to be 200 years old, and No. 28,

BELOW: the (British) Colonial Hote brought a Pal Beach ambience to Nassau wher was built in 1923.

Map on page 144

with its ornate lattice work and traditional dormer windows, probably dates back to the mid-19th century. Devonshire House, or No. 11 Queen Street, was built about 1840 and is an outstanding example of early British colonial architecture.

Farther south on Queen Street is No. 30, which reflects Victorian and Colonial-style architecture and may be 170 years old. The bottom story of this two-story house is constructed of cut squared local stone, while the top floor is of wood. The verandahs, which shade the northeast, east and south sides of the building, are typical of bygone years.

Cumberland Street runs parallel to Nassau Court. In the middle of this wide road stands **Hillside Manor**, once a rambling city residence. Farther south is **The Deanery**, the residence of the Dean of Christ Church Cathedral, and one of the oldest residences in Nassau. Completed in about 1803, this three-storied building is constructed of stone and chamferred quoins. Verandahs of three tiers were orig-

RIGHT: Woodes Rogers guards the entrance to the British Colonial Hilton.

inally built on the north, east and west sides of the house. The fittings of the house, such as doors, dadoes and cornices, some of which have been removed, were typical of the Queen Anne period.

The original kitchen still stands to the west of the house. A one-storied building, it has a fireplace and domed brick oven. The northern end of the building is divided by a thick stone wall with narrow loopholes in lieu of windows. Known as the "Slaves's Quarters," this outbuilding is thought to have housed domestic slaves in the 19th century.

Landmark hotel

Re-entering Marlborough Street, the **British Colonial Hilton Hotel ⓔ** comes in to view. It is said to be built on the site of Fort Nassau, which was constructed in the 1690s. The original Hotel Colonial was made of wood and was destroyed by fire in 1922. The new Colonial Hotel, opened in 1923, is designed in the Spanish-American style imported from Florida.

BOND IN THE BAHAMAS

The Bahamas has been the setting for several James Bond films because of its racy casinos, shipwrecks, and pristine waters, which allow up to 200 ft (61 meters) visibility for filming high-action underwater sequences.

James Bond's fourth movie adventure, *Thunderball*, took him to the Bahamas in 1965. Special agent 007 is called to the British colony when a NATO warplane armed with nuclear weapons disappears into the sea. 007, played by Sean Connery, arrives at Nassau's glittering casinos where he picks up the trail of SPECTRE's number-two man, Emilio Largo, and his mistress, the delectable Domino.

Equipped with "Q's" ingenious range of gadgets, agent 007 saves the day, even battling underwater with Largo's pet sharks. Wrecks created for the films such as the *Vulcan Bomber* off the Nassau coast and the vessel *Tears of Allah* from *Never Say Never Again* are now popular dive sites.

Thunderball and *Never Say Never Again* include scenes filmed at the British Colonial Hilton hotel in Nassau, which has a 007 Suite with film posters and a small collection of Bond films. The hotel's Spy package includes diving lessons at Stuart Cove, where Sean Connery prepared for *Never Say Never Again.* And of course a Martini – shaken, not stirred – is served upon arrival.

Painter's painting

Now probably the Bahamas' best-known artist, Amos Ferguson used to be a house painter. Born on the Bahamian island of Exuma in 1920, he once ran a small farm and helped out with his father's carpentry business. When he later moved to Nassau, he earned a living painting houses. Then – using house paint instead of oil or acrylic – he started creating striking, color-rich folk art *(see page 73)*.

Still using traditional decorators' paint, his thought-provoking themes revolve around biblical and historical images, nature and folklore, and the masks, costumes and music of the Bahamian Junkanoo festival. Instead of canvas, cardboard and fiberboard are his media of choice. However, in recent times he has been known to experiment with ceramics.

Many vacationers were introduced to his early paintings by a Nassau Straw Market vendor named Bea. Along with her hats, bags, beach mats and shell jewelry, visitors

would often purchase one of Ferguson's vivid images. Perhaps in part because Bea was such as good salesperson, she eventually became his wife.

Word began to spread among the world's art-lovers about the bold, yet simple style of this unassuming Bahamian painter. During the 1980s, Ferguson tumbled onto the international art scene. In 1985, a major exhibition of his work began a two-year tour across the United States, traveling from Connecticut on the East Coast to California on the West. His often whimsical works are now owned and treasured by art collectors around the world.

Closer to home, Amos Ferguson's paintings are usually on display in a permanent exhibition in Vendue House, in the capital of the Bahamas. This historic building celebrates Ferguson's roots in both Exuma and Africa. On Bay Street, near George Street in downtown Nassau, Vendue House was originally built around 1796. Until the late 1800s, it served as a marketplace where enslaved Africans were among the "wares" on sale there. (The word *vendue* is French for "sold".)

Today known as Pompey Museum of Slavery and Emancipation, Vendue House was transformed into a heritage museum in 1992. It was named in honor of an enslaved man who led a rebellion of enslaved men and women who refused to be moved from their home on the island of Exuma, which lies south of Nassau. Not only was Pompey able to help put a stop to the forced relocation, but he also won the right for enslaved Bahamians to work part time for themselves. A true victory indeed, at a time before enslaved peoples on the islands were legally emancipated in 1834.

Dedicated to the African experience in the Bahamas, the museum showcases priceless artifacts excavated from former island plantations and objects of African origin used in the islands, while, in the second floor art gallery, there are some of the most powerful works created by Amos Ferguson.

Note: The roof of Vendue House on Bay Street was badly damaged by fire in 2001. The valuable art works and artifacts, which remain intact, will be on display again once the building is repaired.

LEFT: a locall❑ crafted carvi◄

Map
on page
144

It was contracted to Hilton International in November 1999. Once the site of one of the city's major shipping docks, the Hilton is the only hotel property in downtown Nassau with its own private beach. The hotel complex also incorporates the Centre for Commerce, home of the Bahamas International Stock Exchange.

Guarding the entrance to the Hilton is a small statue of Woodes Rogers, the first royal governor of the Bahamas (*see page 32*). Backed by the British Crown, Rogers was sent to the islands, in 1718, to end piracy. Popular folklore claims that several pirates were hanged on the very spot where the statue now stands. The hotel has an attractive arcade, which contains offices and shops on its western side.

Pomp, ceremony and pirates

East of the hotel is one of the oldest buildings in the city. **Vendue House**, a two-story building, most recently occupied by a section of the Bahamas Electricity Corporation, was built in the mid-18th century as a single story arcaded building where traders sold enslaved men and women, cattle and imported goods at public auctions.

Unfortunately, Nassau suffered a devastating fire in 2001, which destroyed a small portion of west Bay Street, and damaged the roof of Vendue House, which is home to the **Pompey Museum of Slavery and Emancipation** Ⓕ. The museum and its priceless exhibits are usually displayed on the ground floor of the building, once also known as the Bourse, one of Nassau's most well-preserved buildings. On the third floor is the **Amos Ferguson Art Gallery** (*see page 150*).

Not far from Vendue House, head south on George Street for a detour to **Christ Church Cathedral**, built in 1837. Standing on the site of a very early church, the new structure is of plain stone consisting of a nave, a center aisle, two side aisles and a western tower. The main west entrance is through a central square clock tower, from which there is an immediate

LOW: surrey drivers await customers near Bay Street.

view of the large and beautiful stained-glass window over the altar.

Almost opposite the cathedral at the corner of George and King streets, is **Pirates of Nassau** (open Mon–Sat 9am–5pm; entrance fee; tel: 356 3759), a fascinating interactive museum with exhibits, historical artifacts and a guided tour that focuses on the golden age of piracy. Visitors can combine a tour of Nassau's forts with a trip to the museum.

Immediately south of Christ Church is **Lex House**, thought to be one of the oldest houses in Nassau. It may have been the home of the commander of the Spanish garrison, which occupied Nassau between 1782 and 1783. The building now houses a law firm. Near the rear of Christ Church, head south on Market Street to **Balcony House** (open 9am–4.30pm Mon–Fri, Sat by appointment only; tel: 302 2621). The house was built of American soft cedar, probably in the late 1700s. It includes a slave kitchen and an ancient staircase, thought to be transplanted from a ship.

Straw street

Turning north again, you can walk down Market or George streets into Bay Street, the main street of the city. Opposite Market Street is the **Nassau Straw Market** . On the site of the old Public Market, which was constructed in 1901 and destroyed by fire in early 1974. The modern market, which was located under the Ministry of Tourism's office building, was razed in 2001.

Temporary stalls stand on the site which will more than likely be redeveloped, not only on account of its historical significance, but also because this is a lively and bustling local market. Bahamians, mostly women, barter their straw work, T-shirts, jewelry, carvings, and other assorted knick-knacks. It is a tough life, but a lucrative one. The market women depend largely on tourists to buy their wares, with straw-work being the most popular. Most of it is made from the top of the thatch palm, known as silver-top, and is made into baskets, hats, table mats and dolls.

LEFT: an interactive experience at the Pirates of Nassau museum. **RIGHT:** browsing through the straw stalls.

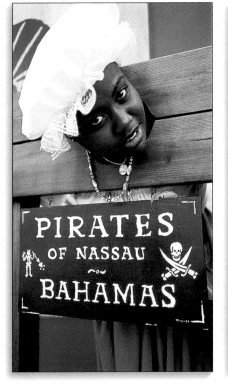

Map on page 144

Plaiting the silver-top was traditionally carried out in Nassau and in many Out Island settlements, especially the Exumas, Long Island and Cat Island. It was customary in the black settlements in New Providence and on the Out Islands for women to weave the silver-top into long bands, which were then rolled into balls to be sold to agents in Nassau. There, other women made up baskets, hats and mats with the plait.

By the wharf

Walking through the market area, or the streets that run parallel, you emerge onto **Woodes Rogers Walk** along the harbor, once the Market Range where mail and sponge boats docked, and where conch, fish and vegetables were sold.

The harbor of Nassau, which has been so important to the development of the city, once came all the way up to Bay Street. To cope with increased shipping in the late 1920s, during Prohibition, the harbor was dredged to 25 ft (8 meters) and

Prince George Wharf ❶ was built. The wharf was named after Prince George, Duke of Kent, to commemorate his visit here in 1928. The former Customs Warehouse on the wharf is now the site of **Junkanoo Expo**, a colorful exhibition showcasing the costumes worn on Boxing Day and New Year's Day Junkanoo celebrations.

Passengers arriving at New Providence by ship land at Prince George Wharf. Some of the world's largest cruise ships make frequent calls here and five piers have been added to the existing seven. Debarking cruise passengers will find inexpensive ferry boats to Paradise Island docked alongside the wharf.

The **Welcome Centre** (open daily 9am–5pm), a long, gazebo-style building, which links the dock to the rear of the straw market area, houses the downtown surrey stall offering horse and buggy rides, a hair-braiding centre and cruise ship visitors' first offering of souvenirs. The inexpensive horse and buggy ride is

well worth it. The guides are well-trained and knowledgeable about the history and buildings in the lively downtown area.

Also worth noting here is a bronze sculpture of a Bahamian woman holding a small child. The statue honors women's contribution to Bahamian society.

Britain on Bay Street

Re-entering Bay Street by Frederick Street, where the historic **Trinity Methodist Church** is located, are some fine shops located in old buildings. Nassau is a mecca for collectors of china and crystal, and the shops are well-supplied by European manufacturers. Visitors can also purchase perfume at bargain prices, and sweaters of lambswool and cashmere.

Also on Bay Street is the **Royal Bank of Canada**, which is the oldest extant bank in the Bahamas. This branch opened in Nassau in 1908 and moved to the ornate structure it now occupies in 1919. Across the street is the **Masonic Temple**, constructed in 1882. Masonic Orders have

met in Nassau since its early days. Farther east on Bay Street is **Rawson Square** (the Public Square), a spacious and well-manicured square, overlooked by the **Churchill Building**, housing the prime minister's and other government offices. There is a bust of Sir Milo Butler, the first Bahamian Governor-General in an independent Bahamas, and a statue of the British Queen Victoria, reminiscent of the Bahamas' colonial past, on the opposite side of the square.

East of town

Leaving Rawson Square in a southerly direction on Parliament Street, you pass the Public Buildings *(see page 146)* and the **Cenotaph ❶**, which displays plaques commemorating Bahamians who died in the two world wars. Opposite is the former Parliament Hotel, a quaint three-storied structure dating back to the late 1930s, which now houses a law office. The Parliament Terrace is a pleasant restaurant serving lunch and dinner on an

BELOW: a policeman keeps watch at Nassau's water tower.

Map on page 144

outdoor patio. On the western corner of Parliament and Shirley streets is **Magna Carta Court**, a building restored by a Nassau lawyer. The exposed cut stones are more reminiscent of St Augustine, Florida, than of Nassau, but it is a fine effort in historic preservation.

During the blockade era (1861–65) Nassau grew rapidly as a result of increased wealth. By 1866, the existing boundaries of the town extended east to Victoria Avenue (originally Culmer Street). Prohibition in America brought further prosperity, followed by tourism, foreign investment and banking. By the early 1980s, the city included Mackey Street to the east, Nassau Street to the west, and Meeting Street and School and Sand Lanes to the south.

Leaving East Street on Shirley Street, in an easterly direction, you reach **Addington House**, the official residence of the Anglican bishop of Nassau and the Bahamas. Given to the diocese in 1876, legend has it that the house had been occupied by the officer-in-charge of the troops stationed at **Fort Fincastle** , situated on Bennet's Hill to the south. To reach the fort, pass the Princess Margaret Hospital on Elizabeth Avenue to the **Queens' Staircase** ⓵. These 66 steps lead to the fort ruins and are said to have been cut in the sandstone cliffs by enslaved people in 1793.

Overlooking Nassau and shaped like a paddle-wheel steamer, Fort Fincastle guarded "all the town and the road eastward where the enemy might probably effect a landing," something that subsequently never came about. Instead, the fort served as a lighthouse and then as a signal tower. Sharing Bennet's Hill with the fort is the **Water Tower**, which maintains water pressure throughout the city. It stands 216 ft (66 meters) above sea level and offers a breathless view from the top. On special occasions, such as a visit by Queen Elizabeth II, the tower is adorned by a crown of lights, enhancing its beauty.

Below the fort is the quaint district

ᏴELOW: built 1793, Fort Fincastle's ramparts never saw battle.

Map
on page
144

known as "Fort Fincastle." Opposite Prison Lane on East Street is the **Police Headquarters**. Erected in 1900 on the site of the old Agricultural Gardens, the buildings are a replica of the Old Military Barracks, which were demolished at the turn of the 20th century to provide the site for the Colonial Hotel. The old **Guard House** has been renovated and preserves much of its original facade.

On the corner of East and Shirley streets is **Zion Baptist Church**, built in 1835. The spacious and popular church was destroyed by the devastating 1929 hurricane and was later rebuilt.

Amerindian heritage

Returning to the corner of Shirley Street and Elizabeth Avenue, you will find the headquarters of the **Bahamas Historical Society** Ⓜ (open Mon–Fri 9am–4.30pm; entrance fee; tel: 322 4231), founded in 1959 to stimulate interest in Bahamian history and to collect and preserve historic materials. Inside is a small museum of art-

ifacts, paintings, photographs and maps. Its prints and paintings include depictions of the infamous pirate, Blackbeard, and sketches of Lucayan Amerindians. The sponge collection gives an insight into the different types of sponges that were the basis of a once important local industry. A few Arawak artifacts are also on display, including pottery shards, stone celts and stone jewelry from various sites in New Providence.

Nassau awake

Modern Nassau, although it has lost some fine old buildings, in some cases replaced by modern office complex and parking lots, retains much of its charm. It is no longer a "quiet, sleepy hollow sort of place" as it was called by the poet Bliss Carman when he visited the town in the late 1880s, but a busy, bustling modern town.

For some nostalgic Bahamians, Nassau has changed for the worse. However, the drive for the preservation of some of the old buildings, originally homes, has taken root. Led by such institutions as the Bahamas Chamber of Commerce, the Bahamas National Trust, the Department of Archives and the Ministry of Tourism, efforts have been made to push for conservation while also welcoming progress.

Plaques giving historic information on buildings and sites have been erected and walking tours launched. Efforts have been made to train taxi drivers and tour guides and to tutor them in the history of the city and its buildings.

The city has upheld the 19th-century dignity Bliss Carman described in the poem "White Nassau." Still to be seen on streets like Queen's Street are the colorful flowering plants and creepers, so vividly captured in some of the paintings of Winslow Homer.

The center of the city is no longer residential. Every morning, thousands of people pour into Nassau to do business. At the end of the working day, the town becomes almost deserted except for police officers and the few tourists who stroll at night. It is then that the mystique and beauty of the historical and charming city of Nassau emerges to the full. ❏

LEFT: Winston Saunders, Nassau playwright, poses before the Dundas Center for the Performing Arts.
RIGHT: tangled gardens of the old Royal Victoria Hotel

Maps:
Area 165
Town 160

NEW PROVIDENCE

Outside the bustle of central Nassau there are quiet coves, country villages and exclusive residential enclaves. Here, too, are lush botanical gardens, tree-lined parks and white sandy beaches

New Providence, small as it is, 21 miles (34 km) long by 7 miles (11 km) wide, is an island full of contrasts. It is the Bahamas' most populous island, and here, if anywhere, among the old British forts and African settlements, walled estates and inviting beaches, may be found the key to the country's diversity, contradictions and beauty.

Only 200 miles (60 km) and a half-hour's flight from Florida, the island is mainly flat but has a ridge of low hills along the north coast, which stretches from Nassau as far west as Love Beach. The Blue Hill Range, farther inland, separates New Providence's two lakes and rises to about 120 ft (37 meters). Prospect Ridge is an extension of the range which can be seen in Nassau. The eastern end of the island has a mainly rocky coast, while the southern coast is flat, often very swampy, with shallow water along its rocky shore.

Western New Providence is known for its pine barren forests (typical of the islands of Andros, Grand Bahama and part of Abaco), potholes and caves. It has two lakes, an inland water hole called Mermaid's Pool, and stretches of fine white sandy beaches. Although there are reefs along the western coast, the water is generally favorable for swimming.

Excursions by car, motorbike or bicycle are the best ways to see the island. Visitors with more time than money might try the buses as well; they are clean, run on time and the drivers are helpful, too.

Outside central Nassau

A good starting point for a tour just outside Nassau's old town is Dowdeswell or Middle Street (so named because it is in the middle of Bay and Shirley Streets). You will notice some fine old houses with traditional verandahs, lattice-work, dormer windows and gingerbread fretwork. One example is the **Carey Home**, constructed

of Abaco pine towards the end of the 19th century. As the area sometimes floods during high tides, the Carey Home, like many on the street, is built on a 3-ft (1-meter) stone foundation.

At the eastern end of Dowdeswell Street is the **Eastern Parade** and **Malcolm's Park** recreational and fair grounds, said to rest on reclaimed swampland. Pan American Airways had an office on the northern side. The airline operated the first passenger service between Miami and Nassau, starting in 1929. Commodore flying boats and twin-engine Sikorsky amphibian craft landed in the harbor, and passengers were taken ashore in small boats. Later, a ramp was laid, and planes discharged passengers directly onshore.

At the end of the Parade is part of an old burial ground, an extension of **St Matthew's Churchyard**. This area contains many old tombs, including one for "John Wells, Esq., late editor of the *Bahamas Gazette*," Nassau's first newspaper. **St Matthew's Church Ⓐ**, the foundation stone of which was laid in 1800, is the oldest church building in the Bahamas. The church is hard to miss because of its distinctive tower and steeple. Its architecture is a strange mixture of neo-Classical forms with Gothic proportions. It was enlarged by the erection of a vestry room, organ chamber and new chancel, consecrated in 1887.

Pondites and Potter's Cay

Near St Matthew's, on Shirley Street, is **Ebenezer Methodist Church**. On the site of an earlier "meeting place," the present church was constructed between 1839 and 1841. Both churches are near to the area known as the **Pond**.

The area was also the site of the **Gym Tennis Club**, which is now located in Winton in the eastern district. The original Gym Tennis Club, established by nurse Florence Wood, was a gym club offering exercises for girls. It opened for ladies and men in about 1928. Until the early 1950s, there was discrimination against black players, who needed special permission to play on the courts of the hotels such as the New Colonial and the Montagu. The Gym Tennis Club produced some leading players in its time, including the Minns brothers and Cyril Burrows.

Not far from the Pond are the two Paradise Island Bridges, and the busy Mackey Street/Paradise Island traffic roundabout. The second bridge was built in 1998 and is used to access Paradise Island, while the old (first) bridge is used to exit the island. Underneath the bridge is **Potter's Cay Ⓑ** dock and a teeming market, where vendors sell conch, fish, fruit and vegetables. This market was formerly held along the Market Range, closer to the center of town, but today New Providence and Out Island fishing boats tie up here to sell their catch, including the Bahamas' special delight – grouper. Conch is also a Bahamian favorite, and is considered to be an aphrodisiac *(see page 118–19)*.

In front of the boats, ladies, and some men, also sell vegetables and fruit. There is a Ministry of Agriculture Produce Exchange at the end of the dock, and an outlet which sells chilled fish. Mailboats from the Out Islands tie up at the dock to take and unload freight and passengers.

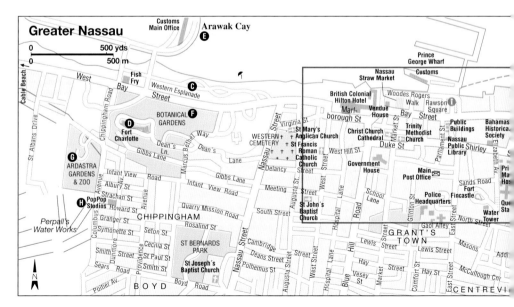

Map on pages 160–61

The bulky wooden boats carry everything from chickens to mattresses, stowed aboard and lashed to the sides.

A treasure trove

Going south on Mackey Street, you soon come to the **Public Records Office, Department of Archives** and **Eastern Public Library**, located in a neo-Georgian-style building constructed in the early 1950s. The archives, established in 1971, has a rich deposit of historical documents and books, and serves as a major research resource in the Bahamas.

Records preserved in the Public Records Office include those of the executive, legislative and judicial branches of government. There are also photographs from the various government ministries and departments, Out Islands, schools, churches, public corporations and private families. Microfilm copies of early original documents held in foreign repositories are also found there. The records held at the archives are a treasure trove for the historian, the economist, the social and political scientist, the genealogist, the student and the general public alike. The Department of Archives sponsors an annual exhibition during the first week in February. Booklets on these exhibitions are printed annually. Other publications include *A Guide to the Records of the Bahamas* and *A Guide to African Settlements in New Providence*.

Next door is the **Salvation Army Headquarters**, which was established in the Bahamas in 1931, the Salvation Army soon built a wooden chapel and made attempts to spread the Christian mission in the Out Islands.

Once residential, Mackey Street is now one of the main thoroughfares running north to south in New Providence. It abounds with small shopping centers, restaurants and various business. It also contains the **Ranfurly Home For Children**, a charitable institution which houses orphans, and the **Dundas Centre for the Performing Arts**, a live theater which stages entertainment all the year round.

West of the old town

At the western end of the old city on West Street, going south, you can explore **Meeting Street**, which received its name from its two Baptist churches, Bethel Baptist and St John's Baptist, which met there in the 18th century. Bethel Baptist Church was founded by a runaway slave, Sambo Scriven, and the land on which the present church sits was purchased in 1801. A

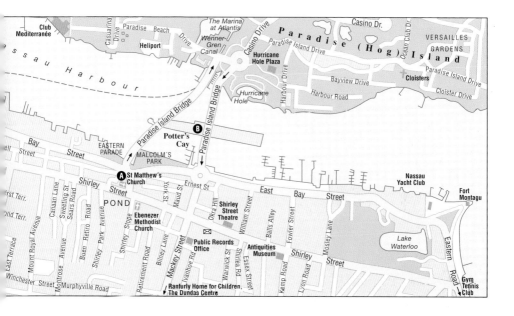

dispute in the church led to the formation of St John's Native Baptist Church, a few hundred yards away in 1832.

Nearby, on Delancy Street, is a delightful old residence, **Buena Vista**, which is one of the Bahamas' finest restaurants and also a hotel.

Farther north, on Virginia Street, is **St Mary's Anglican Church**, first used as a Chapel-of-East to Christ Church. The original church, which was destroyed in the severe hurricane of 1866, was replaced by the present building begun two years later. The church's graveyard borders the **Western Cemetery**, which contains many ancient tombs. One approach to the cemetery is from Nassau Street, which links the interior of the island with West Bay Street.

Cookouts, cannon, cricket

To the west of Nassau Street, **West Bay Street** winds along the seashore. The electric aquamarine color of the water is almost indescribable and can be distracting to the casual motorist. The road first passes the **Western Esplanade ◉**, a popular stretch for "cookouts" where culinary experts sell cool drinks and Bahamian food – often fried grouper, cracked conch or spicy conch salad.

From the esplanade you can see the western end of **Paradise Island** and its picturesque stone lighthouse. Built between 1816 and 1817 from native-quarried stone, the lighthouse served as the signpost to the port of Nassau and warned sailors of the perils of the sea. At first kerosene-fueled, it is now automated.

To the west, West Bay Street passes **Xavier's College**, a private school operated by the Roman Catholic Diocese, a section of the Road Traffic Department and the headquarters of the Bahamas Girl Guide organization.

South, on a hill, is a gunpowder storage unit, and on another hill to the west is **Fort Charlotte ◉**, one of 12 fortifications in the Nassau area and built by John, Earl of Dunmore, governor of the Bahamas from 1787 to 1796. Manned by 42

BELOW: at Potter's Ca[...] fruit from the [...] Out Islands for sale.

Map
on pages
160–61

large and threatening cannons in its heyday, the fort never fired a shot in anger. It stands today as a historic monument on 100 acres (40 hectares) that Lord Dunmore reserved as public lands.

The main part of the fort, named in honor of the wife of King George III, was completed in 1789 when the memory of American revolutionary soldiers' brief occupation of Nassau was still fresh in everyone's mind. The middle bastion, Fort Stanley, came next, and the western section, called Fort D'Arcy, was added later. Cut out of solid rock with the walls buttressed with cedar, a dry moat surrounded the fort. The moat was spanned by a wooden bridge on the northern side.

From the old fort there is a commanding view of **Nassau Harbour**, **The Guns**, a small battery of cannon, and **Arawak Cay ❺**, a man-made island constructed by the government of the Bahamas in the late 1960s. The cay accommodates the customs office and the public service training center. It also serves as a base for

the reception of fresh water, which is brought in by barge from Andros Island.

Locals frequent the mini-community of stalls and eateries on the mainland side of the Cay, where more than a dozen brightly-colored wooden structures – some two-storied, with outdoor patios or awnings – are a great place to get a lunchtime conch salad and freshly fried fish.

The Arawak Cay strip runs from the corner of Chippingham Road and Bay Street, towards downtown almost as far as the Hilton Hotel. It has a police station, a storytellers' porch, and a village green, where festivals and concerts are held, including events that are part of the popular **Junkanoo in June** festival.

Directly across West Bay Street from the entrance to Arawak Cay is Chippingham Road, with the entrance to the **Botanical Gardens ❻** (open daily 9am–4pm; entrance fee; tel: 323 5975) on the left and **Ardastra Gardens and Zoo ❼** (open daily 9am–4.30pm; entrance fee; tel: 323 5806) around the first bend, to the right.

BELOW: conch shells cleaned and shined as souvenirs at Potter's Cay.

Both gardens feature numerous species of tropical plants in beautifully landscaped settings. Ardastra Gardens and Zoo houses over 300 birds, mammals and reptiles and has a fun flamingo show several times per day, except Sunday.

Within walking distance of Ardastra, on the corner of Dunmore Avenue and Strachan Street, is a charming family-owned bed and breakfast, Dillet's Guest House. The original residence built in 1928, retains its Bahamian decor, and is also open for daily tours.

On the same property is **PopPop Studios** (view by appointment; enquire at Dillet's), a gallery containing the oil and canvas and New Age works of artist-in-residence, John Cox. The gallery also exhibits the work of Cox's protégés from the fine arts program he teaches at the College of the Bahamas, the only college in the country with an art institute.

Returning to West Bay Street and còntinuing west you will approach **Saunders Beach**, bordered by large, somnolent casuarina trees. These magnificent trees, which seem like a cross between a pine and a willow, thrive on New Providence, although they were imported from Australia.

The road glides past The Grove, once a sisal plantation. Developed in the 1920s, the Grove is now an enviable residential suburb, as is the adjacent Highland Park.

Rooms with a view

West Bay Street then passes **Brown's Point** or "Go-Slow-Bend," where motorists can catch their first glimpse of **Cable Beach** ❶. So named because the Bahamas' first cable communication with the outside world was made from there to Florida in 1892, the area began to be developed as a resort facility in the 1950s. In 1954 the Emerald Beach Hotel opened; it was the first hotel in the Bahamas to have airconditioning.

A complex of hotels dominates this strip of beach. Superclubs **The Breezes**, built on the site of Westbourne, where Sir Harry Oakes was mysteriously murdered

LEFT: on the beach.

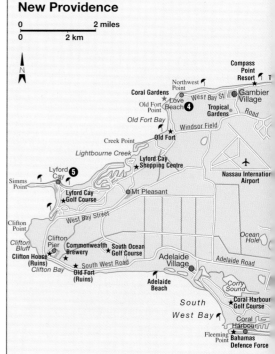

Maps:
Area 165
own 160

in 1943, is the most easterly. Next to it is Café **Johnny Canoe** ❷, a great place for an authentic Bahamian brunch and other local cuisine. The café sits right next to the Forte Nassau Beach Hotel, which lies adjacent to a five-tower complex of gleaming glass, the **Nassau Marriott Resort and Crystal Palace Casino**. It includes a huge gambling casino and a complex of shops.

Less than a mile farther west is the **Sandals Royal Bahamian Hotel**. This elegant pink colonial hideaway, where the cottages have names instead of room numbers, was once a favorite private retreat of the world's elite – including such diverse personalities as the Beatles and Richard Nixon.

Caves and coves

Leaving Cable Beach behind, you soon arrives at **Delaport Point**, and another strip of inviting beach. Near the point is Delaport Village, formerly a plantation. The road continues to hug the coast, providing lovely views of the sea. Very soon it reaches **The Caves** ❸, which developed naturally out of soft limestone. Above them is an inscription commemorating the arrival of the first member of the British royal family to visit the Bahamas: Prince Alfred, Duke of Edinburgh, who landed on New Providence in 1861.

Nearby **Caves Point** is both the location and the name of the oceanfront property which has sprung up in recent years.

Not far from The Caves is Blake Road, which leads to John F. Kennedy Drive and to the airport. A branch of the high-tech modern Doctor's Hospital, a private facility in downtown Nassau, now sits on this short connecting road. Juxtaposed across the street from the hospital is a large storage warehouse containing furniture and other goods belonging to frequent travelers and winter residents.

At the junction of Blake Road and West Bay Street is Conference Corner, where President John F. Kennedy, British prime minister Harold Macmillan and Canadian premier John Diefenbaker planted three trees to mark their meeting here in 1962.

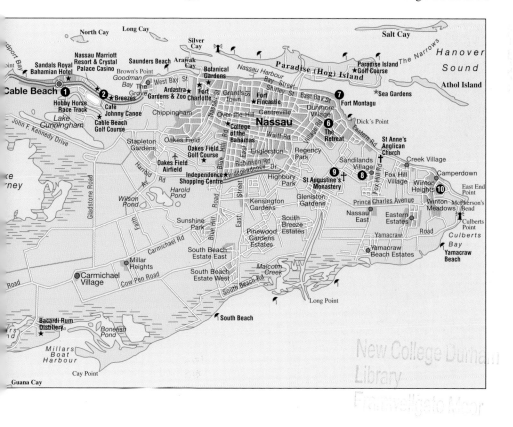

The road then passes Orange Hill, a small hotel and restaurant overlooking a fine swimming beach, which stretches for several hundred yards. The coast becomes rocky near **Gambier Village**, which was settled originally by liberated Africans brought to the Bahamas by the British Royal Navy in 1807. An early settler in Gambier Village was Elizah Morris, a former enslaved man who was involved in the Creole Mutiny which occurred off the coast of Abaco in 1841. The villagers lived mainly by farming and used to sell their produce in the Nassau Market.

Just past the sign identifying Gambier Village, on the right, is the Compass Point Resort. Opened in 1995, the resort has 21 multi-colored units and cottages – some on stilts – beside a swimming pool and restaurant. Guests have included Robin Leach, Babyface, Cindy Crawford and Lenny Kravitz.

Farther west along the coast is **Love Beach ❹**, named after a family of that name and now a fine residential area.

Nearby is Old Fort, originally part of the Charlottesville Estate. An old house remains on the site overlooking one of the best beaches in New Providence.

After passing Lightbourne Creek and the old Waterloo Estate, once owned by William Wylly, a plantation owner and political firebrand in 19th-century Nassau, you reach Lyford Cay.

Exclusive paradise

Development of **Lyford Cay ❺**, once owned by the Loyalist William Lyford, was begun in the early 1950s by H.G. Christie. However, it was a Canadian financier, E.P. Taylor, who turned the wooded area into a rich man's paradise.

This exclusive enclave is the home or second home of the rich and famous, among them shipping magnates and novelists, not to mention (but let's) Sean Connery and Arthur Hailey (*see pages 102–03*). Outside its security-controlled gates is a small shopping center, with shops selling luxurious furniture and bric a brac. Inside are tasteful, sometimes elegant homes along well-paved streets that meander past manicured gardens and canals that enable yachtsmen to dock their vessels literally in their backyards. There is also a luxurious club and hotel, a golf course and numerous tennis courts. The club caters to swimmers, with a large pool, and extensive beachfront, and also promotes scuba diving and waterskiing.

Nearby is a less exclusive suburb, **Mount Pleasant**, where many professional Bahamians have made their homes. Some work at the nearby South Ocean Beach Hotel and Golf Club. On the edge of the club's golf course are the ruins of an old plantation.

Clifton plantation

At the extreme western tip of New Providence is **Clifton House**, on a former plantation once owned by an attorney general of the Bahamas, William Wylly, who also owned plantations at Tusculum (near Gambier) and Waterloo (near Lyford Cay). By 1818, Wylly owned 67 enslaved men and women, who lived on his three plantations. Clifton was the largest. The ruins

LEFT: retrievir a message in bottle.

Map on page 165

of the plantation house are still visible, although, not as extensive as those found in 1891 by a travel writer named J.H. Stark. He reported finding the remains of three large gates and a wide carriage drive leading to a house built on the English plan, along with the remains of a coach house and stables for several carriage horses. He also noticed large slave quarters.

Today, Clifton is the site of the main power plant of the Bahamas Electricity Corporation and also serves as a gasoline storage depot. A large brewery has also been constructed there.

The **Commonwealth Brewery** (tours by appointment; tel: 362 4789) produces Kalik beer. This favorite local refreshment is named for the click, click sound made by cowbells played during Junkanoo.

The rocky coast of **Clifton Point** offers a fantastic view of the deep blue ocean. Clifton was formerly used as a landing place for passenger ships when the weather was too rough for them to enter the harbor at the Nassau Bay.

Adelaide and Carmichael

Beyond the coast road is the South Ocean Beach Hotel's golf course, where the remains of another old plantation can be seen. About 2 miles (3 km) east of this is **Adelaide Village**, named after the wife of William IV.

Situated at South West Bay, Adelaide was founded in 1831 by Governor James Carmichael Smyth. The original inhabitants were liberated Africans, captured from the Portuguese vessel *Rosa*. At that time, slavery had been outlawed in England, so the 157 Africans were automatically freed upon landing in Nassau, a British port. Supplied with hatchets and hoes for farming, they were encouraged to build their own homes in the new village of Adelaide. Some years later a school was founded. In the early 1960s, the village contained a number of simple thatched huts, typical of dwellings built by the Africans in the 19th century. Today, although the village is relatively modernized – it has electricity and telephones – it

BELOW:
Adelaide
Village Church.

retains some of its quaintness and has a comfortable aura of peacefulness.

Not far from Adelaide is **Coral Harbour**, a mainly residential area which also accommodates the Royal Bahamas' Defence Force headquarters. It has man-made canals and fine docking facilities.

Several miles inland to the east is Carmichael Village, originally known as Headquarters. This was perhaps the earliest liberated African settlement founded by James Carmichael Smyth. In the 19th century, many of the Carmichael residents worked as domestics and laborers in Nassau. From around 1825, some of the natives of Carmichael formed a settlement near Nassau, Grant's Town, in order to be nearer to the Nassau Market. Today, Carmichael is a scattered settlement containing many modern residences, subdivisions and farms. Very little of the original village is left.

From Carmichael Village follow Gladstone Road to John F. Kennedy Drive, which runs along the shores of **Lake Cunningham**. Back in the Village take Carmichael Road, turn north on Blue Hill Road to pass the Independence Shopping Center at the intersection with Harrold Road. On the corner of Blue Hill Road and Wulff Road is St Barnabas Anglican Church. To the north, and just west of **Grant's Town**, is **Bain Town**. Originally distinct, the two have now merged.

The original Bain Town was bordered on the east by Blue Hill Road, on the north by South Street, on the south by Poinciana Drive, and on the west by Nassau Street. The area, originally a 140-acre (57-hectare) land grant to one Susannah Weatherspoon, was, in the mid-19th century, sold to a black Bahamian businessman, Charles H. Bain. At the turn of the 20th century, most of the houses in the area were made of wood, with porches and thatched roofs. Today, much development has taken place, and while there are still some small wooden houses, now with shingled roofs, there are also some larger modern buildings, like Woodcock Primary School.

BELOW: checkers contest in Over-the-Hill.

Map on page 165

Over-the-Hill

This area, like Grant's Town to the east, is seething with life. Laid out between 1820 and 1829, it includes the area of land bordered on the east by East Street, west by Blue Hill Road, north by Cockburn and Lees streets and south by the Blue Hills. The entire area, which is densely populated, is a place of sharp contrasts: an area abounding with quaint shops where checkers, dominoes and *warri* (an African game) are still played under shady roadside trees, and where porches, yards and streets are utilized heavily by a bustling and lively population, some of which is migrant from Haiti.

Many prominent people, including Sir Lynden O. Pindling, former prime minister of the Commonwealth of the Bahamas, hail from East Street, one of the main streets of Over-the-Hill. Founded as a suburb for former slaves and freed Africans, Over-the-Hill has always had humble buildings. In its early years it had a market and many trees. Gradually, though, it became more urbanized, so that today it has few open spaces. The people who live there are mostly workers, artisans and shopkeepers, who depend more or less directly on the business generated by Nassau.

Today, Over-the-Hill comprises not only dwellings and small shops, but also is the home of many restaurants, bars, clubs, stores and offices. There are also a variety of churches, including **St Agnes Anglican Church**, first consecrated on April 8, 1848 on Market and Cockburn streets. Not far from St Agnes is **Wesley Methodist Church**, established in 1847. The church stands on the site of an earlier one, which had a thatched roof. Early Methodist services were held in local homes.

Another prominent church in this area is the **Church of God of Prophecy** on East Street. This is the mother church of numerous churches of this denomination that have been established throughout the Bahamas, through proselytizing from its headquarters in Tennessee. Many other churches, including The Church of God

LEFT: High-key colors in a low-key Over-the-Hill shop.

and several Baptist churches are also located in Over-the-Hill.

Progress and preservation

A main artery and the southern boundary of Grant's Town is Wulff Road, which is dotted with various businesses, small shops, eateries and schools.

To the west of Wulff Road is Poinciana Drive, which leads to the College of the Bahamas, established in 1974. The college provides a two-year program that leads to an associate degree in various subjects. Several degree programs are also offered in conjunction with the universities of the West Indies and Miami, which includes a combined internship and academic program in hotel management.

Much further east, Village Road runs from north to south, connecting the interior with Shirley and East Bay streets. It is mostly residential but has a large food store, a plant nursery, a squash club, a few small shops and **The Retreat** ❻ (open Mon–Fri 9am–5pm; tel: 393 1317), the headquarters of The Bahamas National Trust. The property, an 11-acre (5-hectare) estate, contains a cottage, part of which dates to the 1860s, and has some of the rarest palms in the world, collected by the late Arthur and Margaret Langlois, former owners of the estate.

Also on Village road, at No. 18 is **Doongalik Studios** (open Mon–Fri; tel: 394 1886), a showcase of local crafts and fine art set up by artists Jackson Burnside, John Beadle and Jolyon Smith.

Along Montagu Bay

Built from local limestone in 1742 on a point at the eastern entrance to New Providence's harbor, **Fort Montagu** ❼ was built to defend Nassau, and was not very successful at it. It saw action in 1776 when a small force of the American navy attacked the British in Nassau. Its defenses faltered again in 1782, when the Spanish captured New Providence and occupied the capital for a year. Nearby, on Shirley Street, is the derelict Montagu

BELOW: St Anne's Church in Fox Hill.

Map
on page
165

Hotel, built in 1926 to cater to the then fledgling tourist trade.

Turning east onto **East Bay Street**, also called the **Eastern Road**, the route passes **Blair**, a subdivision now but once a large estate. The drive up East Bay Street is beautiful. On the coastline are many fine homes surrounded by large gardens and lush foliage. Most properties are surrounded by picturesque native stone walls and cascades of flowers.

Just past **Dick's Point** is **The Hermitage**, originally built as a country home by Lord Dunmore in the late 18th century. Now it is the home of the Roman Catholic bishop of Nassau. Farther east, the homes on the road's sea side have smaller gardens that are well kept and are reminiscent of the style of houses found in Bermuda.

Joshua, Congo, Nango

Shortly past High Vista is Fox Hill Road. Just opposite the intersection with East Bay Street is the former site of the the 18th century settlement of Creek Village.

Most of the original settlers, who were probably Africans, sold their properties and moved inland after Samuel Fox, a former slave who owned a piece of property in that district.

Later, the then chief justice of the Bahamas, Robert Sandilands, who bought about 1,200 acres (480 hectares) in the **Fox Hill** area, in 1840 laid out a village and made about a hundred grants of land varying from one to 10 acres. Grants were made to various freed Africans who paid either in money or labor to the value of $10. The Africans, who called the settlement **Sandilands Village** ❽, after their benefactor, grew fruits and vegetables which they sold in the Nassau Market. The village was later divided into three towns: Joshua, Congo and Nango.

On the first rise going south on Fox Hill Road is **St Anne's Anglican Church**, a quaint structure, originally erected in 1740. The present church, built between 1867 and 1870, is adjacent to St Anne's School, run by the Anglican Diocese.

BELOW:
the Bahamas'
coat-of-arms,
and students
in Fox Hill.

The Fox Hill/Sandilands area still contains some of its ancient charm as a rural village, with heavily wooded areas and small wooden and limestone and dabble wall houses. Containing many churches, small shops, a public library, fire station and a school, it is also the home of the Boys and Girls Industrial Schools, the Geriatrics Hospital and the Sandilands Rehabilitation Hospital for mentally handicapped individuals.

At the center of the village is **Freedom Park**, opened in 1967. Emancipation Day (August 1) and Fox Hill Day (the 2nd Tuesday in August) are celebrated every year by the residents of Fox Hill on the Village Green and in the park.

Off Bernard Road, one of the main streets in Fox Hill, is **St Augustine's Monastery** ❾ (tours by appointment; tel: 364 1331) and co-educational St Augustine's College. Developed by Benedictines from Minnesota, the two structures were designed by Monsignor John Hawes (or Father Jerome), known also as the Hermit

of Cat Island (*see page 264*). The monastery and the college perched high on a rocky hill near Fox Hill were completed in 1947. Each room opened onto cloisters and had an arched stone roof to match; the floors were cemented and tiled. The long and low structure resembled a fortress.

At the intersection of Fox Hill Road and Yamacraw Road is the region's prison. Turning east on Yamacraw Road, you pass Yamacraw Beach Estates to the south and the southern entrance to Nassau East, a subdivision developed in the late 1960s. It adjoins Nassau Village and Winton Meadows. To the east is **Yamacraw Beach**.

Hugging the coastline with its brilliant sea views, the road soon curves around McPherson's Bend, named after a local resident who was said to park his car there every night to take in the view. Popular lore claims that Harry McPherson was the owner of the island's first real estate company, as well as the island's first car. Park just off the main road here, and a few minutes under the little white gazebo gives credence to the stories that claim this is where Harry proposed to the future Mrs McPherson.

Traveling on East Bay Street towards **Winton Heights** ❿, formerly a large plantation called Lookout, the road passes Solomon's Lighthouse, a candy-striped house built by Fane Solomon, a local merchant. At the top of Winton Highway are the remains of an ancient battery built by Lord Dunmore. **Fort Winton**, as it came to be known, has a commanding view of Nassau, the eastern harbor and Rose Island, which runs almost parallel to the eastern end of New Providence.

West of East Bay Street are Camperdown, once a heavily wooded area, now quite developed, and Sans Souci, a popular subdivision. The eastern end of the island is mostly residential.

New Providence, with its many contrasts, has become one of the western world's popular resorts. Its modern office buildings, fine subdivisions, historic settlements and quaint neo-colonial architecture somehow blend well together – the phenomenal growth of tourism and finance has not diminished its charm. ❏

LEFT: a Junkanoo ma[...] and a reveller ready for the parade. **RIGHT:** Junkanoo mural of masquerader[...] Over-the-Hill.

Map
n pages
178–79

PARADISE ISLAND
(HOG ISLAND)

*Dominated by a mega-resort, this island is a little bit of paradise for
well-heeled pleasure-seekers. Here is a ritzy casino, a spectacular
aquarium, busy beaches and tranquil, lush gardens*

Since an angry God drove Adam and Eve out of Eden, humans have been trying to regain Paradise. Whether it is a Miltonian heaven or a place of refuge, who is not sure that perfection exists – somewhere? The trick is to find it.

When the Swedish industrialist Dr Axel Wenner-Gren docked his 322-ft (100-meter) yacht in Nassau Harbour in 1939, he had already traveled the world. In two years the *Southern Cross*, which he had bought from Howard Hughes, had carried him over 70,000 exotic miles (130,000 km). According to Dr Paul Albury, who chronicles the island's history in his book *Paradise Island Story*, Wenner-Gren saw low-lying Hog Island while docked in Nassau Harbour. Its fringe of ragged shrubs and trees was visible a stone's throw away from his decks, and it must have whispered to him, "Paradise!"

Paradise found

The tall, handsome magnate bought the Lynch estate on Hog Island. He dredged old Burnside's pond and renamed it Paradise Lake; he dug canals to link the lake with Nassau Harbour and the open sea. He refurbished the already commodious Lynch estate, built only two years before by Joseph Lynch of Merrill, Lynch and Company. Inspired by the imaginary land in James Hilton's 1933 novel *Lost Horizon*, he christened his refuge Shangri-La.

Then the United States entered World War II, and Wenner-Gren's companies were blacklisted. In 1935 he had purchased a major interest in Bofors munitions works. This was the Swedish branch of Krupp, and Krupp, of course, supplied weapons and ammunition to the Axis powers. Rumors flew: the *Southern Cross* carried Bofors anti-aircraft guns; the canals were hideouts for German sub-

marines. None of these tales were substantiated, but by the end of the war, Wenner-Gren was reputed to be one of the richest men in the world. Though he spent much of the war and later years in Latin America, after the armistice he returned for visits to his Hog Island Shangri-la.

Wenner-Gren's utopian dream found a still more ardent supporter when, in 1961, the year he died, he sold his Hog Island holdings to another man of immense wealth, Huntington Hartford – the man who had Hog Island's name changed to Paradise.

Today, Paradise Island is a modern resort linked to Nassau by two concrete bridges over the harbor. The second

RECEDING
.GES:
lying golf
Paradise
and.

FT: a tunnel
casuarina
es.

GHT: a tourist
ts away
m it all.

bridge, a $20 million, 2,000-ft (600-meter) access to the Island, lies 400 ft (120 meters) west of the original bridge, and began operation in 1998. At the foot of the bridge is a toll booth – one dollar and Paradise is yours.

High-rise hotel buildings gleam in a landscape of tropical palms, parking areas and speed bumps and at first Paradise seems to be an island of hotels. This impression is corroborated by statistics. There are over 3,000 hotel rooms, dozens of restaurants, lounges and bars serving food ranging from French to Bahamian to Polynesian, and more Bahamians employed in maintaining this tourist paradise than elsewhere on the islands.

Marooned

As early as the 18th century, Paradise Island, then known as Hog Island, was noted for its delights. A map of 1788 shows a few farm huts, two buildings that were likely a shipyard, and a structure called "Banqueting House." If Banqueting House was once the site of idyllic feasting, its tales remain lost in the sand, but in 1834 an American doctor wrote of being taken by the governor of the Bahamas on a "maroon" at the island's abandoned barracks. There they ate a pic-

nic banquet of salmon, corned beef, pickled oysters, cider and good madeira, in the shade beside a snow-white sandy beach.

When swimming became popular in the 1890s, Hog Island's reputation as a tropical paradise grew. Entrepreneurs capitalized on the fledgling tourist trade and offered boat trips to the island. For one shilling (sterling), Victorian pleasure-seekers received use of a changing room and bathing suit, a swim in the warm waters and a feast of fruit.

As competition grew, enterprising proprietors added attractions: sack races, candy-pulls, high wire walkers and trick-bicycle riders, ventriloquist shows, fireworks and even dancing lessons. The center for much of this activity was Saratoga Beach, renamed in the 1920s **Paradise Beach ❶**. A left turn after crossing the Paradise Island Bridge, and a right down shady Casuarina Drive will take you to this slender crescent of white sand on the northwest end of the island – still a mecca for holiday frolickers.

Although no sign remains of the Victorian bathing houses, circus acts or dancing pavilions, the exuberant commercial spirit of the place lives on. For an entrance fee anyone can enjoy Paradise Beach, where a plethora of rentable mechanical toys crowd

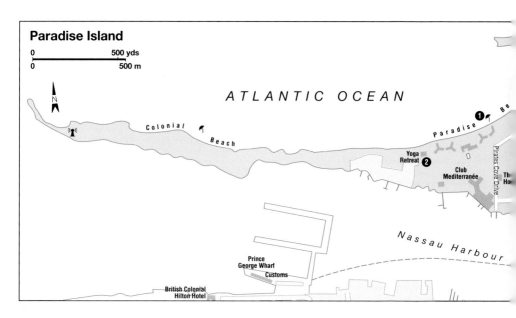

Paradise Island

| 0 | 500 yds |
| 0 | 500 m |

N

ATLANTIC OCEAN

Colonial Beach

Paradise ❶

Yoga Retreat ❷

Club Méditerranée

Pirates Cove Drive

Nassau Harbour

Prince George Wharf

Customs

British Colonial Hilton Hotel

Map
n pages
178–79

the sand: sunfish, windsurfing boards, Hobie 14s, paddleboats, snorkeling equipment, jetskis. The scene on Paradise Beach can resemble a circus, but under the casuarina trees instead of a bigtop.

West of the hubbub of Paradise Beach, the island's narrow western finger extends into a more private realm. In the early 1900s this area became a second home to a small enclave of wealthy Americans who banded together in a group they called the Porcupine Club. By 1930 the club's membership had increased from 11 to 50, and they had moved from their first clubhouse to a larger one. This is not to suggest that the membership requirements grew lax; it was understood that only *multi*-millionaires need apply. Some members arrived in fabulous yachts owned by Mellons, Morgans, or Astors. After World War II many of the original members died off, club enthusiasm waned and many remaining members joined the Lyford Cay Club on New Providence Island. The homes, land and clubhouses were sold.

Swamis and pop-beads

Visible on Casuarina Drive is the entrance to **Club Méditerranée** (Club Med), part of the international resort chain that popularized the "all-inclusive" vacation resort, where incidentals are paid for by popping a bead from a necklace. It occupies the former Porcupine Club land, and though Club Med has constructed some new accommodations, it also maintains the old houses and cottages relatively unchanged. Club Med employees (*gentils organisateurs* or GOs, as they are called) tell ghost stories about a Porcupine Club member's appearance in her old home, now an oceanfront restaurant and employee dormitory.

Other enclaves on Paradise Island's western tip can be reached only by boat. The **Yoga Retreat ❷**, founded by Swami Vishnudevananda occupies four acres donated by one of the swami's grateful students. Chanting, meditation, breathing exercises and vegetarian meals fill the days, which begin with a rising bell at 5.30am. The all-volunteer staff grows produce in the retreat's own gardens, and someone has put up a rustic sign reading "Club Meditation."

Several private homes also occupy the western end, and at the tip is the **lighthouse**, built of limestone quarried nearby. Citizens of Nassau laid its cornerstone in 1816 with great pomp and ceremony. They commemorated the event with speeches, prayers, a phial containing historic

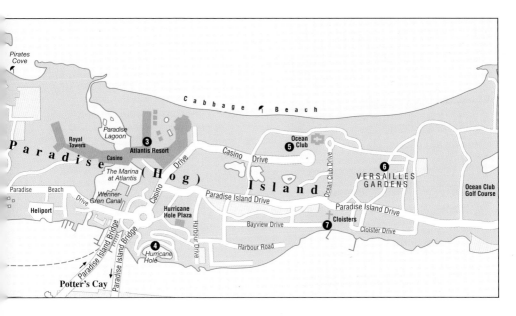

Pirates Cove

C a b b a g e   Beach

Royal Towers

Paradise Lagoon

❸ Atlantis Resort

P a r a d i s e

Casino

The Marina at Atlantis

(H o g)

Casino Drive

Ocean ❺ Club

Casino Drive

Ocean Club Drive

❻

VERSAILLES GARDENS

Ocean Club Golf Course

Paradise   Beach

Drive   Wenner-Gren Canal

Casino Drive

I s l a n d

Heliport

Hurricane Hole Plaza

Paradise Island Drive

Paradise Island Drive

Paradise Island Bridge

Paradise Island Bridge

❹ Hurricane Hole

Harbour Drive

Bayview Drive

Harbour Road

❼

Cloisters

Cloister Drive

Potter's Cay

information, and a few coins and medals that were cemented into the bedrock.

Since there is no road on Paradise Island's western end, the best view of the lighthouse can be enjoyed from a plane or boat. On calm days it is difficult to imagine the many storms the lighthouse and its keepers have endured, particularly the hurricane of 1866, when 60-ft (18-meter) waves surged into Nassau Harbour, their crests level with the lighthouse gallery.

Transformed

The arrival of Sun International's **Atlantis Resort ❸** in 1994 transformed the island's entire landscape. Until then, buildings like the Radisson Grand Hotel dominated the island. Built between the late 1960s and early 1980s in the international style that defines skylines in Florida and California, these older buildings have now been joined – and outshined – by later additions to the Atlantis resort, such as the dramatic **Royal Towers**, built in 1998: 23 storeys high and with more than 1,200 rooms, it

brought investment in the resort to just under $1 billion. Not surprising then that the company owns around 75 percent of the property on the island and the towers are visible from almost any point on the north east coast of New Providence.

The 5,000 sq. ft (500 sq. meter) Bridge Suite between the towers has its own butler and rents for a mere $25,000 a night. Michael Jackson is believed to make hush-hush visits to the suite, which is in the luxury Coral Towers. Basketball legend, Michael Jordan, can often be found on the island's golf course.

Atlantis employs more than 5,000 Bahamians and the self-contained oasis seems a far cry from the Hog Island of its forebears. In its own way – gaudy casino and all – the resort has, some say, redefined the notion of luxury.

Timeshare villas, called "Villas at Atlantis", were begun in late 1999 on the site of the now closed Paradise Island Airport. Tucked away behind screened fences are over 20 tennis courts. Behind a sleek exterior and a plush chandeliered lobby lurks a casino. Inside the hotels' air-conditioned lobbies are plenty of potted palms and tropical rum drinks, and their rear doors open onto commodious swimming pools and the white sand of **Cabbage Beach**. If this is your version of Paradise, look no farther.

Venice to Vegas

Today, at the center of the island, the waters of Wenner-Gren's romantic Paradise Lake no longer reflect a rich man's dream. "Buy one gallon; get one free" was the slogan of the Mary Carter Paint Company, an American firm determined to put Paradise Island on the map as a major tourist resort.

In the late 1960s the paint company built the 1,500-ft (460-meter) **Paradise Island Bridge**, Atlantis-Paradise Island Hotel and a half-acre Casino (now Atlantis Resort), which was expanded to 60,000 sq. ft (5,600 sq. meters) soon after its acquisition by Sun International. Subdued lighting, whirring slot machines, clicking chips, the rattle of roulette wheels, plush carpet and glass sculptures: the casino is reminiscent of Monte Carlo minus the foreign accent.

LEFT:
Hurricane Ho

Map on pages 178–79

Plain sailing

Facing the Atlantis is the $18-million marina at Atlantis, with more than 60 slips accommodating yachts of up to 200 ft (60 meters). An underground tunnel was also built to link vehicular traffic to the Royal Towers of Atlantis.

Wenner-Gren's sparkling little Paradise Lake has become waterfront property for several restaurants, the tennis courts and landscaped pathways. The aging industrialist standing in his boathouse, greeting guests as they sail up his canal, is but a distant memory.

That past seems less remote on the eastern end of the island. After crossing Paradise Island Bridge you will see to the right a narrow road that leads to **Hurricane Hole ❹**, a haven for luxury yachts. Built in the early 1960s, it was a project of Huntington Hartford, the man who succeeded Wenner-Gren as the island's visionary. The marina underwent a $60-million renovation and expansion project in 2001, with upscale harborfront condominiums.

Grandson of the founder of the Great Atlantic and Pacific Tea Company (A&P), Huntington Hartford II was born in 1911 to enjoy the wealth of what was for a time the fifth largest corporation in the United States. The popular press portrayed him as an incorrigible playboy who married a cigarette girl, and later as an irrepressible art critic and patron who viewed most 20th-century art, particularly abstract-expressionist painting, as a scourge.

In 1959, while married to the second of his four wives, he bought a house and two acres on Hog Island. Hartford became friends with Wenner-Gren, who spent winters at his estate, Shangri-La. His finances running low, the older man could no longer dredge lakes, build guesthouses or otherwise augment his private paradise. Hartford, however, was rich in cash and artistic fervor. In a celebrated deal that began in an agreement signed on the back of a dinner menu, Hartford bought Wenner-Gren's extensive Hog Island properties for $9.5 million.

Hog wild

A sybarite and a capitalist, Hartford must have dreamed of finding both pleasure and profit in Hog Island's sunny beaches and sylvan glades. Its name he saw as an impediment. "Hog is an ugly name – the island should be called Paradise," Wenner-Gren reportedly declared, perhaps inspiring Hartford. So, Hartford saw that Hog Island became Paradise Island by decree on May 23, 1962.

A right turn on Paradise Island Drive leads to the heart of Hartford's dreams. The road passes several condominium and time-sharing developments, then glides past a small unobtrusive sign that says **Ocean Club** ❺. A turn up this narrow, shady driveway leads to a pale pink Georgian-style mansion with white verandahs and, likely or not, a limousine purring under the carport. It is not a private mansion but Hartford's Ocean Club hotel, the centerpiece of his many projects. A doorman in livery opens the front door; you sweep into the hall, across its polished floor, perhaps up the gently curved staircase. If it is dinner hour, on one of the balconies above the inner courtyard a jazz band bops and wails: candles flicker at tables around the pool.

Surrounding the hotel, Hartford's elegant **Versailles Gardens** ❻ seem fresh from France via Hollywood. From behind a screen of trees you hear the bounce-pop of a leisurely tennis game. Inspired by Louis XIV's gardens at Versailles, Wenner-Gren initiated the landscaping, and Hartford completed it. Grassy terraces stretch for a quarter-mile (500 meters) in an unbroken vista; shady niches off the terraces shelter bronze statues, not of Venus or Apollo, but of David Livingstone and Franklin Delano Roosevelt, two of Hartford's heros. There are also statues of Napoleon and Josephine, Hercules, and a 1920 bronze called *Mother and Child*.

From the garden's highest terrace you can cross Paradise Island Drive to the **Cloisters** ❼. Brought from a monastery near Lourdes, France, by the American

BELOW: Gothic mystery of the Cloisters.

Map
on pages
178–79

newspaper baron William Randolf Hearst, the pieces of this 14th-century cloister languished in crates in Florida until Hartford purchased them. Hartford had the Cloisters reconstructed stone by stone – a process which took a year because there were no instructions.

Today, the graceful columns and worn, delicately carved capitals form approximately the same serene square they did in France, though now roofless, with manicured grass growing between the paving stones. It is a romantic spot and serves as the ideal setting for wedding pictures of countless Nassauvians. The Cloisters overlook the eastern end of Nassau Harbour, with New Providence Island visible across the water.

Hartford invested $10 million in improvements to Paradise Island, building not only Hurricane Hole, the Ocean Club and Versailles Gardens but an 18-hole golf course, riding stables, a restaurant, and installing a water-taxi service from Nassau, with a dockside garden. He also trans-

formed Wenner-Gren's boathouse into an elegant French restaurant. It remains open to diners today, with candlelit terraces overlooking Paradise Lagoon.

When these extravagant plans did not pay off and severely strained even Hartford's considerable resources, he finally sold it all – lock, stock and barrel – to the Mary Carter Paint Company, who obtained a gambling permit.

Sand traps and solitude

East of the Cloisters, Paradise Island Drive leads to the 18-hole championship **Ocean Club Golf Course**. Originally built by Hartford, the clubhouse retains the intimate poshness he so obviously valued. Along the southern boundary of the golf course runs a shady, romantic drive with views of the water. Like the far western end of the island with its private homes and yoga retreat, the eastern end retains something of the spirit and enchantment that first made people think of Hog Island as Paradise. ❏

BELOW: *Mother
and Child* in
Versailles
Gardens.

GRAND BAHAMA ISLAND

A detailed guide to Grand Bahama, with principal sites
clearly cross-referenced by number to the maps

Floating like a green iguana on its back at the bottom of the Little Bahama Bank, Grand Bahama is regarded by many as a maverick cousin to the rest of the Bahamas. Largely developed by American commercial interest in the 1960s, it's sometimes thought of as non-Bahamian. But continental drift has not made it a part of Florida – yet.

After New Providence and Paradise islands, Grand Bahama is the most popular tourist destination in the Bahamas, and with good reason. Miles of sandy beaches, layers of comfortable hotel rooms in soaringly ambitious hotels, gambling casinos and world-class scuba diving make it a favorite long-weekend vacation spot for neighboring Floridians. Among the modern shops and offices of Freeport, the suburban neighborhoods of Lucaya and the good-natured opulence of the large hotels, most Americans will feel right at home. Visitors from further afield will not be disappointed either. Travel beyond the wide, landscaped thoroughfare of Freeport/Lucaya, and you will find that the island has even more in store…

A popular stop for cruise ships sailing through the Caribbean islands, it's not all shipping and shopping, or glitz and glamour. Eco-friendly activities are increasing, and the fruits of sea make for excellent fishing and remarkable opportunities to swim with dolphins. On dry land you can commune with nature in one of the island's parks or lush exotic gardens, where cascading waterfalls and mature trees provide welcome relief from the intense heat of the day. Sandy beaches away from the busy resorts are not just for sun-worshippers, they are also the location of friendly evening fish frys, complete with music and dancing – a Grand Bahama-style night out.

A network of fascinating limestone caves at the Lucayan National Park, blue holes, piney forests, East End and its nearby cays – all these offer a taste of the "old" Bahamas, and a tranquil "Out Island" atmosphere. On Grand Bahama you will not get away from it *all*, but you will surely find some special treasures. ❏

PRECEDING PAGES: Garden of the Groves.
LEFT: Lucaya's best advertisement.

Map
on page
191

FREEPORT

The busy center of Freeport has shopping, casinos and lively bars while in Lucaya and the southeast luxury hotels line the beaches and visitors snorkel, swim with dolphins and enjoy parks full of exotic flora and fauna

In the late 1980s, a forest of scrub pines was converted into the second city of the Bahamas, Freeport. What was first a clearing in a pine forest some 5 miles (8 km) from Hawksbill Creek, later became more like a frontier construction camp; and today, despite condos and country clubs, there is still a certain rawness to the place. Indeed, it is no coincidence that its principal streets are named for adventurers, settlers and pioneers.

A bold plan

Freeport was the brainchild of Wallace Groves, a Virginian financier. Groves bought a lumber company in 1946, and at his island retreat, Little Whale Cay, in the Berry Islands, he pondered the island of Grand Bahama.

It seemed to have much going for it. It was large and unencumbered by private owners; it was near the United States, and it had large reserves of ground water in addition to the natural resource of lumber. If that wasn't enough, it was a British colony with a benign pro-business government. As an additional bonus, it has abundant sea, sand and sun.

To make his dream come true, Groves needed a concession from the government, but he knew it would not be forthcoming unless he could offer something in return. So to the government he went – represented by his lawyer Sir Stafford Sands, who was at that time the Minister of Tourism – with a bold plan.

Groves's proposal was the development of a free port on Grand Bahama. He asked for, and received, concessions on the importation of duty-free materials and guarantees that there would be no taxes of any kind. He also signed a lease purchase agreement for 50,000 acres (20,000 hectares) of land. In return, he promised to dredge a deepwater harbor, encourage industry, pay for all government personnel

employed within the Port Area (as the land became known) and to reimburse the government for all other government services. These promises were the basis of a contract signed into law in 1955.

Early development was slow, but Groves was fortunate that shipping tycoon D.K. Ludwig had the unlikely notion that he would like to build large ships near the Caribbean. Ludwig paid for the development of a commodious harbor in exchange for 2000 acres (800 hectares) of land. The harbor was never used for shipbuilding and Ludwig continued to purchase his ships in Japan, but at least Freeport had gained a harbor.

The first major industry was a shipbunkering terminal, which fitted nicely

LEFT: straw market.
RIGHT: English are at Churchill Square.

with the deepwater harbor. Due to a quota imposed by the US government on all residual fuels imported into the United States, it was worthwhile for shippers to bunker in Freeport. The strategic location of Freeport brought a bonanza, and in one month alone the terminal exported nearly 1 million barrels of duty-free oil. Other industries were small, catering mainly to the service sector, but in 1961 work began on a giant cement plant on the western side of the harbor. Foreign entrepreneurs and workers poured into the island.

The birth of Lucaya

Five years into the venture the Grand Bahama Port Authority, the company founded by Wallace Groves, found that things were good and could be even better. The original agreement had envisioned an industrial community on Grand Bahama, but Groves realized that there was potential in tourism. So he went back to the government with another plan. The result was an agreement recognizing that the Port Au-

thority had performed as agreed under the principal agreement, and that it now required the port to build a luxury 200-room hotel and permitted it to purchase more land, which became known as Lucaya.

The luxury hotel called the Lucayan Beach Hotel was completed on schedule and opened its doors in 1963. The hotel was different from other hotels in the Bahamas of the time, for it had a large casino. The certificate of exemption required for the gambling license had been furtively obtained from the white minority government.

When the government changed, a commission on gambling studied the manner in which the certificate was obtained and pointed out that there was strong evidence to suggest that undesirables had been involved in the operation and that "skimming" seemed likely; and it further expressed concern "that the consultants who were members of the council (government) should have allowed themselves to be put in a position where conflict of interest would surely have arisen." The slap on the wrist was merely for the record, for under black majority rule it was highly unlikely that former council members would ever hold political office again.

In 1965, when lawyer Lynden O. Pindling (who would later become the first Bahamian prime minister under majority rule) threw the speaker's mace out of the upper-floor window of the House of Assembly *(see page 48)*, the Port Authority and foreign interests noted the mood of the country with apprehension.

For a time it was business as usual. A $100-million oil refinery was built shortly thereafter in Freeport, but by 1970 things started to come unglued. The recession in the United States sent a shock wave through the local economy, and due to the government's Bahamianization policy, foreigners found that their re-entry permits were called in, and that they were charged for new permits. Some were not reissued. For a time the licensees of the Port Authority were in revolt and threatened to challenge the government. But the challenge did not last long. The new prime minister, Lynden Pindling, wanted the licensees to

LEFT: Wallace Groves, global magnate and founder of Freeport.

Map on page 191

"bend or be broken." Many foreigners realized they were destined to play no part in the new Bahamas, and they left.

The Port Authority meanwhile looked overseas to diversify, but unsuccessfully, and the foreign real estate ventures were sold off with small financial gain. In 1970 Wallace Groves, in his 70th year, retired as chairman of the Port Authority. When the Bahamas gained its independence from Britain in 1973, the Bahamians from other islands who had sought to make a new life in Freeport found that they needed to make considerable adjustments to their previous lifestyle.

Company town

The unprecedented birth of Freeport as a foreign "company town" put several characteristics in place which carried over, even though with independence there was a fundamental change in the complexion of the city. The open planning of Freeport does not encourage "street society." With wide streets and liberal yards it is not easy to hail your neighbour; there are no corner shops, almost no neighbourhood bars and, perhaps most regrettable of all, few people walk anywhere anyway. This is a mobile society, completely reliant on the automobile.

Visitors from other islands have few places to socialize publicly, and, without family or friends in Freeport, feel the place to be alien, non-Bahamian somehow. Despite this, they can't help noting that the streets are clean, and that water, electrical and telephone services seem to function without a hitch. Charitable commentators find Freeporters "private," "urbane" even. Other, less charitable observers say they are "cold and indifferent." Because of the employment opportunities, Freeporters are sometimes seen as "materialistic" and "competitive," and they demonstrate more variety than other Bahamians in their choice of lifestyles.

For many years the island was unable to receive Bahamian television from Nassau, so the islanders tuned into US TV stations, especially those based in Florida, or

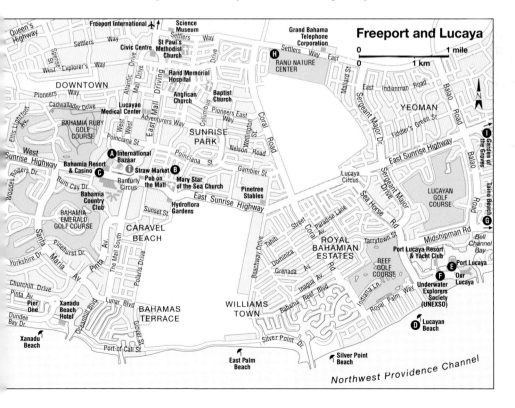

picked up a myriad of programs on back-yard dish antennae. This in turn makes Grand Bahamians more aware of the world (especially the US) and its ways – they have even been accused of being less nationalistic than other Bahamians.

Today, this island's residents have television and internet connectivity which rivals that of any first world community in terms of affordability and reliability. A Freeport resident will shrug off the image of being less patriotic than other Bahamians, suggesting instead that they are more comfortable in their day-to-day contact with internationals – involved with both tourism and the island economy.

Welcome to the bazaar

If you travel by car you will almost certainly enter Freeport by circumnavigating Independence Circle, which bears a sign proudly praising the islands. The Grand Bahama Promotion Board qualifies this sign with one of their own that states more simply, "It's nice to have you here."

Proceeding down the Mall ("Keep left except when overtaking," the sign says, but nobody on the dual carriageway heeds its message) you will pass the Civic Centre site, which contains a court house and several government offices. Next, three Canadian-owned banks occupy the west (right-hand) side of the road, with the main post office just visible behind the Royal Bank of Canada. (Canadian banks hold 80 percent of all deposits in the Bahamas.)

The next set of traffic signals marks the intersection with Pioneers Way, the center of the city. On the left, in a pseudo-colonial building painted lurid pink, the Grand Bahama Port Authority has its headquarters.

A mile south is the **Ranfurly Circus**, a traffic circle named for a popular British colonial governor of the 1950s. Located here is the International Bazaar and several city hotels. This area is a must-see for visitors, if only for the sake of curiosity. The **International Bazaar**  is an

BELOW: the International Bazaar.

Map
on page
191

architectural melange that was better when it was new. Every shop now seems to be touting cheap T-shirts, and the "merchandise-to-fit-the-architecture" rule is largely ignored. Nevertheless, the Bazaar retains some charm. In the words of Jay Mitchell, a local musician:

> *"down to the Bazaar*
> *get what your hearts desire*
> *because it Freeport, Freeport/Lucaya*
> *down to the Bazaar*
> *all the places you want to go,*
> *we got Spain, France, Africa...*
> *we even got Mexico!"*

Cameras and photographic equipment are available at the Ginza in the Oriental section, and a great selection of emeralds and jewelry may be bought at Colombian Emeralds. There is even a free walk through the workshop for anyone interested in seeing the dirty fingernail side of jewelry making. The French Quarter bears a French facsimile street sign, *Place des Wallons*, and features Café Michel, a French-style sidewalk cafe with a lot of atmosphere. An energetic steel drum band sometimes plays nearby. The Spanish section isn't very Spanish, though Casa Miro sells Spanish leather and porcelain.

On the Churchill Pub side of the Bazaar, a Bahamian **Straw Market** Ⓑ is a hive of commercial activity. The straw vendors are always busy sewing on pom poms, chasing their children and hawking their wares, often all at the same time. Locally made straw products are good souvenirs, but a lot of other less appealing merchandise, not made locally, has slipped in. The bazaar area is now the venue for a European-style motor race.

To the west of the Bazaar is the tower of the **Bahamia Resort and Casino** Ⓒ (formerly the Bahamas Princess Resort and Casino). A $50-million hotel refurbishment project is transforming the complex, which comprises two hotel buildings on either side of a spectacular one million-gallon fresh-water "sand pool", with a crescent-shaped man-made white sand beach and two golf courses.

LOW:
eeport's
terfall, at
hamia.

The Moorish-style **Bahamia Casino**, next to the Bazaar, represents the worst of paradise for some. But if gambling is for you, the gaming hall has it all.

Part of West Sunrise Highway has been pedestrianized to allow guests to cross safely between the hotel buildings. On the opposite side of the Highway from the casino is the 565-room **Country Club** at Bahamia. Its rooms are arranged like the spokes of a wheel around a delightful plaza, with hot tubs and a fanciful swimming pool, including a waterfall. Adjacent is the **John B**, an open-air dining room and bar, a charming place to dine or to sip an evening rum punch.

Private Xanadu

West of Ranfurly Circus, past D.K. Ludwig's Bahamia and the 18-hole championship golf courses north and south, are the refinery and the deepwater harbor. On the channel entrance to the harbor is Pier One, built on stilts over the water like a New England fish warehouse, which is a pleas-ant place to dine and watch the cruise ships dock. Continuing straight down the mall you see the ocean for the first time, and **Xanadu Beach Hotel** – formerly the private domain of Howard Hughes, who lived on the sealed-off 12th and 13th floors in total seclusion until his death in 1976.

Travelling east from Ranfurly Circus you will pass the English-style Pub on the Mall, a shrine at **Mary Star of the Sea Church**, erected by Wallace Groves, the small Sunrise Shopping Centre (open after the downtown supermarkets are closed), and the Freeport High School.

Lucayan sand and sun

Another mile and another circle, this time Lucaya Circle, and you reach the Groves/Chesler area of Lucaya. A right turn (south) will bring you to the **Lucayan Beach** . Here, situated on a beautiful white-powder sand beach, are the principal beach hotels of the island.

This area has undergone massive development since it was taken over by a

LEFT: an encounter with a dolphin is a unique experience.

SWIMMING WITH THE DOLPHINS

The Dolphin Experience is situated at Sanctuary Bay, a 9½-acre (4-hectare) lagoon, a short ferryboat ride from the UNEXSO (Underwater Explorers Society) dock at Port Lucaya, along the south shore of Grand Bahama Island. Various programs allow visitors to interact with Atlantic bottlenose dolphins in their marine environment.

As well as an in-water encounter with the mammals, participants can learn about the dolphins, including the gestation period, which is 12 months, weight and life cycle. Most calves stay with their mother for up to two years. The dolphins at Sanctuary Bay are considered to be ambassadors for the marine environment. Visitors to the Experience not only have lots of fun, but also walk away with a heightened awareness of dolphin physiology, and many become conservation advocates.

Although Flipper, the world's most famous dolphin, lives off Nassau and here, Sanctuary Bay has its fair share of celebrities. Four of the group were involved in the feature film *Cocoon*. Other dolphins, such as Kela and Ribala, have appeared in the motion picture *Zeus and Roxanne*, *In the Wild* series with Robin Williams, and Jack Hanna's *Animal Adventures*. The dolphins have even featured in a Bee-Gees music video.

Map
on page
191

large conglomerate, Hutchinson Lucaya, in 1997. Some of the old resorts have been completely demolished to make way for the **Our Lucaya** complex – Harbour Plaza Hotels and Resorts' three-hotel community in Lucaya. It comprises two golf courses, a casino and a sprawling resort with more than 1300 rooms.

A short stroll from Our Lucaya is the festival marketplace at **Port Lucaya ⓔ**. With 85 shops and ongoing entertainment, it is very popular, and there is a refreshing emphasis on Bahamian ingenuity. **Count Basie Square** in the center of the marketplace is a hub of activity, especially during the evening, when there is usually live local entertainment. The bars and restaurants that surround the square and overlook the marina buzz with activity.

To the north, across from the hotels, is an extensive man-made canal system, with several small waterfront hotels and the largest yacht basin on the island, the **Port Lucaya Resort and Yacht Club**. A stone's throw away are two 18-hole golf

courses, Our Lucaya's Reef Course and the Lucayan Course. The **Butch Harmon School of Golf** (tel: 373-1333) is on the Lucayan course. Designed by the man who teaches pro golf sensation, Tiger Woods, it offers hourly and daily golf classes for first timers and professionals.

The Lucayan Beach area is where most of the action is. In the daytime there are organized boat trips for fishing and snorkeling, and the **Underwater Explorers Society** (UNEXSO) **ⓕ** (tel: 373-1244) offers splendid facilities for scuba divers and the chance for an in-water encounter with dolphins. If just sitting in the sun is not enough, you can parasail or hire a Boston whaler, windsurfer or Hobe Cat.

East of the hotel strip and Bell Channel is tiny and pristine **Taino Beach ⓖ**, which offers an authentic experience that is a world away from the nearby luxurious resorts. Under a thatched roof, cooking his famous roast conch, is Tony Macaroni (a.k.a. Anthony Hanna). Several days a week he serves conch (sometimes lobster)

BELOW:
low tide at
Taino Beach.

roasted in a blend of lime and secret seasonings. Though the meal is served in foil and you'll be eating with a plastic fork, this is likely to be a delicious introduction to Bahamian cuisine and hospitality. Don't bother trying to extract the secret recipe from Tony Macaroni. Instead, pull up a deck chair and prepare for a lesson on the history and culture of the island.

Taino Beach is also the location of weekly fish fries. Locals and vistors converge on Taino Beach on Wednesday for a friendly and relaxed evening of dancing, fuelled by delicious Bahamian fare.

Flamingo pink

If you'd prefer a quieter, more contemplative mood, do not despair. Taxi and bus operators will take visitors around Freeport, identifying "Mr Grove house" (now owned by a wealthy German industrialist), the Sir "Union" Jack Hayward abode, some upper-middle-class housing and a glimpse of downtown. Some of these trips end up with free drinks and the

opportunity to sign on the dotted line for time-sharing privileges. Others take the adventurous to the small settlements engulfed by Freeport or to the pleasantly tranquil Taino and Fortune beaches.

Map on page 191

The **Rand Nature Center** ❶ (open Mon–Fri 9am–4pm, Sat 9am–1pm; entrance fee; tel: 352-5438) is worth seeing. Near the center of Freeport, the reserve has interesting nature trails, and a knowledgeable Bahamian guide can explain the flora and fauna of the island. Run by the Bahamas National Trust, the 100-acre (40-hectare) national park, located off Settler's Way, has a variety of wildlife, including a flock of West Indian Flamingos.

Continuing east from Freeport and Lucaya you come to the 12-acre (5-hectare) **Garden of the Groves** ❶ (open Mon–Sat 9am–4pm, Sun 10am–4pm; entrance fee; tel: 373-5668). Located at the corner of Midshipman Road and Magellan Drive, this is a spectacular botanical garden, which opened in 1973. Created for the Bahamian people by Georgette and Wallace Groves, the garden has exotic (and labeled) trees, plants and shrubs from all over the world. There are also cool, cascading waterfalls, flamingos and a lush fern gully, that make it a popular venue for wedding parties and picnics. There is also a small chapel and a zoo which has African pygmy goats, Vietnamese pot bellied pigs, alligators, macaws and cockatoos. Guided tours of the garden are available.

The **Grand Bahama Museum**, on the same site as the Garden of Groves captures the history of the island with reconstructed caves, a marine exhibit and audiovisual presentations. There are also Lucayan Amerindian and pirate-era artifacts. In the small garden attached to the museum is a native house reconstructed from local pine lumber. The wood was actually cannibalized from the first airport terminal of Freeport. On the way out, note the driving wheels of a steam locomotive that once served the lumber industry of the island.

Freeport, in its short existence, has certainly known the boom-and-bust cycle that has typified much of Bahamian history. More may yet come. ❑

LEFT: pretty in pink flora.
RIGHT: pink plumage at the Garden of the Groves.

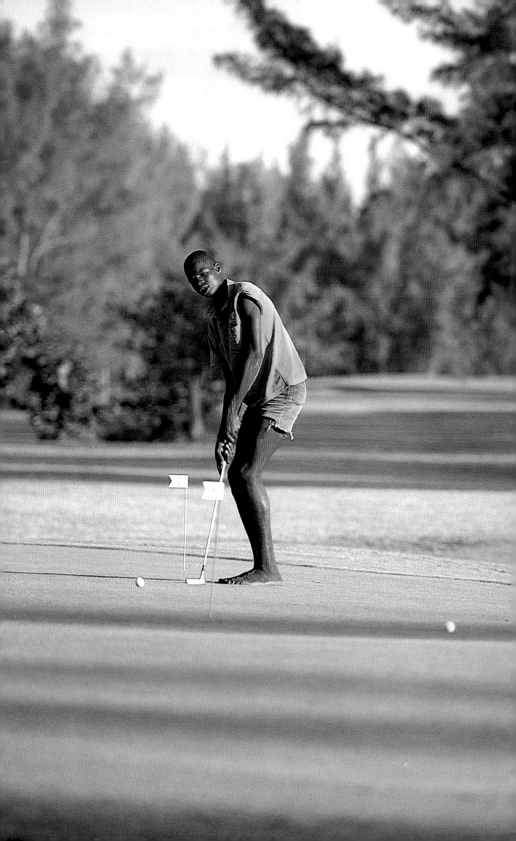

Map on page 200

GRAND BAHAMA

This is an ideal place for escapists, with miles of white sandy beach,
a remarkable reef rich with marine life, fabulous fishing,
and fragrant forests and mangroves

With the arrival of the Hutchison Whampoa Container Port in 1997, and the subsequent opening of the mega-resort, Our Lucaya, few will argue that there has been a major resurgence in the economy of Grand Bahama.

This is not a place with wild nightlife, though lively bars do exist. Instead, be prepared for miles of sandy beach, dozens of places with exceptional cuisine, and a real respect for the environment evidenced by the wide variety of ecotourist activities.

With a maximum elevation of 50 ft (15 meters), Grand Bahama does not have the visual impact of many of the world's great volcanic islands. The island, part of a lime-stone platform thousands of feet thick, had rather a more peaceful genesis.

Wrecking and opportunism

Grand Bahama is the most northerly island of the Bahamas and is thus the first island most visitors from the north will see. In early times it was a place to avoid. Before lighthouses and modern naviga-tional aides were introduced, there was constant danger of shipwreck on the outer fringes of the Little Bahama Bank. The island of Grand Bahama lies along the southern boundary of this vast expanse of shallow water, some 10 to 30 ft (3 to 9 meters) deep.

Seaborne traffic around the Bank, and especially through the 65-mile (106-km) wide Straits of Florida, was plagued by numerous wrecks. Indeed, for over a cen-tury, salvaging wrecks was a way of life in the Bahamas, the government regulating the occupation. And if faulty navigation – aggravated by deliberately confusing beacons – was not the cause of a wreck, there was the constant danger of pirates. With the decline in piracy, the building of lighthouses, including the Great Isaac Light in 1859, and improved charting of the seabed, the dangers lessened.

The people of Grand Bahama returned to subsistence living, but, always astute in the ways of the world, they soon reaped a bonanza by acting as a supply depot for Confederate forces in the American Civil War. Later, they tried their hands at spong-ing, at providing liquor to the United States in the 13 years of Prohibition, and as a well-placed conduit for the supply of illicit drugs to North America.

The original settlers of the Bahamas were the Siboney, a primitive stone-age culture which disappeared with the arriv-al of the Lucayan Indians. The Lucayans were a branch of the Island Arawak Indian group, who first colonized the Turks and Caicos Islands, then later the entire Bahamian archipelago. How many lived

LEFT: a caddy resting out the green.
RIGHT: where to get off in Eight Mile Rock.

on Grand Bahama we do not know, but when Ponce de Leon visited Grand Bahama in 1513 he found only one old woman "*la vieja*" at or near what is today West End. The remainder of her people had probably died from diseases brought by the white man to which they had no immunity, or they had been transported to work in the mines of Hispaniola and Cuba, where certain death awaited them.

Ponce de Leon left two men on the northern island to look for the fabled "Fountain of Youth" while he continued on to what he called Florida (for *Pascua Flor-ida*, the Easter Day of Flowers or Easter Sunday). He returned to Puerto Rico and then traveled onto Spain, where he received the title of *Don* and *Adelantao* of Florida and Bimini, which presumably included the island of Grand Bahama.

Treasure ships

Grand Bahama takes its name from the Spanish *gran bajamar* (the great shallows or, literally, the vast underwater). The Spaniards had reason to note the shallows, for the reefs and shoals on the island's outer edge were to be approached only at grave peril. Later, the entire country derived its name from these shallows.

The Grand Bahama islands may have been the only land base many pirates ever knew. They lived their harsh, cruel lives aboard ship, but from time to time they needed to refit their vessels. Remote, uninhabited islands such as Grand Bahama would make passable havens, even though safe channels and anchorages were minimal.

In 1628 a Dutch privateer made an audacious raid at Matanzas Bay in Cuba and carried away several treasure ships. For reasons unknown, one of the prize ships broke away and sank in shallow water off the south shore of Grand Bahama. It was found in 1965 and con-tained 10,000 silver coins, valued at any-where from $2 to $9 million.

In 1655 a large convoy set sail from Cartagena en route to Spain. It refitted and

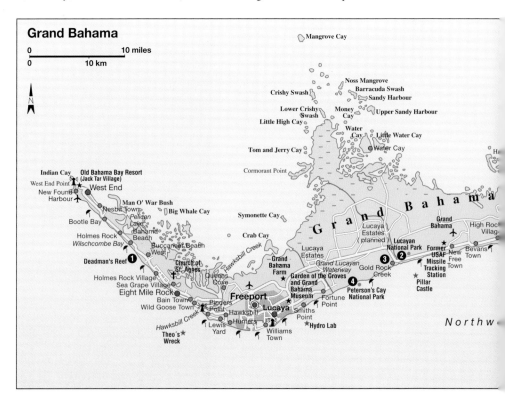

Map below

sailed from Havana on January 1, 1656. Three days later *Nuestra Señora della Maravilla* sailed into shallow water near Memory Rock, north of West End, and tried to warn the other ships of the dangers. In the confusion that followed, the *Maravilla* was struck by another ship and started sinking in 50 ft (15 meters) of water. The winter weather had turned foul, and salvage operations were delayed for six months. It was estimated that only a quarter of the treasure was recovered. The *Maravilla* was rediscovered in 1972 and became the richest treasure found in the Bahamas in recent history. Salvage work began anew on the site in 1984, continuing through 1988.

Governor Phenney, writing in 1721, confirms that Grand Bahama had no population but noted that the island had fine timber (indeed the island is today largely covered by pine forest) and "white land" along the south coast which, he predicted, would yield fair crops of corn. In 1772 a sale of 240 acres (96 hectares) was record-ed, and the island started to be permanently inhabited in the early 19th century.

First settlement

By 1836 the island had a population of 370. **Golden Grove** became the administrative center of the island, presumably because of its central location and the small channel entrance which could accommodate skiffs but not much else.

Almost a century later the population was just 1,700. Then Prohibition was introduced in the United States and West End became an important center for trans-shipment of liquor. The boom ended in 1933 when Prohibition ended. The Commissioner who had been relocated to West End to "administer" the busy nest of boot-leggers was moved to Eight Mile Rock, near the mouth of Hawksbill Creek.

West End's main street is lined with bars, shops and houses. There is a service station, a small clinic and a straw market. This is a good place to hire a boat to go bonefishing *(see pages 125–7)* – a pastime

GHT: a jewel ashed up on ore.

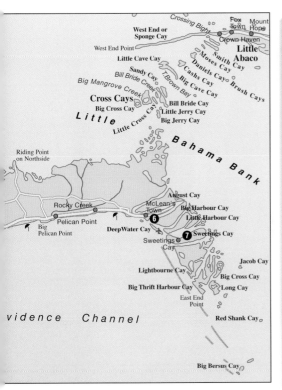

especially reserved by the government for tourists. Mountains of empty conch shells suggest the principal food staple of the inhabitants of West End.

At the western end of the coastal road are the remains of Jack Tar Village. Once this was one of the most self-sufficient hostelries in the Bahamas, with its own private jetport, marina, PGA-ranked 27-hole golf course (with nine links holes) and commissary.

The original buildings were constructed by Sir Billy Butlin (of British holiday camp fame) in 1948. In a master stroke of foresight, Butlin located his "holiday camp" on the nearest point of Grand Bahama to the United States. For a time it seemed that West End would enjoy the kind of tourist surge that Nassau was attracting. But with construction delays, a devaluation of the British pound and finally jittery creditors, the hotel was closed down a year after it opened.

"Welcome to that perfect piece of the world," states the sign at the entrance to the former Jack Tar complex, which has been re-born as the **Old Bahama Bay Resort**. A 45-minute drive from Freeport, it has a 70-slip marina and diners can enjoy a drink or a meal al fresco at the waterfront restaurant and bar. The upscale resort also has a snorkeling program, and trail guides are available for adventurous guests who want to explore the surrounding area. The elegant suites in one of six pastel-colored, two-story bungalows face either the marina or the beach.

Rocks and caves

The other settlements between West End and Freeport are positioned along the government road or **Queen's Highway**, its proper name. Just after leaving West End you come to Bootle Bay, a small canal development which is partly developed. Not so the other "subdivisions", farther along this route, which are rapidly being reclaimed by the bush. A good place to stop for lunch is Harry's American Bar, which occupies a beachfront site and also offers

BELOW: a roadside stal in West End.

Map on page 200

rooms for rent. A mile farther east is the **Buccaneer Club**, the best restaurant on the island outside of Freeport.

There is good diving off the cays at **Deadman's Reef ❶** near Holmes Rock. Close by is Paradise Cove, ideal for visitors wanting to get away from it all. This small, family-owned collection of simple apartments and cottages sits on a sheltered stretch of well-kept beach that fronts the reef. The Cove, which is a just a short distance from the Buccaneer Club, offers watersports, and the reef provides hours of spectacular underwater sights.

From Holmes Rock there is almost continual development of a more modest sort all the way to the Freeport "bonded area" boundary.

The small Catholic **Church of St Agnes**, just south of Sea Grape Village, is worthy of note and farther down the same road, **Peace and Plenty** on the seafront provides excellent Bahamian cuisine. It is wise to telephone before visiting.

Eight Mile Rock is exactly that: 8 miles (13 km) of rocky foreshore stretching east and west of **Hawksbill Creek**. It is, in actuality, a dormitory suburb of Freeport, though it is now home to the commissioner for the west end of the island. Across the Hawksbill Creek Causeway are Pinders Point, Lewis Yard and Hunters, the eastern half of the 8 miles (13 km) of rock immediately south of Freeport.

"Towns" in the Bahamas can consist of as little as two houses which often bear the names of the incumbents. Traveling along the oceanfront you will see an interesting "**boiling hole**" next to the coastal road. Boiling holes are entrances to subterranean cave systems, and differ from "blue holes" since the water coming out of them is under pressure and appears to "boil." Visitors to the boiling hole are invited to see the bottling and packing process of the water, here.

Hunters has a good Bahamian restaurant called Freddie's that serves dinner. The ambience is ho-hum but the food is usually excellent. Offshore is another boiling

LOW: clutter conch shells Hawksbill eek.

hole, the **Chimney**, which creates a vortex in both directions depending on the tide. Below is an extensive cave system, but viewing is best accomplished in the company of a qualified cave diver.

Williams Town and **Russell Town** occupy a beautiful stretch of beach just south of Freeport, at the southern end of Beachway Drive (a road much used for trekking by equestrians from the Pinewood Riding stables).

Nearby, a cemetery contains the mortal remains of many of the villagers. Just outside the cemetery is a simple monument surmounted by a cross that reads: "In memory of our twenty-one Haitian brothers and sisters who died at Sea 19th, July 1973. Ke pose yi." The unfortunate Haitians drowned just off Williams Town while trying to sail to the United States as would-be immigrants.

The small beachfront communities **Smiths Point** and **Mather Town** are geographically in Freeport but outside the "bonded area." The White Wave Club is the place for a cool drink in Smiths Point. The Caribe Club in Mathers Town, on the other side of the canal entrance, has good local food and fronts rights onto a gorgeous white sand beach. It is an excellent place for brunch.

Excursions

A worthwhile excursion might be a visit to Water Cay, situated just east of the bulge in the north coast of Grand Bahama. Access is difficult. If you have a boat you can get there from Hawksbill Creek or via the Grand Lucayan Waterway.

Another, less sure way of gaining access is to drive through the Lucaya "country" subdivisions to the north shore dock. With luck, a returning resident or an alert boatman might pick you up. A trip to the cay is worthwhile, since it is the most unspoiled settlement of Grand Bahama, with simple dwellings, luxuriant vegetation and no motor vehicles.

About the only point on the north coast that is easily accessible is Dover Sound.

LEFT: a bird keeps watch. **RIGHT:** a parrot at Lucayan National Park

Map
n page
200

To the parks

A less arduous and very rewarding side trip is to **Lucayan National Park** ❷ (open daily 9am–4pm; entrance fee; tel: 352 5438). It is only 13 miles (21 km) east from Freeport's Garden of the Groves *(see page 196)*, but the journey through the pine forest may seem endless.

As you continue along the main road towards the Lucayan National Park, stay alert for the sign. Once there, pull off into the parking area and consult the visitor orientation signboard, which illustrates the pathway system and gives some background information on the park. Yes, that's right, "the largest explored underwater cave system in the world" is right under your feet.

The park has an extensive "figure eight" pathway system which takes visitors into two caves and up to a lookout point. (The second cave opening has yielded some Lucayan Amerindian artifacts and human bones, now preserved in the Grand Bahama Museum close to Freeport.)

The 40-acre (16 hectare) park contains nature trails along which visitors can explore rich forests of tropical vegetation such as cedar and mahogany, and dense healthy mangroves that are populated by abundant birdlife.

The route to the national park will take you over the **Grand Lucayan Waterway**, a $30-million canal bisecting the island and a monument to the confidence the early developers had. When the straight road through the pine forest finally curves south (right) look out for a film studio on your left-hand side. The studio was stillborn when the Freeport bubble burst in the late 1960s.

At the next bend in the road – this time left – take the turn-off for Old Free Town. The villagers were removed when their land was purchased by the Port Authority and were relocated in New Free Town. All that is left are a few walls, a hibiscus bush or two and some fruit trees. Of primary interest in Old Free Town are the **blue holes** located near here.

LOW:
orkeling
hts.
HT: blue
e, Lucayan
tional Park.

Left of the turn-off road is a long and innocent looking swamp, which is actually the entrance to a cave system. Nearly a mile west of the cutoff road is a concealed pathway to **Mermaids Lair**, another surface opening to an underwater cave system. Farther inland (and joined to Mermaids Lair by water-filled caves) is the bell-shaped **Owl Hole**, a "cenote" of impressive proportions. The mouth of this hole is 35 ft (11 meters) above the water, and the walls dumbbell inwards with small limestone stalactites hanging down.

South of the road leading to the park the pathway leads to a bridge which crosses **Gold Rock Creek ❸**. A trip by canoe down this 2-mile (3-km) long creek has to be one of the most memorable inland sights of Grand Bahama. Once across the bridge and through the mangroves, the sea and the small islet **Gold Rock** become visible. The dunes are among the highest on the island and the deserted beach is exquisite – proof that it may indeed be, as the locals claim, "Better in the Bahamas."

A Bahamas National Trust property worth visiting is **Peterson's Cay National Park ❹**. This is located a mile or so east of the entrance to the Grand Lucayan Waterway. You will need a boat, a mask and snorkel. The reef around this cay is spectacular. Opposite the cay is **Barbary Beach** and the uninhabited hermitage – originally a church, built in 1901, which was occupied in the early days of Freeport by a former Trappist monk.

Eastern rocks

On leaving Lucayan National Park and the eastern boundary of the port area, for a moment you are in a US military base. This is Gold Rock Missile Tracking Station, and, though it is not overly active nowadays, the base shows evidence of its former importance when it was the first down-range station from Cape Canaveral. This general area is called **Gold Rock** (formerly known as Golden Grove) and incorporates a small village of relocated islanders, **New Free Town**.

BELOW: domino playe at High Rock

Map on page 200

The most impressive structure in New Free Town is the "Baptis (*sic*) Church, Ded. September 13, 1981, Rev. Cleveland Cooper Pastor," according to the sign. A little farther down the road is the remaining facade of Zion Baptist Church. Groceries in New Free Town may be purchased from "Chicken Man."

Down the road is Bevans Town, with the Three Sisters Restaurant and the Star Club. Most important here is the service station – the only place where vehicle repairs are possible in eastern Grand Bahama.

The administrative center for the east end of the island is at **High Rock ❺**. This is a charming little village situated on a low bluff above the sea some 5 miles (8 km) east of the Port Area. The sign says it all:

Welcome to High Rock where the scenery is beautiful and the people peaceful and friendly so enjoy your stay with us. —*The residents*

Ezekiel Pinder's Oceanview Restaurant is the place to eat. If you wish, you can carry your meal across the shore road to a palm thatch hut and look at the sea while the waves crash on the rocks below you. Some of the older frame houses are worthy of note at High Rock. Also note that the settlement has a police station, a public library, a cemetery and a side-by-side public "john." From High Rock the road eastwards gets progressively worse.

End of the road

Cast your eyes upwards for a moment and you may see Fat Albert, the World War II barrage balloon, peeping through the clouds in the service of the Drug Enforcement Administration. The balloon is tethered at the Burmah Oil Transhipment Depot which, in more optimistic times, was intended by the government to be the nucleus of another industrial area on the island. **Pelican Point** is situated on what is probably the widest beach on the island. This is also the last place that gasoline is available for sale.

Leaving Pelican Point, a graded road serves the east end of the island. The

LOW: a colorful country fruit stall.

beach track is much more interesting, but check that the tide is not high, and avoid it if there has been recent rainfall, unless your vehicle is a four-wheel drive.

It is easy to miss the turn-off to **Rocky Creek**. This would be a pity because the settlement consists of three or four small houses, but more significantly, includes a **blue hole** in an inlet off the sea. The blue hole is a natural sea aquarium for many species of marine life.

Just cracking

Finally, or almost, the intrepid explorer arrives at **McLean's Town** ⓺, the last mainland settlement on the east of the island. Whereas West End has a thriving deep sea fishing industry, McLean's Town claims to have cornered the island's specialist and flourishing (for tourists) bone-fishing market. This small community has good shallow water anchorage and is famous throughout the islands for its lively **Conch Cracking Contest**, held every year on Columbus Day.

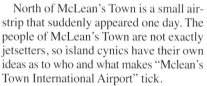
Map on page 200

"Cracking" a conch is a three-step process. First, the conch has to be hit with an axe or similar object at exactly the right spot to break the shell where the animal is attached. This leaves the characteristically oval-shaped hole seen on most conches not in their customary marine habitat. Then the conch is "jewked" (removed) from the shell by grasping the "claw" or foot (actually an operculum). Finally the slimy foot-long (30-cm) animal is cleaned and dumped in a bucket. An expert conch cracker can dispose of about 20 in five minutes.

North of McLean's Town is a small airstrip that suddenly appeared one day. The people of McLean's Town are not exactly jetsetters, so island cynics have their own ideas as to who and what makes "Mclean's Town International Airport" tick.

Farther exploration from this part of the island must be by boat. Just across Runners creek is the **Deep Water Cay** development, which has some small guesthouses and a bush airstrip.

The most easterly habitation of the island is at **Sweetings Cay** ⓻, a neat and tidy place. It was settled when sponging was the primary industry of the Little Bahamas Bank. There are a few places for refreshment, including the Travellers Rest and the Seagarden Bar. Nearby is a small tourist development which offers cottages for rent. Like on Water Cay, there are no vehicles on this tranquil "out island" cay.

Exploring Nature's bounty

Sweetings Cay, Lightbourne Cay, and Water Cay have begun developing birding excursions for the growing number of ecotourists who visit the Bahamas because of its naturally rich marine and birdlife. Brown pelicans, blue herons, egrets and laughing gulls live in the forests and mangrove swamps at this end of the island.

As Grand Bahama's population of around 30,000 continues to grow, it retains the spirit of a new frontier. Meanwhile, its occupants bask in the serenity of spaciousness, replete with all of the perks of a modern high-tech society. ❏

LEFT: jewking a conch. **RIGHT:** conch meat and shells.

THE OUT ISLANDS

Perfect for getting away from it all, these remote islands are the Bahamas' best-kept secrets – nature flourishes, the people are friendly, the pace of life is relaxed, and sandy beaches are lapped by clear seas

You've survived the storm; your ship is battered, but you finally limp into a quiet, deserted cove and drop anchor. On the shore you see a hand-lettered sign: "Columbus landed here." The scene is imaginary, but not impossible, for the paths of early explorers indeed crisscrossed these islands – Columbus, eyes peeled for the gold and spices of Cathay; Ponce de Leon in search of the Fountain of Youth; pirates needing secluded landfalls to rendezvous, take on water and hide treasure.

Called the Family Islands during the 1980s, but now more commonly referred to by their original name, the Out Islands are remote, beautiful and mysterious. To many people they are the real Bahamas,

the heart of this complex and diverse country. They are hardly "out" for travelers with a sense of adventure.

It would take years to discover all the secrets and pleasures of these islands – the friendly settlements of the Exumas; the piney woods of Andros; sunbaked Bimini; the trim, seafaring villages of the Abacos.

We start the coverage of the Out Islands with the Biminis, the islands closest to the United States, and travel in a leisurely fashion to the farthest, the strange and fascinating island of Inagua. It is doubtful, however, that any but the most hearty yachtsman would wish to visit the Bahama islands in this order. Travelers with a week or two to spare should concentrate on one or two islands. Today, just

PRECEDING PAGES: shade of a Marsh Harbour evening. **BELOW:** Hope Town, Elbow Cay in Abaco.

Map
on pages
136–37

as throughout the Bahamas' history, island hopping, or a whirlwind multi-island tour, is not a practical enterprise.

Clear as well water in a china cup, borrowing dappled ribbons of color from the blue of the sky, the pristine sea around the Bahama islands is a thin skin covering treacherous reef, bars and shoals. Covering more than 90,000 sq. miles (230,000 sq. km), it makes every island a castle – surrounded by a moat with no drawbridge.

Linking the chain

For most of the Bahamas' history, communication and commerce between the islands was difficult and sporadic. The Out Islands were truly "out," and in the mid-19th century even Nassau did not enjoy regular steamship connections with New York. (An act of parliament in 1851 offered an annual bounty of £1,000 to anyone who would provide a "good, substantial and efficient" steamship service between New York and Nassau.)

Sailors knew how to read these waters –

sandbars, grassy patches, deep channels are all described by the sea's color – and, if they didn't, they joined the many shipwrecks in the Bahamas' "Davey Jones' locker." Boat-building was both art and industry in the Out Islands, but the best sailing skills could not keep these islands from being chronically isolated. The words of the old spiritual, "In the sweet bye and bye, we will meet on that beautiful shore," must have had a temporal as well as a religious significance. To sail from Miami or Fort Lauderdale to Bimini took (and still does) a good 12 hours; from Nassau to Long Island, several days.

When a man named Arthur Burns "Pappy" Chalk began flying a three-seat Stinson Voyager between Florida and the Bahamas in 1919, a new era in Bahamian travel began. Pappy's chief customers on the Voyager and a Curtiss HS-2L floatplane were bootleggers; the cargo was whiskey and rum to slake the thirst of American Prohibition. No one suspected that Chalk's Airlines would still be in

BELOW: wildlife
Allan's
ys, Exuma.

operation decades later – the oldest continuously operating airline in the world.

By 1933, when Prohibition was repealed, Pappy Chalk was still in business, with headquarters on Miami's Watson Island. Judy Garland, Errol Flynn and Howard Hughes flew Chalk's seaplanes to the Bahamas – taking off in a foamy wake, droning low over the water, landing with a splash. A flight to one of Chalk's three current destinations – Bimini, Cat Cay and Paradise Island – can be a sightseeing tour in itself. Fishing boats, reefs, fish and starfish glide by beneath the wings.

With its near perfect safety record (except for one hijacking to Cuba in the early 1970s) and reliable adherence to schedules, barring weather conditions that might make flying unsafe, Chalk's Airlines is a top choice for Bahamian travel.

For travel to most of the Out Islands, Bahamians opt for the national carrier, Bahamasair. A sight more common than the elusive flamingo is one of Bahamasair's blue and yellow Hawker-Siddeleys.

These British-made planes carry up to 48 passengers, and they're almost always filled with businessmen, grandmothers, children, tourists, suitcases and cardboard boxes. When the two propellors start to whir, get ready for a ride over some of the world's most colorful seas on what is essentially an inter-island bus. The conventional wisdom warns that only the first flight of the day is on time. (Like most adages, this one has a basis in truth.) Bahamians will tell you, "If you have some time to spare, be sure to fly Bahamasair," adding that the airline's safety record is excellent. These workhorse planes fly from 7.30am until night (sometimes only until sunset), linking the islands with a little confusion and a lot of goodwill.

Tying loose

Old-timers, however, remember when travel to another island meant not "taking off" but "tying loose." In the early part of this century, Bahamian-built two-masted schooners plied the turquoise seas, serving

BELOW: a Chalk's seaplane splashes dow

Map
on pages
136–37

as mother ships for fleets of sponge-fishing dinghies. In the 1920s they made rum runs to the US. Single-masted fishing smacks, 20–40 ft (6–12 meters) long, also sometimes carried travelers between the islands. Fish voyaged to market in watery darkness in live wells in the hulls, while above them seven to 10 passengers and crew cooked, ate and slept on the open deck.

The government mailboats provided the only regular service to most Out Islands – first by sail, later by diesel power. Today, these battered boats with their peeling paint and roughneck crews are still the link that gets the mail sack, cars, chickens, diesel drums and foodstuffs to the far flung islands. *Bahamas Daybreak, Bimini Mac, Current Pride, Eleuthera Express, Captain Moxey* and others make weekly trips between Nassau and one or two of the Out Islands, and if the old *Lady D* or *Lady Gloria* is carrying you home or on an adventure, she can seem like a goddess.

One of these goddesses can be yours for close to US$50 for a one-way ticket, which can be purchased at the harbormaster's office at Potter's Cay, Nassau. The price is hardly cheaper than Bahamasair, and the boats' safety record is not as good, but that is the price you pay for adventure. You can look over the boats and crews at Potter's Cay dock, where they all begin and end their journeys, and where you will soon learn that these sometimes fickle ladies are not wedded to a fixed schedule. A bunk to sleep in and store belongings are the only amenities guaranteed to passengers, but on some boats you will have clean sheets, home-cooked Bahamian food, congenial companionship, and always the sea and the stars.

However you reach the Out Islands, the first thing to remember is that these are the islands most Bahamians call home. Ask a Bahamian, whether in Nassau, Freeport or New York, "Where are you from?" and in the response you will almost always hear a note of pride and nostalgia. "I come from Eleuthera," or Mangrove Cay, or Marsh Harbour. ❏

BELOW: unloading the mailboat's cargo.

Map
on page
225

THE BIMINI ISLANDS

*A popular vacation spot of the rich and famous since the 1930s,
these islands still offer some of the world's best sport fishing.
Some believe the waters here hide a link to the lost city of Atlantis*

The Bimini Islands are the only group in the Bahamas whose deep-water "weather" side faces west. In the long summer of 1935, Ernest Hemingway told friends that the discovery of Bimini was one of the great events in his life, and he got these islands down on paper in the novel *Islands In The Stream* – no less true, he might argue, for its being fiction.

At the closest point they are less than 50 miles (80 km) from Florida; and from North Bimini on a clear night you can see the glow of Miami's lights. Since the 1930s, the rich and talented from Key West to Wall Street have made Bimini their lawless vacation suburb – a place where Ernest Hemingway fought, drank, brawled, bullied, fished and wrote his way through several seasons.

The islands are as flat as bonefish, and the string extends 28 miles (45 km), with large North Bimini and South Bimini on the top, running down to Turtle Rocks, Piquet Rocks, Holm Cay, Gun Cay, North and South Cat Cays, Sandy Cay and Ocean Cay. Seen from the air the upper arm of North Bimini looks like a giant gray-green crab claw floating low on the surface of the sea.

Alice Town

Wearing a girl's name is all that is feminine about **Alice Town ❶** *(see page 224)*, a flea-bitten, raucous, but charming town where a good boat, a good catch, or, lacking that, a souped-up Mitsubishi pickup truck, will get you farther than any sweet talking. Whether docking by boat or flying in by seaplane to **North Bimini ❷**, the first street you see in Alice Town will be the narrow, dusty King's Highway, where the bars outnumber the shops, and traffic is two-way only if both drivers are willing. Local people have discovered the freewheeling eco-friendliness of the golf cart, which they overload with oil drums, shop-ping and children. The effect is charming by day, alarming by night, when most drive without lights whilst under the influence.

King's Highway takes a lot of its character from the time of day: in early morning the town seems empty, the sandy street golden, the shuttered buildings (mostly pastel except for the rust-colored Red Lion Pub) contrite. A sunburned man in a T-shirt walks by carrying an ice chest. Someone has started the coffee in **Captain Bob's Conch Hall of Fame** and a few people are inside at the lunch counter. By the time the sun's full up in the sky the fishermen are out on their boats; the town can daydream or go back to sleep as the sun heats up the street.

Later on, women come out to sell fruit

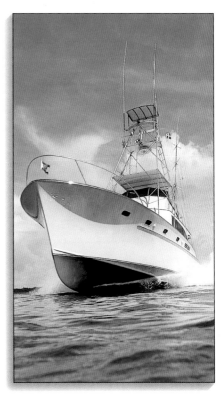

and straw baskets in the shade of the tin-roofed marketplace. The children are in school, and the potcakes (Bahamian hound dogs) move from sunny doorsteps to lie in the shade.

When the Chalks seaplane roars in from Florida on schedule, winging over the island and landing with a splash in **Bimini Harbour**, it's like Big Ben chiming in the afternoon. A few new tourists arrive; Biminites head for the terminal to pick up packages, to pick up a cab fare, to greet arriving friends or relatives.

In *Islands In The Stream* Ernest Hemingway wrote: "It was cool [in the bar] and almost dark after the glare of the coral road and [he] had a gin and tonic water with a piece of lime peel in the glass and a few drops of Angostura in the drink. Mr Bobby was behind the bar looking terrible. Four Negro boys were playing billiards, occasionally lifting the table when necessary to bring off a difficult carom... Two of the crew of the yacht that was tied up at the slip were in the bar and as Thomas Hudson's eyes slip adjusted to the light it was dim and cool and pleasant."

The **End of the World Bar**, with its sand floor and back door open to the harbor, would be a good place for the first drink, or a good place to wait for people to come in off the boats. When the sun starts to set, the fishing boats come in with their sunburned, beer-bellied fishermen, and once it's dark the mosquitoes come out, and then the town begins to hop.

Compleat Angler

The hotel where Ernest Hemingway used to stay is not content to remember; it likes to live up to its reputation. The bar in the **Compleat Angler**, with its polished wood walls, red leather-cushioned stools and captains' chairs, is where most visitors to Alice Town whoop it up. Personalized auto license plates decorate the wood panelling, and the rows of bottles behind the bar beckon yachtsmen.

It's after dinner when the walls begin to shake, so if you're early you might check

BELOW: a view of Bimini as you arrive by air.

Map on page 225

out the library-cum-museum dedicated to Hemingway memorabilia – snapshots of the writer posing beside monstrous fish, smiling in gracious camaraderie with friends, sophisticated sportsmen and women of the 1930s. These are scattered on panelled walls that gleam with varnish like the most fastidious sea captain's cabin, amid cracked leather upholstery, a pair of backgammon tables and a few tattered volumes. It's an outdoorsman's library no question – though, sadly, most of the books have been removed by human magpies.

Back in the entrance hall, a local band – calypso, rock, amplified – is setting up, and tough luck for anyone who thinks he's going to hole up in the library or climb those polished wood stairs and get some sleep in the rooms above the bar.

A wild night out

The local action at the **Hy Star Disco** is heating up. If you're not up for that, you might pop into the **Red Lion Pub** for a bowl of conch chowder beneath framed newspaper articles on world-record size marlin and signed photos of Miami Dolphin football players. The tables and walls are the battered sort where you might find some boozy fisherman has carved his girlfriend's name.

Back out in the wild night, a few yachtsmen are relaxing on their boats at the dock. It wasn't that different in Hemingway's day: "It was a fine night and after they had eaten dinner they sat out in the stern with coffee and cigars, and a couple of other people, both worthless sporting characters, came over from one of the other boats with a guitar," Hemingway wrote. "There was quite a lot of celebration going on at Bobby's place and you could see the lights… over the water."

Don't forget, as you revel in the haze of a warm, festive night, that the people out on the docks are the reason for most of the action on Bimini. By sunrise most of them will be up, and sport fishing will once again be the island's king.

GHT: divers enjoy the nance of e deep.

BIMINI ROAD

The fascination with the lost city of Atlantis dates back to Plato in 300 BC. For centuries it was accepted as a Mediterranean story, centered on a volcanic explosion which destroyed most of the Greek island of Thira. The resulting tidal wave is said to have inspired the Bible story about Noah and wiped out the entire Minoan civilization.

In the 1930s, American Edgar Cayce, known as the sleeping prophet for his ability to slip into hypnotic trances, predicted that an Atlantean temple, dating from 50,000 BC would be discovered off the coast of North Bimini.

Cayce was dismissed as a fruitcake until the 1960s, when an airline pilot reported distinctive geometric bands of color in the water near Paradise Point.

Dr. Manson Valentine, curator of the Miami Science Museum, was prompted to lead an exploration team. They found hundreds of flat rocks, 8 ft (2 meters) square and 2 ft (1 meter) thick, weighing 10 tons each, stretching in an orderly row, half a mile long. Geological tests revealed that the stones were not made of rock occurring in the area. This led to the supposition that they were brought to Bimini by Atlanteans. Some claim they were laid down by extra-terrestrials. Today, the stones, known as the Bimini Road, attract only a trickle of visitors interested in myths.

Hemingway in Bimini

Before Ernest Hemingway discovered Bimini in 1935, the island was not unknown – as some of the writer's fans, and perhaps Hemingway himself, liked to think. Sportsmen in the know, mainly ones with a good deal of money, fished the Gulf Stream and stopped off for rest and relaxation on this little island throughout the 1930s.

According to Hemingway's biographer Carlos Baker, the inimitable writer-adventurer heard of Bimini in 1933 or 1934 when he was spending time at his home in Key West, Florida. But he needed a boat to get there So, in 1934 he bought the *Pilar*. She was a 38-ft (12-meter) diesel-powered cruiser that could do 16 knots on a flat sea; her cabin slept six, with room for one more in the cockpit. She was painted black.

On the first trip to Bimini, on April 7, 1935,

ERNEST HEMINGWAY WITH TWO SAIL FISHES

Ernest Hemingway set out on the *Pilar* with John Dos Passos and four others. They trolled on the way, and when Hemingway hooked a large shark he brought it alongside the boat and blasted its head with a barrage of bullets. As he fired, the gaff broke, Hemingway slipped, and he shot himself in both legs. In Baker's words: "Instead of Bimini, Ernest went to bed."

Hemingway arrived in Bimini a week later and spent much of that spring and summer there. He reeled in a 785-pound (355-kg) mako shark and boasted to his editor, Maxwell Perkins, that his expertise had changed the "whole system" of sportfishing on Bimini. He also indulged in his passion for boxing, offering $250 to any black man who could stay in a ring with him for three three-minute rounds. Despite several challenges, he held on to his $250. He was not above fistfights with the rich sportsmen whose yachts crowded the harbor. The tale of his knockout victory over wealthy publisher Joseph Knapp was memorialized by a calypso band whose improvised lyrics lauded "the big fat slob" from Key West.

Hemingway could also have earned celebrity status for his amazing fishing prowess. When, in 1936, he sailed into the harbor with a 514-pound (233-kg) tuna, hooked off Gun Cay, south of the Biminis, it is said the whole population came out to admire the fish. This excitement aside, he was still Hemingway the writer, and in June 1937 he was also at work in Bimini, revising the manuscript of *To Have And Have Not*. His lifestyle in Bimini did everything to enhance a career that put a generation in what biographer A.E. Hotchner called "Hemingway Awe."

In the novel *Islands In The Stream*, which remained unfinished at the time of his death in 1961, Hemingway captured in fiction the seedy charm of Alice Town, North Bimini, and the mysterious power of battling a big fish in the Gulf Stream. The novel's central character, Thomas Hudson, is calmer and more peaceable than "Papa" Hemingway was himself in those Bimini years, but the novel, which was published in 1970, still served to prolong the spell he cast over the island. Though he did not "create" big fishing in Bimini, it never would have been the same without him. ❑

LEFT: Hemingway t sportsman.

Map on page 225

LOW: ptain Bob in s restaurant.

Bimini big game

The center for fishermen is the **Bimini Big Game Fishing Club**, where the good-sized swimming pool, expensive, subdued restaurant and liveable rooms are all secondary to the action on the docks and the walk-in freezer for the day's catches. At dawn the bleary-eyed fisherman can take inspiration from a mural on a wall near the pool which commemorates some Bimini greats, including Bonefish Willie, a seasoned, genial boat captain who is also a minister. Sequestered from King's Highway by a discreet wall, the club is almost sufficient unto itself. You could go from dock to hotel to restaurant without seeing another bit of Bimini.

The prime season for bluefin (giant) tuna is May 7 to June 15. The ultimate opponent for sport-fishermen, they swim fast, live long and grow up to 1,800 lbs (900 kg), spending their winters off New England. June and July are best for blue marlin, summer and fall for tarpon, so there is almost always a big fish to chase here.

For true bluefin and billfish aficionados, no visit to the Bimini Islands would be complete without a visit to the southern Biminis. It was off **Gun Cay**, 9 miles (14 km) south of Bimini Harbour, that Ernest Hemingway caught with rod and reel the giant bluefin tuna that he claimed galvanized Bimini fishing. In the middle of the Depression, Louis Wasey founded a club on **North Cat Cay**, where he and a few friends could get away for golf on the nine-hole course, formal banquets in the tudor-style mansion and cocktails at the Kitten Cay Bar. Still a private club today, North Cat Cay is a place where the fishing goes on in style with His and Hers Tournaments and evening yacht parties.

At the far southern end of the Bimini chain, man has added to nature's work by building **Ocean Cay**. Aragonite, a pure lime sand, is dredged here from the ocean floor, to be used in the making of cement, fertilizers, glass and other products. Tall cranes and other equipment make it a landmark for yachtsmen.

Back in port

Alice Town is easily explored in an after-noon on foot. At the far south end of the King's Highway is a roughly painted sign indicating that beyond the fence, one should fear for one's life. So that is as far south as you can go. (You can see South Bimini and some homes along its shore from here.) Nearby, to the west, over-grown with a spongy, grass-like moss, is a small graveyard with some of the older headstones sunk deep, only their tops showing. The pink stucco **Government Complex** north of the Big Game Fishing Club, along King's Highway, was dam-aged by fire in the late 1970s. Today, it houses the island's administrative offices, the police, the post office and the Ministry of Tourism.

Down King's Highway is a lagoon shaded by coconut palms and fenced by chain link, a number of small shops and bars, and an impressive outdoor patio extravaganza with lots of tables, trees, and gently swinging lanterns.

Literary inspiration

At the **Anchorage**, the Cape Cod clap-board building at the highest point on North Bimini, is a pleasant restaurant with windows overlooking the water. It was the home of Mike and Helen Lerner. Mike Lerner, who was a friend of Hemingway, was a philanthropist whose projects included the Lerner Marine Laboratory in Alice Town, a branch of the American Museum of Natural History. From its opening in 1947 until its closing in 1974, scientists at the lab studied the behavior of sharks, dolphins and fish and made signif-icant contributions in the fields of micro-biology, icthyology and marine ecology. With its commanding location and sea views east and west, it was undoubtedly the Lerners' home that inspired Thomas Hudson's house in *Islands in the Stream*.

The Anchorage, on its knoll, has added guest rooms in a modern wing, part of the Bimini Blue Water Resort. No one with a day to spend on Bimini should miss the beach on the deepwater side. It has coarse

BELOW: end of the hunt.

Map on page 225

white sand, starting below the Anchorage and extending in either direction. The waves here are large enough for body surfing and can make visibility for snorkeling rough unless you swim beyond them.

On the pathway above the beach, you will find trim, white and green clapboard **Wesley Methodist Church**, founded in 1858. Its French doors open onto a clean, simple nave with polished pews. There's a small belltower on the roof with dusty, old-fashioned loudspeakers aimed outward.

A walk north on the path above the beach ends up at **Bailey Town ❸**, 2 miles (3 km) north of Alice Town. This is where most of the population of North Bimini lives, and on a walk there at dusk you will see children on shiny bicycles playing outside old wooden homes, well-kept churches and at least a dozen ambitious frame houses or duplexes freshly painted beige, yellow or tawny brown. At some of the houses, cars fill the short driveways and curtains cover the windows. In the dusk, people pass on foot, on bicycle or motorbike on their way home; in the air is a trace of marijuana and aftershave.

Burgeoning Bimini

There is money on Bimini, and it's hardly a secret where it comes from. North Bimini has a narrow mangrove-tangled creek, leading from the open sea to a safe natural harbor, which is blatantly depicted on maps as the Drugs Channel. A fast boat can carry a cargo of marijuana, or cocaine, to Florida in a matter of hours. The temptation is too great for a few local men, and some women have had to become the breadwinners whilst their partners spend lengthy "vacations" in a Miami jail. Thanks to such ill-gotten gains the island pulses with mega sound systems and shiny new cars. In 1986, motorcycles with horsepower above 125cc were banned from Bimini, but there are plenty of guys in sunglasses who manage to make driving a golf cart look cool.

Today, most islanders fill their bellies, courtesy of the tourist dollar, but they are

LOW: nefish Willie, teemed mini boat ptain.

wary of big developers. So far, Bimini has escaped the clutches of the big chain hotels, but that looks set to change. **Bimini Bay 4** at the northern tip of North Bimini is a popular picnic spot for both locals and visitors with wild desolate beaches, seagrape trees, pines and mangroves. It was bought by an American-Cuban property developer for an undisclosed sum, with the ambitious plan of building a 600-room hotel and casino.

Sceptics say it will never amount to much, but a drive up to the Bay reveals teams of giant earthmovers, ploughing up and down the beach seven days a week. Many local people are devout Christians who strongly oppose the casino. Some welcome the promise of jobs and the high-spending visitors it would bring to Bimini, but all agree that such a large development would irreversibly alter the character of the sleepy sister islands.

At **Paradise Point 5**, nearby Bimini Bay, lies an underwater rock formation known as **Bimini Road**. Some claim the

rocks are part of the lost city of Atlantis *(see page 221)*, and local fisherman are happy to earn a few extra dollars by taking people out. Though not spectacular, the rocks are easily visible in the looking glass clear water and the snorkelling is good.

As well as some deserted white-sand beaches, visitors taking the two-minute inter-island ferry from North Bimini can test the rejuvenating powers of a pool called **Healing Hole**.

Map on page 225

Side trip to South Bimini

South Bimini 6 (North Bimini's neighbor), with a bit of farming, a shark research laboratory and a few vacation homes – owned mainly by Miami fishermen – has been described as a backwater. However, the Bimini Sands Beach Club has breathed new life into the island, providing its first gas station, a marina, condos and a weekly disco.

South Bimini holds fast to the claim that the explorer Ponce de Leon discovered the fabled "Fountain of Youth" here. If you must, you can sip the fetid water from a leaky bucket. The scientific evidence is zero, but the islanders do carry their age well.

Back on the King's Highway

Back in Alice Town you will be able to smell your way to Estella Rolle's fresh bread, which she bakes and sells in a blue wooden hutch about 5 ft (1.5 meters) square and lays out for sale on the doorsill. She makes bread with raisins, regular white bread, and delicious coconut rolls.

Down the King's Highway, someone is dancing on the sand floor of the End of the World Bar. The sun is setting, and the fishermen are back. Barefooted sportsmen pass, carrying open bottles of beer. In the purple dusk, someone is revving the motor of a car. In one of the shops, where they sell T-shirts, local girls are keeping the place open while they plan their evening, and light spills out on the street. You take a few steps starboard to the docks and you're where you want to be. Out on the boat, if it weren't for the dock lights, you could see the stars. It's no wonder people keep coming back to Bimini. ❏

LEFT: cruising the King's Highway. **RIGHT:** smiling schoolgirls.

THE BERRY ISLANDS

An exclusive enclave for celebrities and the well-heeled,
this collection of predominantly private cays and islands has
bird colonies, white-sand beaches and seas rich with colorful marine life

The Berry Islands lure a special breed to their shores. Low-lying, rocky, with little water or arable soil, these are islands for people who already have everything money can buy.

Except for Bullocks Harbour on Great Harbour Cay, most of the 30 tiny islands – if inhabited at all – are enjoyed by foreigners who have the means to create "worlds" on their own private cays. Other areas remain paradises for wildlife. Terns, pelicans and noddies make them favorite nesting grounds. Beneath the waters, sailfish, blue marlin and giant bluefin tuna roam, tempting sports fisherman to this lovely, desolate chain of cays. They are known mostly to yachtsmen who use them for stopover trips between Florida and Nassau.

Just over 600 souls make the Berry Islands their permanent home. Most of the islanders live in **Bullocks Harbour** on **Great Harbour Cay ❶**. Politically, they are tied to the North Andros constituency, with which they share a representative in parliament. In reality, they seem to float free with the tides and trade winds on the Great Bahama Bank.

The largest of the Berry Islands, at 6 miles (10 km) long and 2½ miles (4 km) wide, Great Harbour Cay saw its first residents in 1836, when Governor Colebrook founded a settlement there for recently emancipated and homeless enslaved Africans and their families. For a 19-century agrarian community, this tiny island offered a harsh life. Poor soil and

BELOW:
abandoned or
Great Stirrup
Cay.

Map on page 229

little naturally occurring potable water left room for hardly more than a bare existence, supplemented only by the abundance of the sea.

Great Harbour Cay has an 8-mile (13-km) sandy beach on the east coast that fans out to **Sugar Beach** in the north and **Great Harbour Bay** in the south. The water that laps the fine sand is cool and clear. Towards the west coast are areas populated by a variety of waterfowl such as egret and heron, which live among the islands' mangroves and salt ponds.

In the past, economic difficulties kept facilities for yachtsmen and other visitors to a minimum. Nonetheless, the Berry Islands are second only to the Biminis for sports fishing, and host back billfishing tournaments every March, April and May. The annual Homecoming Regatta on the Cay offers the chance for fun and festivities in August.

A considerable number of visitors arrive by boat; they head for the marina, south of the main town, which has 80 slips. Great

Harbour Cay also has an airstrip that accepts small aircraft only.

Accommodation on the cay is limited. The Tropical Diversion Resort, near Bullocks Harbour, has villas for rent, and can also recommend guides for visitors wanting to participate in a spot of fishing.

Passing ships

Cruise lines also have seen the attraction of the Berry Islands as a pristine landfall on the way to Nassau. When the great white ship appears on the horizon, **Great Stirrup Cay** ❷ comes to life. Passengers disembark onto the private cay for a picnic, a swim and "native" entertainment (generally non-Bahamian fun like limbo dancing), which contribute to a day of fun on the cay's unspoiled beach.

Great Stirrup Cay also marks the northernmost tip of this hook-shaped chain. Here, a lighthouse beams its white light to passing ships. Less romantic, but more effective, is the red light on the tower of the US Tracking Station, visible to boats

ELOW: a lone **istaway.**

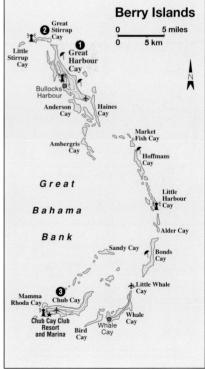

Berry Islands

0 — 5 miles
0 — 5 km

N

Great Stirrup Cay ❷
Little Stirrup Cay
Great Harbour Cay ❶
Bullocks Harbour
Anderson Cay
Haines Cay
Market Fish Cay
Ambergris Cay
Hoffmans Cay

Great Bahama Bank

Little Harbour Cay
Alder Cay
Sandy Cay
Bonds Cay
Little Whale Cay
Mamma Rhoda Cay
Chub Cay ❸
Whale Cay
Chub Cay Club Resort and Marina
Bird Cay
Whale Cay

as far as 18 miles (30 km) from shore. To the west is another, smaller private cay, **Little Stirrup Cay**, that is also on the cruise ship route.

Exclusive enclave

At the southernmost end of the chain, tiny **Chub Cay ❸** sits on the very edge of the Great Bahama Bank, overlooking the deep sea trench, the so-called Tongue of the Ocean. Here, you will find the semi-private and exclusive **Chub Cay Club Resort and Marina**. A popular celebrity hideaway because of its seclusion, the cay also provides enthusiastic snorkelers and divers with a delightful opportunity to view a myriad of reef fish and open-water marine life.

Founded by a wealthy Florida horse-breeder, Chub Cay and its club became a favorite gathering place for sportsmen and women with the time and money to pursue the big fish. Some people call Chub Cay the billfish capital of the Bahamas, but it is interesting to note that the founder

and first owner of the club was an avid bonefisherman whose research into the habits of bonefish led him to this spot. Visitors can charter a big-game fishing boat here, or hire a boat and guide for bonefishing. Non-members with deep pockets can also enjoy the club facilities, such as watersports and tennis. In July, fishermen swell the ranks when they arrive to compete in the annual Chub Cay Blue Marlin Tournament.

Sun-worshippers will be delighted by the crescent-shaped beach with its powdery sand, and, for those with a little more energy, the sea water close to shore is home to turtles and stingray.

The reefs around the Berry Islands are so rich with sea life that one of the most popular is protected by the Bahamas National Trust. The **Mamma Rhoda Reef**, south of Mamma Rhoda Rock and Chub Cay, is part of a marine park that has shallow-water elkhorn and staghorn coral, populated by colorful moray eels, eagle rays, trumpetfish, snapper and sharks. Dive excursions to the reef can be arranged on nearby Chub Cay.

Private paradises

Between Great Harbour Cay and Chub Cay, many of the cays are privately owned; landing on any of these is strictly by invitation only. **Bird Cay**, with its plantings of tall coconut trees, casuarinas and fruit trees, shelters several luxurious homes. **Whale Cay** is being developed as a private resort.

Frozen Cay and **Alder Cay** are a paradise for birds – and bird lovers. At sunrise and sunset the air around them fills with terns. Pelicans and brown noddies also nest here, marking off their own "private property." Visitors to the two cays can help to preserve these natural sanctuaries by treading carefully and leaving them free from litter.

On **Little Whale Cay**, Wallace Groves (and his family), namesake of the beautiful Garden of the Groves in Grand Bahama *(see page 196)*, had an elegantly landscaped estate with an airstrip and aviary for exotic birds, including flamingos, pheasants and peacocks. ❏

LEFT: a school of curious fish. **RIGHT:** the colorful reefs are rich with sea life.

Map
on page
237

THE ABACOS

East of Grand Bahama, this island and its chain of cays
have a rich heritage of boatbuilding and farming. Today, tourism
is also creating additional wealth for the local population

A lovely group of islands, situated approximately 106 miles (170 km) north of Nassau, and about 200 miles (320 km) northeast of Miami, the Abacos are the most versatile of the Bahamian island groups. Thoroughly saturated with the quaint and harmonious atmosphere which is a trademark of the Out Islands, the Abacos also offer the visitor some of the conveniences of "city" life in Marsh Harbour, the third largest town in the Bahamas.

In the Abacos you can take a yacht out to sea by day and dine onshore in a fine restaurant at night. You can let your hair down and enjoy the islands thoroughly, but if you want to recapture a chic appearance for the trip home, there is a hair-styling boutique at your service. From Walker's Cay in the north all the way down to Hole-in-the-Wall in the south, the Abacos simply offer visitors a unique experience.

The Abacos was a prime shipbuilding center, but with a fine agricultural tradition, too; the islanders have always been self-sufficient. They have long had the reputation of being some of the most ambitious people in the country. So proud are Abaconians of their own abilities and their islands that at one point, in the early 1970s, many supported a move to secede from the rest of the Bahamas.

Abaconians like Bunyan Key and the late Albert Lowe built such sleek craft that they became something of a legend in their time. Both learned boatbuilding from older relatives in the early 1900s. The Abaconian three-masted schooner, when completed, was a vessel of tremendous beauty and typified the craftsmanship of the Abaco boatbuilder.

When the government officially announced plans for the Bahamas to become an independent nation, a great number of Abaconians were quite upset. The controversy split the people of the Abacos virtually in half, with one group advocating going it alone as a small nation, and the other preferring to remain a part of the Bahamas.

But the conflict did not dampen the enterprising spirit of the Abaconians. They continued to strive and develop the islands, and today, with boatbuilding and farming taking a back seat to tourism, the Abacos have perhaps the highest employment rate in the Out Islands.

A number of attractive marinas have made the Abacos a popular resort area. All year, and especially during peak season, the **Conch Inn Resort and Marina** and **Green Turtle Yacht Club and Marina** are filled with an absolutely dazzling array of sailing and fishing boats.

PRECEDING PAGES: pastel clapboards on Green Turtle Cay.
LEFT: the girl next door gets married in Hope Town.
RIGHT: children and their bicycles in Hope Town.

Early settlers

Many of the people of the Abacos are descendants of the British Loyalists, who, left the United States following the Revolutionary War and arrived here in the 1780s; but, they were not the only early settlers. Putting down roots here around the same time were a group of Harbour Islanders (whose forebears had been among the first settlers of the Bahamas 150 years before). Some say it was the pretty Loyalist girls that attracted these Harbour Island men, plus the prospect of a developing area with plentiful resources. Prior to the Loyalists' arrival in the Abacos, these islands were a cruising ground for pirates, and before that, home to Indians, who gave the island its early name of Yucayonequi.

It was the Loyalists, however, who should be credited with starting the agricultural tradition in the Abacos. Thanks to them, farming gained a strong foothold, and from that time to today, agriculture has been able to supplement other means of survival for the Abaconians.

When the Harbour Islanders arrived in the Abacos they married into the Loyalist families. Soon life in the Abacos was an amalgam of old island ways and "modern" Loyalist ambitions, with the old ways growing stronger all the time. The settlements on the mainland were not successful, and soon almost everyone was living on the cays, engaged mainly in boat-building and fishing.

In a country where more than 85 percent of the population is of African descent, some 50 percent of the residents of the Abacos are white. Some historians say that this is simply because the more prosperous Loyalist families (who were of European descent) stuck together and helped each other out. Others believe that it was by design – that poorer, black Bahamians were deliberately kept out in large numbers.

Travel to the Abacos by air and you will land at either Treasure Cay, on the north end of **Great Abaco**, or at Marsh Harbour, in the island's center. Both towns

BELOW:
Man-O-War
Cay, ship
shape as a
New England
fishing village

Map below

are near the site of one of the earliest Loyalist settlements; the first arrivals stepped ashore not far from Treasure Cay.

Carleton site

Records indicate that about 600 Loyalists – both black and white – left New York City in around 1783 and arrived on **Treasure Cay ❶** with the intention of establishing a self-sufficient township. They named their settlement Carleton, a tribute to Sir Guy Carleton, a noted representative of the king and the top royal official in all of North America. The settlement was supposed to evolve into a great community for those whose continued allegiance to England had made them outcasts after the American revolution.

The Loyalists must have felt some of the same kind of uncertainty that Christopher Columbus knew 300 years before when he first came to Bahamian territory. The difference between Christopher Columbus and his crews on the *Niña*, *Pinta* and *Santa Maria*, and the Loyalists

is that the former were a group of explorers looking to find new discoveries for Spain. The Loyalists, on the other hand, were a rather desperate group of people, some in a more dejected state than others, hoping to begin a new life that would wipe out the sad and bitter memories of the American Revolution.

Various conflicts developed among the Loyalists, and their plans met many obstacles, including a devastating hurricane that totally destroyed their first settlement. Nothing of Carleton remains today, but a mile or so north of Treasure Cay is what's believed to be its site.

Treasure Cay (which is not a cay, but on the mainland of Great Abaco) is perhaps the most modern, complete resort facility in the Out Islands. Started by a native Abaconian in 1959, when the site's principal attraction was a lovely 3-mile (5-km) beach, the resort, northwest of Marsh Harbour, now features a hotel, the only golf course on the island, shops, and well-landscaped roads, along which a

GHT: a fruit ndor at arsh Harbour.

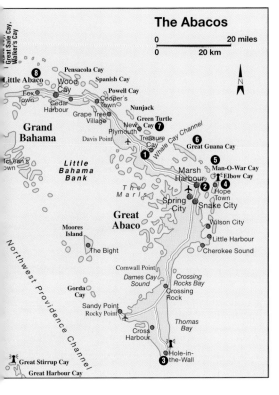

number of Americans have vacation homes. Jets fly directly from the US to Treasure Cay; yachts from Florida and ports farther afield tie up in the marina. One of the resort's slogans is "60 minutes from Florida… a million miles from cares."

From a historic point of view, the Loyalists who settled in the Abacos were hardly a million miles from cares. Fortunately, not all suffered the same fate as the Carleton group. Some of the first Loyalist settlers split up from the original Carleton group, and traveled south to found the settlement of Marsh Harbour.

Land of water

More than one-third of the island of Great Abaco is marshland along the western coast, making it difficult to judge where the water ends and the land begins. Therefore most of the settlements of Great Abaco dot the solid ground of the east coast with **Marsh Harbour ❷**, the island's commercial center, smack in the middle. Available in downtown Marsh

Harbour are modern food stores, carrying everything a chef could desire. There are department and hardware stores, several banks, restaurants, a beauty salon, an exclusive dining room, gas stations, a plush motel and time-sharing facilities.

Two adjoining communities, **Murphey Town** and **Dundas Town**, complete the spectrum of life in Marsh Harbour and give it a population of about 3,000 – making it the third largest town in the Bahamas. Despite this distinction, it is still a relatively quiet place, sprawled out along the large harbor.

The road linking the towns of Great Abaco was built in 1959 by the Owens-Illinois Company to transport logs from Abaco's forests to their mill in **Snake Cay**. This operation, plus an earlier lumber operation in **Wilson City**, caused the principal development of the area south of Marsh Harbour. From having two licensed cars in 1959 to having more than 2,000 in 1970, Abaco sped into the automobile age, and Marsh Harbour, and for a

BELOW: triplets at Treasure Cay.

Map on page 237

time the area south, rather than the off-shore cays, became the hub of activity.

South of Marsh Harbour, **Spring City** and Snake Cay were built by Owens-Illinois to house workers for their lumber and sugar cane enterprises. These were not the first "company towns" in the Abacos, for in 1906 an American company developed Wilson City, which attracted workers from all over the Abacos and the Bahamas, and produced large amounts of lumber until 1916. Later on, the work was carried on by the Bahamas Cuban Company and the Abaco Lumber Company, and finally by Owens-Illinois.

Today, in these old lumbering areas abandoned by Owens-Illinois in 1970, the few residents devote themselves mostly to farming and fishing. **Cherokee Sound** and **Sandy Point** are basically fishing settlements. There are no settlements south of Sandy Point, but the lighthouse at **Hole-in-the-Wall ❸**, in the far south, is one of the most important navigational lights operating in the Bahamas.

Until the construction of the main highway on Great Abaco, the Abaco cays were the island's hubs of activity. None was more important than Hope Town, on **Elbow Cay**, which was the life of the Abacos and the seat of the islands' Commissioner until 1960.

Hope Town

Located a short ferry ride across the water from Marsh Harbour, **Hope Town ❹** is a picturesque village of pastel-trimmed clapboard houses. Orange, pink, and purple bougainvillea and other blossoms tumble over stone and picket fences enclosing trim yards. The red-and-white striped Hope Town harbor lighthouse is probably the most photographed in the Bahamas, and the small town of about 350 residents, mostly descendants of the original Loyalist settlers of the Abacos, is one of the most fascinating. A quiet pride in the past permeates this town, where a few families – the Russells, Lowes, Bethels, Sawyers and Malones – have dominated for

BELOW: candy stripes at Elbow Cay's landmark lighthouse.

Boatbuilding

The pine forests, the watery distances between the cays and the ambitions of the first settlers all contributed to turning the Abacos into the first boatbuilding center in the Bahamas, and also the most famous. Marsh Harbour, Cherokee Sound, New Plymouth, Hope Town and Man-O-War Cay are all names that sound long and clear throughout Bahamian nautical history. Dinghies, smacks, sloops and even large cargo schooners built in these settlements have cut wakes through the Atlantic for over 150 years.

Presently, the majority of the boatbuilders on Man-O-War Cay turn out sleek fiberglass boats, but old-fashioned boatbuilding, made with local lumber and hand tools, persists. But while the traditionally-crafted wooden boats are still very much part of the Bahamian boatbuilders' repertoire in Man-O-War Cay, the modern fiberglass vessels are being produced to meet the demand for faster, lighter motor-powered boats.

Throughout the Abaco chain, and beyond, boatbuilders have created their own styles, which means that sailors can often tell who built a particular boat on sight. The crafting and carpentry skills have passed from father to son, from generation to generation. From the early settlers in the 18th century up to the present day, the same group of families has dominated the island boatyards.

The island sailing regattas and races offer opportunities to watch some of the finest Bahamian crafted boats in action. During the summer there is the annual Abaco Regatta, a series of races around the island and cays.

There are several steps involved in building the famous Abaco dinghy the traditional way. First, the builder selects and cuts the wood for the boat's frame. He usually uses corkwood trees, which are plentiful near Hope Town, but the hardwoods madeira (mahogany), dogwood and horseflesh, which also grow in the Abacos, were traditionally used. He works without plans, making use of the crooks of trees for the frame, the natural curve of the wood providing the structure with extra strength. He imports pine boards for the planking, though in former years Abaco pines provided this material. He tamps cotton into the seams, paints and applies caulking; for sailing models he constructs a rudder, mast and boom. The finished boat is one of the prides of the Bahamas – eminently seaworthy, simple and yet very beautiful.

The dinghy is a modest creature compared to the creations of the early part of the 20th century – two- and three-masted schooners which were both glorious achievements and something of an anachronism in their time. Born in 1886, Jenkins Roberts was perhaps the most famous of these master builders. He built the twin-masted *Albertine Adoue*, which served as the Abacos' mailboat until the 1920s, and in 1922 he launched the 130-foot (40-meter) *Abaco, Bahamas*, – the largest ship ever built in the Abacos.

Many other Abaconians – Edwin Carey, Dickie Roberts, William Albury, Albert Lowe and others – made their marks as skilled shipbuilders during the years when travel and commerce in the Bahamas made voyages by sea part of daily life, in the same way that journeys by road, and more recently by air, are for most communities today. ❑

LEFT: *Rough Waters*, a famous racer built on Man-O-War Cay.

Map
n page
237

two centuries. They have preserved a taste of the early life in the **Wyannie Malone Historical Museum**, which occupies an old Hope Town house on Bay Street. Named for the widow Wyannie Malone, whose four children formed the basis for much of Hope Town's later population, it contains a fascinating melange of old furniture and artifacts collected from residents. Catching the museum open is another story, since the hours tend to be erratic. However, learning about the history of this friendly town is as easy as chatting with a store owner or someone unloading a boat at the dock.

Cars are not allowed on the streets of Hope Town; this contributes to the impression that on making the short trip from Marsh Harbour you have made a voyage into the past.

In the old days residents farmed, fished and won occasional windfalls from the practice of "wrecking." The reefs around the Abacos proved dangerous to passing ships, and as soon as one ran aground on a reef the Abaconians were out on the water to rescue the luckless mariners and seize the cargo. By law the cargo was sold in Nassau, with a certain percentage of the receipts paid in tax to the government, a large portion to the wreckers, and the remaining bit to the hapless ship owner. The natives of Hope Town depended so much on this source of livelihood that they went so far as to sabotage the construction of the **Hope Town Lighthouse** in the 1830s. Today, the lighthouse is important for tourism, particularly since it is one of the few in the Bahamas that has not been automated. Be sure to climb the 100 stairs to the top for the view.

A number of foreigners have found Hope Town a delightful place to build second homes, and today more than half the houses on Elbow Cay are owned by non-Bahamians. Several inns provide rooms for visitors. Along with the attractive town, the main attractions on this narrow island are the long, ivory beaches, some backed by dunes.

OW: boats
bing in the
er at Hope
vn harbor,
ow Cay.

Man-O-War

Elbow Cay's next door neighbor, **Man-O-War Cay ❺**, is famous for shipbuilding, which peaked in the 19th century. Through the years, locals have proven their ability to design and produce first-class vessels, whether large ocean boats or dinghies for harbor.

With a slightly more disciplined atmosphere than Hope Town, Man-O-War is a ship-shape settlement. Proud of their heritage and determined to preserve it, Man-O-War residents have allowed no hotels to be built on their island, and, until fairly recently, they allowed no black people to remain on the island overnight. No liquor has ever been sold there. The people are known for their efficiency and ingenuity, and many yachtsmen from the United States have their craft regularly hauled up for painting and repairs on the Cay.

One enterprising Man-O-War citizen changed the face of life in the Abacos by instituting **Albury's Ferry Service**, which is the main mode of transportation between the Abaco cays. Travel in the Abacos has always been by boat, and some Out Islanders say the Abaconians could not help but develop a special talent for producing seaworthy boats. Yet, though Abaconians had been ferrying themselves and their families to visit relatives to and from the cays and islands for years, an actual ferry service for visitors did not take root until the late 1950s. As ironic as it may seem, the opening of two airports, in Marsh Harbour and Treasure Cay, actually inspired ferrying as a business.

Inter-island travel

Prior to the opening of the airports, sea planes landed twice a week at Green Turtle and Man-O-War cays. When larger planes started landing at Treasure Cay and Marsh Harbour, the seaplane service became obsolete. Yet there was still a need for mainland people to get to the cays, especially when tourists began landing in Marsh Harbour and Treasure Cay. So Marcel Albury, from a distinguished line

BELOW: Green Turtle Cay Yacht Club.

Map
n page
237

of Abaconian boatmen, purchased a vessel and started the Albury Ferry Service, a venture soon to be duplicated by several other locals who were perhaps more at home in boats than under the roofs of their homes.

Twice a week Albury's Ferry travels to **Great Guana Cay ❻**, where about 100 people live, mostly fishing and farming for a living. There is a hotel, the Guana Beach Resort, and many deserted beaches.

Green Turtle

New Plymouth, on **Green Turtle Cay ❼**, once rivaled Hope Town as the hub of the Abacos. Like the other cays, Green Turtle was known for boatbuilding; the residents also had a reputation for growing delicious pineapples. Today the pineapple industry is no longer, and New Plymouth on Green Turtle Cay is primarily a quaint fishing village. The New England-style saltbox houses – sometimes brightly painted – seem to belong to another century.

New Plymouth's quaint and friendly atmosphere has attracted foreigners to build homes, as they have in Hope Town. Also like Hope Town, New Plymouth has an interesting small museum.

In 1984, the **Albert Lowe Museum** (open Mon–Sat 9–11.45am and 1–4pm; entrance fee; tel: 365 4094), housed in a 150-year-old building on Parliament Street, formed a partnership with Treasure Cay Resorts and a group of archaeologists in order to locate and excavate the first Loyalist settlement, Carleton. Visitors to the museum will find interesting models of Abaconian ships, built by New Plymouth native Albert Lowe, displays of Loyalist artifacts and early photographs.

More of the past is celebrated at the **Memorial Sculpture Garden**, northeast of the museum and across the road from the handsome New Plymouth Inn. This tranquil garden honors residents of the Abacos who have made important contributions to the Bahamas. Busts sit on pedestals commemorating the accomplishments of all kinds of Abaconians from Albert Lowe to Jeanne I. Thompson – a

OW: the
ert Lowe
seum in
v Plymouth.

black Bahamian, who was a contemporary playwright and the country's second woman to practice law.

New Year's Day is a special time on Green Turtle Cay, when everyone celebrates the capture of Bunce – a character who, according to local folklore, lived in Abaco's pine forests. Residents and visitors can enjoy a parade and festivities.

Yachtsmen make Green Turtle Cay and its lively restaurants and bars a favorite stop. For land-based travelers there are several charming hotels. Those who like a lot of action should plan well ahead to be on Green Turtle Cay for the regatta, sponsored annually by the Green Turtle Yacht Club. Ferries make the trip from a dock near Treasure Cay to Green Turtle Cay.

Toward Little Abaco

The north end of Great Abaco, north of Treasure Cay, and the adjoining island of Little Abaco are little visited, but the cays offshore are a favorite cruising ground for yachtsmen. North of Green Turtle Cay, the

nearest mainland settlement is **Cooper's Town** on Great Abaco.

Map on page 237

Just five miles (8 km) north, across a causeway bridge, is the island of **Little Abaco ❽** and the villages of Cedar Harbour, Wood Cay, Mount Hope, Fox Town and Crown Haven. Neither Cooperstown nor the settlements of Little Abaco have deepwater harbors, so the inhabitants long lived in relative isolation from the rest of the Abaco chain.

Since the road was built connecting them with Treasure Cay, some of the residents have taken jobs at the Treasure Cay resort; others have found prosperity in the booming business of crawfishing. Unlike those on the Abaco cays, the primarily black settlers were brought into the islands with the Loyalists in the 18th century.

North of Green Turtle Cay, only two cays are inhabited – Grand Cay and Walker's Cay – and the sailing between them is breathtaking. **Powell Cay** is a private property, but uninhabited. According to the *Yachtsman's Guide to the Bahamas*, there is a fine anchorage off its high bluffs and, the beach is beautiful, but the mosquitoes are unusually voracious. The mud flats and mangrove roots along the edges of the harbor on **Great Sale Cay** are home to barracuda, sand sharks, bonefish, snappers and other fish.

Some yachtsmen use **Grand Cay** as a base for fishing. A number of the people living in Grand Cay commute to work – by boat – to the resort at **Walker's Cay**. Here, on the northernmost point in the Bahamas, the Walker's Cay Club caters mainly to fishermen from the north who fly in to the private airstrip or sail in on yachts. Perched on a bluff, the club offers fabulous views of the sea.

From Walker's Cay it's a short step to the Mantanilla Reef, then off the **Little Bahama Bank** and into the Gulf Stream. It's a step Abaconians have taken in the past, for jobs and opportunities in the US and beyond, yet today more are returning and remaining. Whereas New Providence and Grand Bahama had tremendous outside influence in their development, the people of the Abacos have made their strides largely on their own. ❑

LEFT: Abaconian memories a the Albert Lowe Muset **RIGHT:** Abaco sails.

Map
on page
250

ELEUTHERA, HARBOUR ISLAND AND SPANISH WELLS

These historically important islands are tranquil havens for travelers, who stroll through charming towns decorated in pastels, explore the rich fruits of the sea, and enjoy a friendly Out Island welcome from the locals

In 1649 a group of religious dissidents from Bermuda set out to sea. Information is sketchy as to whether Eleuthera was their intended destination, but when their vessel was wrecked just off the northern end of the island, they went ashore. Taking shelter in a limestone cave, they faced fear, hardship and privation on the island of Eleuthera.

These first settlers, like the Puritans who colonized New England, were British subjects fleeing religious persecution at home. They called the island Eleuthera – from the Greek word for freedom *(see page 30)*. They later split ranks and settled on Harbour Island and Spanish Wells as well.

The population of these islands grew when colonists in Bermuda exiled both free and uncooperative enslaved Africans to Eleuthera. These were the first black people to live in the Bahamas, and they arrived as free men and women. In the 18th and 19th centuries, British loyalists from the new United States of America joined these first settlers. Some brought enslaved Africans with them.

Today, the descendants of the Eleutherian Adventurers (as they were called), the freed Africans and the Loyalists can be found throughout the island of Eleuthera and the adjacent cays – but nowhere is the melting pot of cultures, old and new, as delightful as on **Harbour Island ❶**.

Harbour Island to Briland

With its fine natural harbor, Harbour Island (also called Briland) is thought by some historians to have been the intended destination of the Eleutherian Adventurers. Located just off the northeast coast of the island of Eleuthera, it is well protected from rough weather by the treacherous reefs that destroyed the Eleutherian Adventurers' ship. More of the Adventur-

ers eventually settled on Harbour Island than on Eleuthera. The hardy nucleus of Eleutherian Adventurers was bolstered by the arrival of British loyalists from the American colonies. Bringing with them expertise in shipbuilding and agriculture, the Loyalists helped launch the prosperous economy that the Bahamas enjoyed in the late 18th-century.

From the 18th century until World War II (1939–45), ships built on Harbour Island plied the seas of the world. By the 19th century, the island's main settlement, **Dunmore Town ❷**, was the Bahamas' second city, exceeded only by Nassau in population and wealth. Islanders built

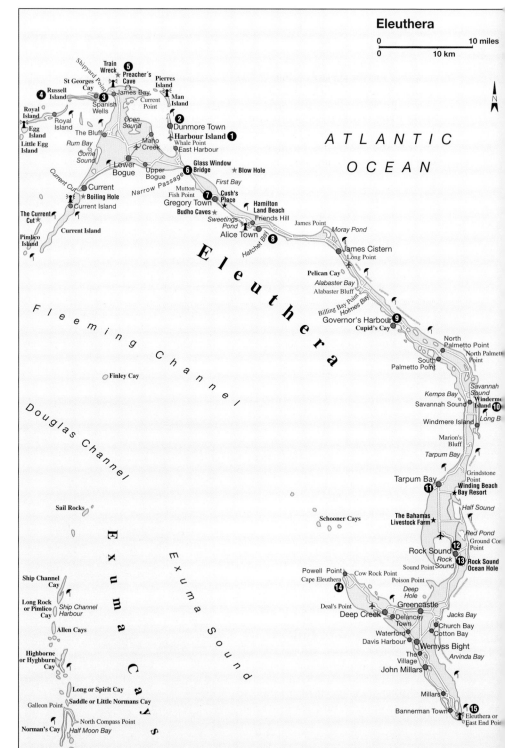

Eleuthera

0   10 miles
0   10 km

Train Wreck
Shipyard Point
St Georges Cay
Russell Island
Royal Island
Egg Island
Little Egg Island
Royal Island
The Bluff
Rum Bay
Corrie Sound
Preacher's Cave
Pierres Island
James Bay
Spanish Wells
Open Sound
Lower Bogue
Upper Bogue
Current Point
Man Island
Dunmore Town
Harbour Island
Whale Point
East Harbour
Glass Window Bridge
Blow Hole
Maho Creek

ATLANTIC
OCEAN

Current
Boiling Hole
Current Island
The Current Cut
Pimlico Island
Current Island
Narrow Passage
Current Cut
Mutton Fish Point
Gregory Town
Budho Caves
Sweetings Pond
Alice Town
Hatchet Bay
First Bay
Cush's Place
Hamilton Land Beach
Friends Hill
James Point
Moray Pond
James Cistern
Long Point

Fleeming Channel
Finley Cay

Pelican Cay
Alabaster Bay
Alabaster Bluff
Billing Bay Point
Holmes Bay
Governor's Harbour
Cupid's Cay

North Palmetto Point
North Palmetto Point
South Palmetto Point

Douglas Channel

Sail Rocks

Schooner Cays

Savannah Sound
Kemps Bay
Savannah Sound
Windmere Island
Windmere Island
Long B
Marion's Bluff
Tarpum Bay
Grindstone Point
Tarpum Bay
Winding Beach Bay Resort
Half Sound

Exuma

The Bahamas Livestock Farm
Red Pond
Ground Cor Point
Rock Sound
Rock Sound Point
Rock Sound Ocean Hole

Ship Channel Cay
Long Rock or Pimlico Cay
Ship Channel Harbour
Allen Cays
Highborne or Hyghburn Cay

Exuma Sound

Powell Point
Cape Eleuthera
Deal's Point
Deep Creek
Cow Rock Point
Poison Point
Deep Hole
Greencastle
Delancey Town
Waterford
Davis Harbour
Jacks Bay
Church Bay
Cotton Bay
Wemyss Bight
The Village
John Millars
Arvinda Bay

Long or Spirit Cay
Saddle or Little Normans Cay
Galleon Point
North Compass Point
Norman's Cay
Half Moon Bay

Millars
Bannerman Town
Eleuthera or East End Poir

Wax Cay

E l e u t h e r a

Map on page 250

everything from dinghies to swift three-masted schooners.

A striking measure of Dunmore Town's prosperity and subsequent decline are the population records, which list 2,500 residents in the 1870s and a little more than 700 in 1943. Today, Harbour Island is a sleepy community of about 1,000 people, far removed from the hustling and bustling era when trading was a by-word.

It is an island for passing the afternoon on a shady porch or on the lovely pink sand beach, for chatting with a neighbor over the garden fence, for watching the many flowers bloom. Fishing and farming occupy the time of some of the population, while others are employed domestically or by the government. There are also ferry operators who transport people to and from North Eleuthera.

Island character

Friendly Willie Gibson, a Harbour Island native, provides perhaps the best description of his home: "Harbour Island is a place of native peace, a place of joy, a place of harmony with lots of friendly people." Gibson is the prototype of modern island life. A fruit vendor, he hits the street for short periods each day with his trolley, but mainly he sells from home, where he can be found, just relaxing the time away.

Then there is Earl P. Johnson, the local justice of the peace. He strolls around the island visiting residents and processing legal documents when the Commissioner of the Island is out of town, or otherwise just giving advice and reliving the aristocratic Harbour Island past. "This was the first capital. The seat of the Governor was here and this town (Dunmore Town) was named after Lord Dunmore. When I was a young man, there were certain levels, and you had to live up to them to earn a certain respect. There is great history in this place. When our men went to Nassau and took it over from the Spaniards who had gained possession, that was the finest achievement of a group of Bahamians at the time. That incident will forever live in our history," Johnson said.

Today, the only evidence of the "fighting spirit" of the men of Harbour Island are some of the old-style wooden-frame houses which served as headquarters for the military. They stand as sturdily as the determination of those soldiers who sailed into Nassau two centuries ago under Colonel Andrew Deveaux, and drove the Spanish conquerors away, liberating the city and taking control for the British.

Today, in Dunmore Town you will find a remarkable mix of characters and colors – pastel clapboard cottages, several small hotels and restaurants, and the 3-mile (5-km) beach famous for its pinkish sand, created by crushed coral and shells. This is the place for days on the beach, twilight strolls along the harbor, or perhaps a noonday ride on a bicycle or in a golfcart, to explore the island's 2 sq. miles (5 sq. km) at greater speed.

As one of the oldest settlements in the Bahamas, Dunmore Town has many quaintly beautiful buildings. Those along the harbor are especially noteworthy, some of them carefully restored. A house two centuries old has been converted into a

well-loved bar. Along Bay Street, the main drag, the pastel colors of the buildings glow in the late afternoon sun. Canadians and Americans own most of these homes; some are available as vacation rentals.

Fig trees, coconut palms, and wispy tropical pines shade Harbour Island's streets. On Sunday, clusters of people dressed to kill chat outside churches before and after services. Two of the Bahamas' oldest churches are found on Dunmore Street: **St John's**, the oldest Anglican house of worship, erected in the mid-eighteenth century, and **Wesley Methodist**, built around 1846.

For vacationers, life in Dunmore Town is one of evenings in bars, lunches by the pool, dinner in a terrace or by candlelight, rooms with ceiling fans. For everyone it is a place where bougainvillea and hibiscus bloom along white picket fences, and the pace is friendly and leisurely. This island easily has the most distinctive group of small hotels in the Bahamas. All with fewer than fifty rooms, most of Harbour Island's accommodations sit on a bluff overlooking the rosy beach or offer wonderful sunset views of the harbor.

The **Romora Bay Club**, with its ancient tropical garden, is a favorite among visitors, as are **Runaway Hill Club**, **Pink Sands Resort** and **Valentine's Yacht Club**. Divers come especially to enjoy the nearby reefs. **The Landing**, a charming bed and breakfast overlooking the harbor, pairs jazz and gourmet cuisine with breathtaking views from the patio.

What Tingum Village lacks in views, this family-run hotel makes up for in delicious home-style food in its popular patio restaurant. Another local favorite, Angela's Starfish, perched on a hill above the harbor on Nesbit Street, serves some of the best cracked conch and peas and rice around. (Go easy on the hot sauce, though.)

Devil's Backbone

The sharp reefs off the coast of North Eleuthera snagged the Eleutherian Adventurers' ship, and have been the nemesis of

BELOW: relaxing on Pink Sands beach.

Map
on page
250

dozens more. So it is easy to see why one reef earned the name Devil's Backbone. Divers, however, will find them a paradise. Parrotfish, giant groupers and angelfish glide through the hulk of a 250-ft (75-meter) freighter. Divers can also explore the train wreck, the remains of a barge which ran aground as it was carrying a train locomotive to Cuba in 1865. There is also an 1890s passenger steamship that sank on the reef during a tropical storm.

Spanish Wells

Even for experienced yachtsmen, a sail along the north coast of Eleuthera, between Harbour Island and Spanish Wells, is a treacherous one. Sailors making the trip for the first few times will probably need the help of a local pilot. But this should not deter anyone who visits Harbour Island from making the trip to **Spanish Wells ❸**. (Visitors who arrive by plane in North Eleuthera have an easier time of it. It's a short taxi ride to the ferry and then a 10-minute ferry ride to

Spanish Wells.) Here, you will hear traces of a British accent and diction centuries old, spoken by the descendants of the original Eleutherian Adventurers, who settled here in the 17th century.

Spanish Wells is unique to the Bahamas: in more than 300 years the makeup of its population has hardly changed. The people still make a living mostly from small farms and the sea. However, unlike Harbour Island and the rest of Eleuthera, the insular community here is not especially friendly to outsiders.

Rich sea

The people of Spanish Wells are unique in another significant way. They form the richest society in the Commonwealth of the Bahamas.

In Spanish Wells a youngster at age 22 could very well be a millionaire. The fishing business is extremely lucrative, and young men learn fishing habits from an early age. Lobsters are the prime catch and biggest money maker, and boats from

BELOW:
Spanish Wells,
between the
sea and sky.

Spanish Wells scour the Bahamas in search of them. Some divers call these lobsters "bugs," but a better name would be "gold bugs." So lucrative is the business, and so much has it influenced the entire community, that educators have a difficult time convincing the young children to stay in school.

Many young people, by the time they are 14 or 15, have opted to skip classes in favor of fishing trips, which can earn them as much as $20,000 each. The situation is a source of great frustration for teachers in the local schools.

"If you talk to the captains of the boats and you hear the figures they talk about, you would wonder why we are sitting down teaching at school instead of all being out there on the water," says the headmaster of one school. "The money filters right on down the line. The children who stay in school have to deal with the sarcasm from their former classmates who throw jeers from their new car or the back of a motorcycle. 'You're still in school, but I've just been paid $20,000.'" Some of his students triple his earnings as a school principal.

But life on Spanish Wells has not always been so easy. The settlement, which got its name from the Spanish galleons stopping to take on water, bred a people nurtured in the ways of the sea because their lives depended on it. The first settlers, the Eleutherian Adventurers, endured great hardship to survive on this cay, which is less than 2 miles (3 km) long and a quarter-mile wide. Later, during the American war for independence, British loyalists from the American colonies joined the original inhabitants. But those who enslaved Africans were turned away, it is said, because of the original settlers' abhorrence of slavery.

Tropic Cape Cod

Like their counterparts in New England, the Puritan settlers in Spanish Wells built ship-shape Cape Cod-style cottages, many now painted blue, yellow or pink. Blond,

BELOW: a golfcart and clapboard houses, familiar sight

Map n page 250

blue-eyed and hard-working, most natives of Spanish Wells are Methodist or Anglican (belonging to an offshoot called the People's Church). Out of a population of 700, a large proportion share the surnames Pinder, Albury, Higgs or Sweeting, and tangled family trees. In this quiet, insulated utopia, hardly a newspaper is delivered (people get the news from television), hardly anyone locks their doors or even takes the keys out of the car ignition.

For visitors there are bicycles for rent (but no cars). Needless to say, the fishing is excellent off Spanish Wells. A number of men there are available for hire as fishing guides to waters off nearby Royal and Russell islands in the south.

On **Russell Island ❹**, the island's nearest neighbor, a small group of Haitians live and grow produce that they sell to the people of Spanish Wells. It's interesting to speculate that perhaps they endure many of the hardships known to the area's earliest settlers, who toughed it out on the tip of North Eleuthera a couple of miles away.

LOW:
spoken
maraderie
Governor's
rbour.

Preacher's Cave

When the Eleutherian Adventurers lost their ship and supplies to the winds and waves, they found shelter ashore in a cave. For months they lived on food foraged from the land and sea, until their leader, Captain William Sayle, set off in a small shallop (boat) with eight men to obtain help from the Puritan settlers in the colony of Jamestown, Virginia. When he returned with supplies, they were able to survive for two years longer until, desperate, they appealed again for aid from the colonists in Massachusetts. (These were the "Pilgrims," who landed at Plymouth Rock in 1620.)

The New Englanders generously sent supplies, and the Eleutherians thanked them by returning the ship loaded with hardwood. They asked that proceeds from the sale of the wood should be used to benefit Harvard College.

Throughout these early years, **Preacher's Cave ❺** was used first as a makeshift shelter, then as a place of worship (from

which it derives its name). You can travel there today by a rocky, unpaved road that leads north from the settlements of **North Eleuthera**, a journey of about 10 miles (16 km). In the cave you will see a large rock that the settlers roughly shaped to approximate a pulpit. Light filters gently down from holes in the cave roof. This quiet spot might be said to be the location of the first government of the Bahamas, where the Adventurers breathed the first air of democracy in this part of the world.

Eleuthera developed slowly but steadily through the centuries, and on the northern part of the island the settlers hung on to life by tenaciously farming the rocky soil. Today, Eleuthera tomatoes and pineapples are synonymous with quality in the Bahamas.

South from Preacher's Cave are two small farming settlements, Upper Bogue and Lower Bogue. From here it is not far to one of the most stunning land formations of the Bahamas, the **Glass Window Bridge ❻**. Here, Eleuthera nearly be-

comes two islands. The bluffs of North Eleuthera and the rest of the island break apart in a steep drop, connected only by the thinnest of threads at sea level. A bridge links the northern and southern bluffs. On the eastern side of the bridge waves crash against the rocks, while on the western side the sea may be smooth as glass.

A few miles south of the Glass Window is **Gregory Town ❼**, a quaint fishing settlement that attracts young American, Canadian and European surfers. It was also a pineapple growing center in the 19th century and more recently the site of a pineapple canning factory, but is known more enduringly for production of a pineapple rum known locally as "Gregory Town Special."

Several more miles along is **Hatchet Bay ❽**, which naturalists find interesting for its bat cave. Here, thousands of leaf-nosed bats roost in the midnight black cave, waiting to fly out at night to search for food. In the 1930s and 1940s Hatchet Bay was one of the major workplaces in the country with a large poultry and dairy industry. When the company closed down the economy practically died. Today, it is on the upswing due to a government farming and produce exchange.

Old mortality

A fading Victorian beauty, **Governor's Harbour ❾**, in the center of the island, was once one of the Bahamas' most prosperous towns. Founded by some of the original Eleutherian Adventurers, with the arrival of the Loyalists it became a hive of activity. Ships loaded with pineapples and other fruit set sail for Baltimore and New York, to return with the fruits of America's burgeoning 19th-century industries – food and building supplies, cloth, tools and household items. Women traveled from Nassau to Governor's Harbour to buy the latest fashions.

Today, large casuarina trees, poincianas and bougainvilleas shade the quiet streets of one of Eleuthera's oldest settlements. With beautiful, wide pink beaches, hilly Governor's Harbour is considered a real find by visitors seeking peace and quiet with few tourists around.

LEFT: stunning views from Glass Window Bridge.

Map on page 250

Across a little bridge, west of the center of Governor's Harbour, is **Cupid's Cay**, where the colonial homes are charming, if a bit tattered by the years of use.

Touring the south

A few miles south and off the mainland is **Windermere Island ⑩**, once ruled by the preppie, understated Windermere Club. The well-heeled vacationers here have included Princess Diana and Prince Charles, the Duke and Duchess of Abercorne, Countess Mountbatten and Edwin Moses, the American Olympic gold medalist track star. Although the Club is now closed, private villas on the island can still be rented. With names such as Cherokee, Dolphin House, and Beaumaris, these luxury homes line the main road, overhung with tall pines whose branches form a shady canopy. You can reach the island by bridge from the small settlement of **Savannah Sound**.

Several miles south of Savannah Sound is **Tarpum Bay ⑪**, an old settlement which had its heyday when Eleuthera was a booming exporter of pineapples. The then Assistant Resident Justice, Joseph Culmer, even composed an essay on the pineapple industry in 1904. "Select good men as cutters and draggers out of the field, avoid the injurious practice of breaking off the pineapple from the stem by pressure of the knee, cut the stem at the base of the fruit; pass the pineapple over to the attendant who will lay them carefully at the fence or margin of the field..." he instructed. Regrettably, this care was often taken for naught, as pineapples were packed by the thousands in the holds of large schooners, and those on the bottom did not always arrive in the best condition.

Throughout the 19th century, Eleuthera led the Bahamas in pineapple exports and know-how, and is credited with introducing the crop to Cat Island and Long Island. It was largely pineapples that gave life to towns like Tarpum Bay, where today the dock no longer bustles with activity. In the words of an Eleutherian

LOW: rpum Bay, ɔpared for ristmas.

Map on page 250

pineapple grower: "It was from the Bahamas that the Americans took pineapples to Hawaii and it was from Hawaii that the Bahamas received most of its competition which ultimately led to the decline of the industry." Today, the ramshackle gingerbread houses and shady casuarina trees make Tarpum Bay a pleasant place to stroll the quiet streets.

Farther south, **Rock Sound** ⓬ was another pineapple center, where, as recently as 1964, Bahamas Best Products was canning sliced pineapples and pineapple juice. Today, Eleuthera pineapples are still delicious, but they are grown mostly for consumption within the Bahamas. Rock Sound is an enjoyable place to visit, with a modern shopping center. There are also several restaurants in town and the **Cotton Bay Marina and Golf Club**, with an 18-hole championship course.

Just over 1 mile (1.5 km) east of Rock Sound, down a narrow road, is **Rock Sound Ocean Hole** ⓭. Like other inland "ocean holes" or "blue holes" in the

Bahamas, this pool is reputed to be so deep it has no bottom. Actually, it is connected by underground caves and passages to the sea. Seagoing fish like grouper and yellowtail travel the watery ways to swim around in this "lake."

From Rock Sound, one has the option of traveling either to **Cape Eleuthera** ⓮ or **Eleuthera Point** ⓯, like the opposite tips on the tail of a fish. Though hard to reach, Eleuthera Point is worth a stop for its beautiful beach and excellent diving.

In between the tips, along the bottom of the fin, are several small quiet villages: Deep Creek, Delancey Town, Wemyss Bight, Bannerman Town and Millars. There are no resorts along this "tail" of the island, but bonefishermen will find blissful fishing in the many creeks that are favorite homes for those wily fish.

Same as it ever was

In the villages here and in the other villages farther north on the island – Upper Bogue and Lower Bogue, Gregory Town, Alice Town, James Cistern – life ambles on much as it has for years throughout the Out Islands. A middle-aged man, with the experience of many years, deftly skins a goat that hangs from a tree beside the road. Fresh "local mutton" will soon be on the dinner tables in his settlement. A child stands outside his modest thatched home overlooking the sea, he eats fresh fish and conch and is robust and healthy. An elderly woman pats two loaves of dough into an iron pan and, using a stick of wood, guides the pan into an outdoor stone oven, which she claims will bake the tastiest bread anywhere in the hemisphere.

In the larger settlements, like Rock Sound, Tarpum Bay and Hatchet Bay, friends greet each other in a shop. In old Governor's Harbour, dusk is falling, and the lights in the houses begin to come on. Off Spanish Wells an experienced seaman guides a sloop safely between the reefs towards port in Harbour Island. In Dunmore Town a girl plucks a hibiscus flower. At the Glass Window Bridge, deep water surges around the rocks on one side, while the water on the other side is calm and peaceful. ❑

LEFT: girls in Tarpum Bay.
RIGHT: spectacular starfish.

CAT ISLAND

Colorful stories of pirates and magic reveal a land that is steeped in traditional African-Bahamian culture. Ruined plantation houses dot the landscape and sweeping remote bays offer peace

Imagine walking down a country road on a sun-washed morning, the sky above blue, the air soft and fresh, the day ready to unfold. A lunch in the shade of tall casuarina trees beside a deserted beach, then exploring a ruined plantation house where the walls are green with vines. Imagine the perfect summer day.

Then think of watching clouds scuttle across the moon and the roar of wind in the trees. Imagine the thick darkness of a night beyond the edges of the scientific, citified world.

Shrouded in mystery, bathed in sunlight, Cat Island is the sixth largest and among the least known islands in the Bahamas, and also the least traveled. Most Bahamians know little about this long-forgotten island, except that it is about 50 miles (80 km) long and shaped like a pirate's boot or a lady's stocking. The summit of one of the hills, as every Bahamian will tell you, is the highest point in the Bahamas. Cat Island is a stone's throw away from Eleuthera, to its north, and 130 miles (209 km) southeast of the nation's capital, Nassau.

Pirates and island magic

The island was named after a pirate, Arthur Catt, who used to rendezvous here at Port Howe with his friends Henry Morgan and Edward Teach (also known as Blackbeard). Stories about Cat Island concern buried gold and jewels. Some years ago a yacht came into Port Howe,

PRECEDING PAGES: an exhilarating way to travel between the islands. **BELOW:** bird's eye view of Fernandez Ba[

Map below

goes one story, and the yacht captain got into conversation with a very old woman on shore, who told him that her father had been overseer at the Richman Hill-Newfield plantation, and that he had told her where some treasure was buried. She described the location, they organized a treasure hunt, and they found an old chest full of silver coins. The captain took the chest away and left the woman to mourn: "They gave me only one piece."

Many other stories concern ghosts and the supernatural powers of spells and curses. Though most Cat Islanders are zealous church-goers, around the island are trees with bottles hung in the branches. Graveyard dirt, hair, fingernails and other articles inside the bottles are meant to protect the owner's property from robbers. Known throughout the Bahamas as a big Obeah island, Cat Island is inhabited by powerful Obeah men and women – practitioners of this traditional Bahamian form of witchcraft or magic who can "put a witch" (hex) on someone. Potions cre-

ated by practitioners can be used to curse or cure. The island abounds with tales of illnesses, deaths and retribution meted out by the powers of Obeah, of hands coming from nowhere to strangle in the night, *sperrids* (spirits) and zombies rising out of graves. Originating in West African folklore, Obeah is still practiced in the Bahamas and some Caribbean islands, although few people openly admit to it.

First landfall

Another story islanders like to tell is that Cat Island is where Columbus first set foot on the New World. It is indeed true that old deeds and maps name Cat Island "San Salvador," which was Columbus's first landfall, and call the present San Salvador "Watling's Island." (Watling, like Catt, was a pirate.) The large lake at the ankle of the boot and the huge bay on the island's west side of Columbus's enigmatic journal descriptions of "San Salvador" also fit the geography of the current San Salvador. The huge bay,

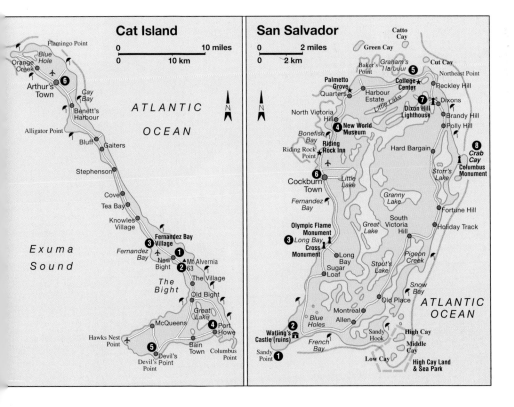

which was perhaps the one Columbus meant when he wrote of a harbour that could hold "all the ships in Christendom," would make a fine place to begin an exploration of the foot of this boot-shaped island – this could take the better part of a day, or more.

The Bights

Called **The Bight**, the immense bay laps on the shores of two villages, New Bight and Old Bight. In **New Bight** , the administrative center, are small shops for groceries and supplies, the commissioner's house and the Catholic Church, built by Father Jerome, who also built the hermitage on Mount Alvernia *(see page 265)*.

South, on the Queen's Highway, **Old Bight** is more quaint; it lies inland from a beautiful, lazy curve of beach. Not to miss along the north end of the Bight are the ruins of **Pigeon Bay Cottage**, a plantation house dating from the early 19th century when, for a few short years cotton was king on the island. Now, white goats wander amid the tumbledown walls, and the two-story house on the graceful rise above the road clings to but a glimmer of its proud past.

When Britain's abolition of slavery and the cotton-eating chenille bug combined to put an end to the plantation way of life, most plantation owners abandoned the island. A man named W.E. Armbrister remained, however, and put his field hands to work growing fruit, vegetables and sisal. Midway down the road along the Bight, in a settlement called **The Village**, W.E. Armbrister had a small factory to extract the fibers from the sisal plant, which was then shipped to foreign ports to be made into rope. A narrow gauge railroad, the remains of which can be seen here, carried sisal from the fields on the other side of the island.

Holy solitude

On the calm, western side of the island, above the village of New Bight, is a spot with a gorgeous view. In the early part of

BELOW: it's a steep climb to Mount Alvernia.

Map
on page
263

the 20th century a man named John Hawes, who later took the name Father Jerome, built churches throughout the Bahamas – notably two on Long Island and St Augustine's Monastery in Nassau. He converted from Anglican to Catholicism, retreating toward the end of his days to Cat Island. A tall man, he slept in a short, narrow bed to mortify his body; he wore sandals and a long robe in all weathers.

It seems that he was humble in everything but the choice of a site for his **Hermitage**, which he built on the highest point in the Bahamas.

Looking down from **Mount Alvernia ❷** you feel like you are on the top of the world. At 206 ft (63 meters), the hill offers both eastern and western views of the ocean. Getting there involves a short drive on the dirt road that begins next to the commissioner's house in New Bight, and then a steep climb past the stations of the cross that Father Jerome carved by hand.

From a distance, the chapel, bell tower and adjoining buildings of the hermitage seem three times their actual size; up close they form a small, Italian-style monastery. In fact, only two or three adults could sit in the chapel; the living quarters consists of three main rooms, none much larger than a closet, with small windows with glimpses of the sea. From a covered outdoor passage, between the stone arches, the dusky green of the north island and the bright blue of The Bight are visible.

About 3 miles (5 km) north of New Bight is **Fernandez Bay Village ❸**, a small, gracious resort with several guest cottages built of local stone among the casuarina trees. In each cottage, large glass doors open onto the sandy curve of beach along Fernandez Bay. At dusk, the sinking sun fills the whole bay with gold and silver-blue, as if it were a giant turtle shell filled with all the gleaming fish in this warm, shallow sea. A fine place for dinner is the dining room of Fernandez Bay Village, where you can dine on fresh fish caught earlier that day in a paneled room beneath mahogany beams.

BELOW: the Hermitage, a monastery in miniature.

Plantation legacy

To the south east, along the Atlantic coastline of windblown shrubbery, crumbling cliffs and sea views, are the ruins of the Richman Hill-Newfield plantation, Port Howe and the Deveaux house. East from the Cutlass Bay Club are the villages of Bain Town and Zonicles. Past Zonicles, the gray stone ruins of **Richman Hill-Newfield** plantation are just visible from the road. The walls were once part of the overseer's house. The road to the plantation is totally overgrown; under better conditions you could see garden walls, what remains of the slave quarters and the main house. The plantation's lands encompassed 2,000 acres (800 hectares), stretching from the lake that lies just inland from the ocean.

A couple of miles from the plantation ruins is **Port Howe ❹**, known for the delicious pineapples grown round about it each summer. In the past it was known for wreckers, who used to lure ships onto the offshore reef by shining false and confus-

ing lights. When the ships floundered and broke up, they reaped the bounty of the cargo. These wreckers were among the earliest settlers of the island. In 1768, Governor Thomas Shirley, describing the population of the island, declared that there were "in all supposed to be 30 people who have gone thither [to Cat Island and Exuma] to make a trial of the soil and for the convention of wrecking."

A more illustrious early citizen was the famed Colonel Andrew Deveaux. He received grants of land on Cat Island as a reward for capturing Nassau from the Spanish in 1783 and built himself a fine house near Port Howe, where he lived as lord-of-the-manor. The *Bahamas Gazette* in April 1799 reported in an "Extract of a Letter from a Cotton Planter" that "the best specimen of practical rural economy that has met my observation is afforded by the elder Mr. Deveaux's plantation in St Salvador [Cat Island]... His is a plantation of Georgia cotton without bugs; and his crop is gathered, in the barn, clean and

BELOW: the faded splendo of the Deveau mansion.

Map on page 263

white. Indeed, the dreadful outcry against Georgia cotton on account of bugs must be silenced by the actual state of nearly all the St Salvador plantations."

Deveaux and his family lived in fairly grand style in a two-story plantation house with a detached kitchen and a smaller one-story addition next door. In the 1930s, when two Catholic priests lived there, the house still had its balconies, a staircase and random width plank floors.

Today, shrubs grow through the open floor, and in the kitchen a tree has strung its twisted roots around the fireplace. In the parlor, only a ghostly trace remains of the once elegant staircase, a faint stain that rises up the wall, step by step. In the afternoon, the faded pink walls catch the last of the sunlight before slipping into the shadow of the school that has been built next door.

To the heel and sole

BELOW: boating the waters off Cat Island.

The coast near Port Howe affords splendid views. Cliffs drop sharply to the sea; the low, thick undergrowth shines waxy green in the bright light. A couple of American business magnates have built second homes here. Though no road goes there, about three miles from Port Howe is the easternmost point of the island, the heel of the boot. It points towards Spain and is called **Columbus Point**.

Along the road west via Deep South Roundabout is a fine view of the ocean at **Devil's Point ⑤**, in the south west; this ragged, pretty village on the sole of the boot is the southernmost point on the island. As in many Cat Island settlements, the thick-walled stone houses are painted white, yellow or pink, with roofs made of palmetto thatch.

Journey north

A trip up the leg of the boot is a fine outing for another day. There are no hotels on this long, skinny shin of the island. The road north along the water passes one quaint settlement after another: **Tea Bay**, with wooden dinghies pulled up on the beach beneath the tall coconut palms;

Bluff, with its outdoor stone ovens white-washed like miniature houses; **Bennett's Harbour**, one of the island's larger and oldest settlements.

At the north end of the island, **Arthur's Town** ❻ lacks the charm of the other villages, but it has a perfectly paved 7,800-ft (2,400-meter) airstrip, several provisions stores, and a telephone station. It was the childhood home of Sidney Poitier, the award-winning actor and a Bahamas Ambassador, who relates some fond memories of his parents and Cat Island relatives in his book *This Life*. Like many Cat Islanders then and now, his parents were farmers.

Using the traditional cut-and-burn method to clear the ground of undergrowth, farmers create small plots, usually no larger than one or two acres (less than one hectare), where they grow mostly tomatoes and pineapples, but also pigeon peas, bananas and melons. Plots are often a considerable distance from home, and the long trip is often made on

Map on page 263

foot, though horses were sometimes used in the past.

Fishing supplements the very small profit gained from farming, and some people have been known to keep a Cat Island turtle *(Pseudemys felis)* in the bottom of a well as insurance against hard times. Islanders call these turtles "peters," and consider their meat delicious. These freshwater turtles have experienced hard times of their own throughout the Bahamas, and Cat Island's muddy, shallow ponds are the last refuge of this particular species.

Island heritage

If ever there was an island meant for heritage tourism, Cat Island is surely it. Old world ways meet new in a delightful way at the annual **Cat Island Heritage Festival**, held in May. The brainchild of Pamela Poitier, daughter of Sidney Poitier, this summer festival is a weekend celebration that enlivens Arthur's Town.

The festival provides an opportunity to experience traditional African-Bahamian culture, featuring all things Bahamian from quadrille dancing to rake and scrape music competitions and lectures on the mysteries of obeah. Also in May/June is the annual Rake and Scrape competition, and in August the **Cat Island Regatta**, held on Emancipation Day.

At times it seems Cat Island is a distant, sheltered, hidden pool, not for turtles, but for an old Bahamian way of life. But time has not stood completely still here. A few satellite dishes have sprung up. Yet some things remain much the same. In the villages, farmers set out in the early morning for their fields – leaving behind their thatched houses, their whitewashed outdoor ovens, their children studying in a one-room school.

On the long afternoons, the coconut palms, casuarina trees, palmettos, pineapple plants and the rocky limestone soil seem to lie beyond time, warming in the tropical sun. As the rest of the world moves on, grinding through the day's momentous and trivial events, life on Cat Island shuffle steps through its age-old dance, readying for evening, for night. ❑

LEFT: Sunday best. **RIGHT:** a Cat Islander and his kid.

SAN SALVADOR

First came the Lucayans, then Christopher Columbus. Now tourists are attracted by the island's pristine reefs, populated by colorful sea life and littered with shipwrecks, and with expanses of beach

Map on page 263

On the decks of the three Spanish vessels, men were tense. The day had been exciting; they had seen land birds overhead and green branches floating by. It was 10 o'clock when all hands were awakened. A shout came from the masthead: "A light, a light!" To Christopher Columbus's elation, another person had seen the flickering light, which he had been afraid to tell himself was not just another mirage.

At two o'clock the white cliffs of High Cay were clearly visible. With a prudent mariner's skill, Columbus ordered his fleet to heave-to until daylight, when the rising sun would reveal dangerous coral reefs connecting High Cay to its sisters, Low Cay and Nancy Cay. These small cays, visible from San Salvador's southeastern shore and easily reachable by small boat, are now the graveyard of numerous ships whose captains were not as skilled as Columbus.

The deep south

Continuing westward, Columbus skirted **French Bay**, missing the reef break leading into a safe winter anchorage. Visitors today find French Bay well worth a visit. Shelling and tidal pools attract beach walkers; outstanding elkhorn coral reefs beckon snorkelers and scuba divers; and the ruins of Watling's Castle encourage the enthusiastic history buff.

South along the west coast of the island on the Queen's Highway is the Government Dock on French Bay. For more vigorous swimmers and divers, a trip to the western tip of **Sandy Point ❶**, where the fringing reef across French Bay attaches itself to the headland, is a must in calm weather. Reached from a small road off the Queen's Highway parallel to the bay, this pristine reef consists of massive stands of elkhorn corals and numerous varieties of reef fish.

On the hill overlooking French Bay are the ruins of **Watling's Castle ❷**. Although the island tourist trade has promoted the legend that the pirate John Watling built this "castle" here in the 1600s, the ruins are in fact the remains of a Loyalist plantation. Following the American Revolution, many southern planters who remained loyal to the British crown migrated to the Bahamas and re-established cotton plantations worked by enslaved Africans. This migration played a major role in populating San Salvador, since emancipation in the 1830s resulted in the landowners leaving their land on the island in the hands of the people they had once enslaved.

Watling's Castle, more properly called

the Sandy Point Estate, consisted of numerous stone buildings, including several for industrial or storage purposes as well as a main house and a cookhouse for the master. Curious visitors can climb the hill to the west of the Queen's Highway and walk among the ruins of these buildings. To the east of the highway are what remains of the slave quarters, which were small, one-room stone dwellings with no distinguishing features. It is difficult to visualize what the entire plantation looked like in its heyday because of the dense vegetation covering some of the buildings that are still standing, but a visit is worthwhile for anyone interested in the history of the Bahamas.

Landing at Long Bay

As Christopher Columbus rounded Sandy Point, he prudently avoided the outer reef, anxiously seeking a break in the coral for passage to the sandy shoreline. Eventually he succeeded, bringing his three vessels into what is now **Long Bay ❸**.

Columbus brought his boats as close to the beach as he dared, thus providing cannon support for a landing party. A bronze monument is now located under the sea at Long Bay, to mark the spot where Columbus anchored in 1492.

On shore, Columbus knelt and gave thanks, declaring the land to be the property of the king and queen of Spain, and naming the island San Salvador. Today, a large white cross, erected in 1956 by Columbian historian and artist Ruth Wolper, marks this spot.

The Amerindians who welcomed Columbus, came from a village near the shore, the remains of which have been excavated by archaeologists. Artifacts unearthed include bronze buckles, glass beads, and pieces of European crockery, all items Columbus, in his notes, described his men trading with the Amerindians. These original inhabitants of the island, which they called Guanahani, were Arawakian speakers related to other Amerindians who lived in the Caribbean

BELOW: "Watling's Castle", in fact a ruined plantation house.

Map
n page
263

and South America. Specifically, they were Lucayan *(see page 21)*, a peaceful people who lived by fishing and the cultivation of manioc or cassava.

Explorations

Columbus described the rocks along the shore to the north as "suitable for the construction of government buildings." These rocks are still visible today, though we now know that their composition precludes their use in construction. Because these rocks seem to move in and out of the water during wave and tidal action, they have been termed **Riding Rocks**, and gave their name to the long established hotel on San Salvador, the **Riding Rock Inn**. The hotel is just north of Cockburn Town, the main community and government center for the island's 1,000 residents. Club Med Columbus Isle opened in 1992 and was located on a stunning beach near Riding Rock. This snazzy resort provided a choice of accommodation before it closed, once again making

the Riding Rock Inn the only game in town for vacationers. It still attracts avid scuba divers and visitors looking for a Bahamian atmosphere. Guest rooms and small stone cottages are simply furnished.

To explore the island, Columbus used his long boats, rowing northward along the coast. On rounding a point on the northwest corner of San Salvador, he described a group of Amerindians coming from their homes. Archaeologists have located a Lucayan Amerindian settlement here and named it **Palmetto Grove**. Artifacts from this site and others on the island are now housed in the **New World Museum ❹**, located near this point and the present North Victoria Hill near the northwest coast. Viewing of the museum is free but by appointment only; there is no telephone, so ask at your hotel.

A northeastward course brought Columbus into Graham's Harbour, which he said "would hold all the ships of Christendom." To the east he beheld **North Point**, a long spit of land jutting northward. The end of

OW:
cate skin
he water.

the point Columbus felt would make an excellent place for a fortification, since it could be easily separated from the mainland by digging a moat. Nature itself later provided the moat, separating **Cut Cay** from North Point sometime in the last 500–600 years. And, in fact, a fortress may have occupied this site at one time, since a cannon was brought up from the sea near Cut Cay and cannon balls have been unearthed along its shore. A leisurely walk along North Point reveals the vast contrast in the ocean, with the calm waters of **Graham's Harbour ❺** on one side and the fierce, crashing waves of the open ocean on the other.

On the hill overlooking the western end of Graham's Harbour is the grave of the first priest to bring Catholicism to San Salvador, Fr. Chrysostom Schreiner, probably best known for his extensive Columbian research, which resulted in the name of the island being changed from Watling's Island back to Columbus's original, San Salvador.

Fossils and missiles

A large complex of buildings located along the beach of Graham's Harbour is the **College Center of the Finger Lakes' Bahamian Field Station**, which studies the island's biology and geology, and its history. This consortium of United States colleges and universities provides housing, laboratories, and related support facilities for scientists and students throughout the world to study and learn in this unspoiled and unique environment.

The facilities of the CCFL Bahamian Field Station were originally built by the United States Navy in the late 1950s and early 1960s as a submarine tracking station. Also built during this same period were the US Pan American Base and airport, on the northwest side of the island, and the US Coast Guard Station, on the northeastern corner of San Salvador. These military bases were constructed on what was then British land. When these facilities became obsolete, they were turned over to the Bahamas government,

BELOW: a fisherman's son.

Map
n page
263

ow: the
ns of *agave
eana*, can
sed as
les.

as was the navy base on Graham's Harbour. Today, the CCFL Bahamian Field Station leases its campus from the Bahamas government.

The effect of this influx of US military and civilian personnel on San Salvador in the 1950s was phenomenal. Before, the island had been accessible only by boat, and transportation on the island was by dirt trails and small boats plying the inland lakes. Today, San Salvador airport, located in the northwest, near Cockburn Town, provides the major link to the outside world, with daily commercial flights from Nassau and numerous air charters from the US. The weekly mailboat brings produce, freight and mail from Nassau.

The departure of the US personnel in the late 1960s also altered the local economy and subsequently the lifestyle. Many young men and women had to leave San Salvador to find employment elsewhere. Those who remained found positions within the rising tourist industry. The small Riding Rock Inn *(see page 273)* had

been built south of the airport in the late 1950s to accommodate relatives and friends of the military personnel. This was purchased by a Florida land development company, which used it as a base while developing large tracts of land at the southern end of the island.

The second landing

Americans, Canadians, and Europeans were brought to San Salvador by the development company, accommodated in the expanded Riding Rock Inn, and sold land. The landscape of the southern portion of the island was greatly altered, with streets, avenues, and a golf course bulldozed into existence. When the roads were finished and the property sold, the land company departed, leaving behind 12 condominiums, 20 private homes, and an overgrown golf course.

The Riding Rock Inn continues to operate under different ownership, catering now to divers and underwater photographers who flock to the pristine reefs of

San Salvador, considered by many to be the best in the Caribbean. The steep submarine canyons off Southwest Point and French Bay are a special attraction.

When not in the water, visitors enjoy walking through the narrow, charming streets of nearby **Cockburn Town ⑥** (pronounced Ko-burn town). Home to about 250 people, this town is easily explored on foot.

Lookouts and salt lakes

Directly east of the Riding Rock Inn, a road leads inland to a **lookout tower**, from which most of San Salvador is visible. A sight of beauty and wonder are the numerous inland lakes that were once the main transportation network of the island, but are now peaceful and seldom visited. Across the lakes to the northeast is the large community of United Estates and the lighthouse, now reached by the paved Queen's Highway that circles the whole island.

The **Dixon Hill Lighthouse ⑦** (donations welcome), which is located south of

Graham's Harbour, was built in 1856 and is one of the few lighthouses still in existence that is entirely manually operated. The light from a small kerosene lamp is beamed up to 19 miles (35 km) at 400,000 candle power by a set of prisms floating on a bed of mercury. The double flash sent out every 25 seconds is controlled by a set of weights and clockworks, which must be wound regularly by one of the two lighthouse keepers. A tour of the lighthouse machinery and a view from the top of Dixon Hill are a must for anyone visiting San Salvador. It is well worth the short, but steep climb from the road.

Eastward from the lighthouse, across a narrow causeway and over several sand dunes, is **East Beach**. This mile-long stretch of golden beach awaits beachcombers, since glass fishing floats and bottles with notes inside often come ashore here. For the venturesome, a walk to the south leads to a rocky outcrop, **Crab Cay ⑧**, on which sits the oldest monument commemorating Columbus' landing on San Salvador in 1492. Overlooking the numerous reefs and rocks along this coastline, one wonders why anyone believed this to be the site of Columbus' first landfall. Yet, in 1892, *The Chicago Herald* newspaper built this monument to celebrate the 400th anniversary of this event.

Returning to the Queen's Highway you can continue south, though the road lies inland most of the way. **Storr's Lake**, a large muddy lake west of the highway, is a good example of the many hypersaline, utrophic lakes which make up the interior of the island. Farther south the road runs parallel to **Pigeon Creek**, an 8-mile (13-km) lagoon whose opening is at the southeast corner of the island, opposite High Cay. Since this lagoon is flushed regularly by tides, it is slowly filling with sand, but it still serves as a calm anchorage for small fishing boats. The mangroves along its shores form a unique ecological niche as a nursery area for numerous species of large fish, including shark.

Offshore, the southern cays that form **High Cay Land and Sea Park** protect the habitats of rare birds and iguanas. ❏

LEFT: bay o[f] discovery.
RIGHT: histo[ric] Dixon Hill Lighthouse.

Map on page 282

ANDROS

Dive in blue holes, enjoy a spot of bonefishing, relax on quiet palm-fringed beaches and see unique crafts. This island has a rich culture, enlivened with tales of strange forest-dwelling creatures and buried pirates' treasure

Andros, the largest of the Bahamian islands, has always been described as a mystery. Lying in the middle of the Atlantic Ocean with its host of sister islands, cays, rocks and forests that are home to mythical beings, Andros is well endowed with everything a visitor could dream of. About 104 miles (225 km) long and 40 miles (64 km) wide, Andros lies west of the Bahamian capital of Nassau, on New Providence, and has the third largest population in the Out Islands.

Divided politically into three sections – North, Central and South – Andros features some of the most interesting sporting life in the Bahamas, in its deep sea fishing and diving.

Tantalizing tales

Columbus called Andros "La Isla del Espirito Santo," the island of the Holy Spirit. No wonder a cloud of mystery surrounds it. The huge island's modern name is believed to be derived from the British commander, Sir Edmund Andros.

The history of the island is as vague as it is tantalizing. There are numerous tales and Amerindian myths relating to it, the most famous being the chickcharnies of Red Bay, North Andros. Possibly, the tale of these odd-looking red-eyed, tree-dwelling birds originated with Seminole Indians, who migrated from South Florida to Red Bay some time in the 17th century.

According to legend, the chickcharnies, birds with beards, are responsible for much mischief and build their nests by tying the tops of pine trees together. They are also said to hang from the trees by their "tails". The chickcharnie's origins can be traced back to before the ice age, when Andros was a plateau 400 ft (120 meters) above sea level and when the entire coastline was riddled with caves. In these caves, it is claimed, lived a human-like owl that was believed to mea-

sure 3–5 ft (1–2 meters) tall. The islanders have reportedly discovered the birds' remains in blue holes. Part of the owl's staple diet was a large rodent called a hutia. When the ice cap melted Andros sunk, and supposedly, the large owl and the rodent disappeared, too.

It was not until the island's dense forest was logged in the 1950s, more than 12,000 years later, that the chickcharnies were reportedly rediscovered. Some of the people working in the virgin forest told frightening tales of a large owl that appeared to them at dusk. Prior to this the creatures were considered to be a creation of Amerindian legends, worshipped as the sacred and mystical gods of the island. Unfortunately, the colorful stories that

form part of Andros island's folklore are slowly being lost as the elders, entrusted with keeping the tales alive, are dying out.

A tricky approach

One of the least known of all the Bahamian islands, in spite of its size, Andros has a great many tricky shoals on the western side, from Morgan's Bluff in the north to Mars Bay in the south, rendering it almost unapproachable by boat. The eastern coastline has the world's longest coral reef outside Australia.

Andros has four small airports for easy travel to any part of the island, which is divided at several points by long, narrow creeks. There are airports at San Andros (serving the north), Andros Town and Mangrove Cay (for the center) and Congo Town for flights to the south.

In addition, there are three official ports of entry: Fresh Creek (central), Mastic Point (north) and Congo Town (south), all servicing boats, aircraft and seaplanes that arrive on a daily basis.

Spectacular dives

Offering a variety of sports, the island has always been popular with scuba divers for its 140-mile (225-km) long **Andros Barrier Reef** ❶. The second longest coral reef in the world (only Australia's Great Barrier Reef is longer) attracts hundreds of visitors throughout the year. Lying on the eastern shore, the reef divides the 12-ft (3.5-meter) waters of the Great Bahama Bank from the depths of a great ocean trench, the **Tongue of the Ocean** ❷. Plunging 2 miles (3 km) into watery darkness, the Tongue of the Ocean is an anomaly in the shallow Bahamian seas. Geologists speculate that it was once a prehistoric riverbed, something like the Grand Canyon in Arizona, USA.

The coral gardens, drop-offs and wall dives here are among the most spectacular in the world. The Small Hope Bay Lodge *(see page 287)* at Fresh Creek is one of the diving centers on the island; there are also instructors and dive masters at Nicholls Town. Deep dives, such as those

LEFT: an inland blue hole.

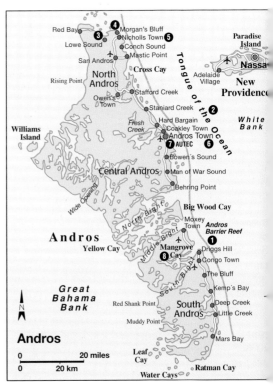

Map on page 282

around the Bahama Bank are recommended for experienced divers, and then only with a reputable local dive operator. Beginners and inexperienced divers can still enjoy the ocean's stunning sights whilst diving in shallower water.

To cap off a breathtaking diving experience, there are numerous blue holes where freshwater springs well to the surface in the middle of the ocean floor. A 1981 exploration of the blue holes of Andros by a team of expert British and American divers was described as one of the most original, exciting and important underwater adventures in recent memory. **Conch Sound**, with more than 3,000 ft (900 meters) of passage, was explored during the expeditions and has been revisited for exploration of more distant passages. Experts described the blue holes as the longest, deepest and most beautiful submarine caves on earth.

Water also wells up to form some spectacular inland blue holes of great depth, where the mirror-like waters reflect the

GHT: a rving of a ickcharnie.

tall trees and sky. Evil spirits called *luca*, which, according to folk legend, resemble octopi, are said to live in these blue holes, lying in wait to pull unsuspecting divers and small boats down to the depths.

Nets and spears

Andros is a well-known diving center and has also established itself as "Bonefish Capital of the World," with miles of flats. The center for this activity is the **Lowe Sound ❸** settlement in North Andros.

In former times the people of Andros used nets to haul in fish, but spearfishing among the reefs has become the most fashionable form of fishing, although reel-fishing from yachts is on the rise too. Offshore reefs attract a large variety of fish, including mackerel, snapper, amberjack, grouper and yellowtail. Inhabiting the Tongue of the Ocean are sailfish, wahoo, dolphin (fish), tarpon, marlin and jack. *(See Hooked on Fishing, pages 117–27.)*

Skiffs, sailboats, sunfish and larger and faster speedboats, such as Boston Whalers

LEGEND OF THE CHICKCHARNIES

The chickcharnie is a mythical creature believed to live on Andros. Half-man, half-bird, it inhabits the island's pine forests and can be found where one set of trees criss-cross over another. In between the branches you may see a giant nest that is said to be the home of the chickcharnie.

Prior to sightings of the creatures in the 1950s, they were considered to be nothing more than a myth from Amerindian legends, by a people who worshipped them as the sacred and mystical gods of the island. Today, many of the stories are dying with the island elders.

One of the stories of the chickcharnies suggests that they protected the Lucayan Amerindians from the invading Spaniards, by giving them the power to become invisible. The legend also states that if you go to a pine forest, make sure that you have only good intentions toward Andros island on your mind, because if you don't the chickcharnies can sense this.

If the chickcharnies discover that you have bad intentions they will turn your head backwards and that will be that. You will never go forwards again in your life, and as one island elder puts it "when you go backwards it's the end of your time."

and Abacos, explore the island's many inlets, bays and creeks. Several small boat marinas are available to fishermen and small boaters. The island has one full service marina, at the Lighthouse Yacht Club in Andros Town. The marina can accommodate sizeable vessels up to 150 ft (46 meters) and has 18 slips.

Pigeon fanciers

Adding further excitement for a few sports lovers is the six-month September to March hunting season, when hunters can take advantage of the island's large wild bird preserves. **Green Cay**, 20 miles (32 km) east of Deep Creek in the Kemp's Bay Area, South Andros, holds the second largest breeding colony of white-crowned pigeons in the world. The pigeons, one of the hunter's prime targets, fly to Andros in search of food and water.

The yearly white-crowned pigeon hunt has been a Bahamian tradition, ever since early times when settlers needed pigeons for food. In the 19th century these birds flocked to the area in such abundance that C.J. Maynard, an ornithologist, counted over 10,000 nests on a single one-acre (half-hectare) cay. He wrote in his journal: "The rocks were mostly covered with a scanty growth of low bushes and with a more luxuriant growth of cacti, and upon both plants and brushes the birds had placed their nests, and some were on elevated portions of rock, while a few were placed on the naked ground. So completely covered was the southern and northern portion of this key that the nests were nowhere over two feet apart, and often nearer than that."

Since Maynard's time the population has been depleted, and laws now protect them (including a 90-day residency requirement for foreign hunters).

Birdwatchers in Andros have also spotted rare types of tern and the rare whistling tree duck. The island's forests, green pinelands and mangroves are inhabited by more than 100 different species, including resident and migratory birds.

BELOW: North Andros forest

Map
on page
282

Nature lovers can explore the various nature trails on the island, especially those in South Andros around Driggs Hill, Congo Town and Kemp's Bay *(see page 290)*. Visitors interested in walking the nature trails can take a tour accompanied by a local guide, who will point out and describe the fauna and flora seen along the way. The flora may include brilliantly-colored wild orchids, bromeliads and plants that have medicinal properties. As for fauna, you are likely to see not only the white-crowned pigeon, but also the yellow crown heron and the brown lizard cuckoo.

Bays and bluffs

North and central Andros offer more variety than any part of the island. At the northernmost tip, close to the Lowe Sound settlement, is **Morgan's Bluff** ❹, believed to be named after the pirate Sir Henry Morgan. It is claimed that he, hid a valuable but as yet undiscovered treasure in a cave aptly called **Henry Morgan's**

Cave, located around 90 ft (30 meters) from the road.

To the west of Lowe Sound, across vast mud flats unreachable except by boat or unpaved road, is **Red Bay**, a small village whose inhabitants are descendants of unions between Seminole Indians and black settlers, believed to have arrived in the mid-19th century as runaway slaves from the United States.

Red Bay is the sponge capital of the Bahamas islands thanks to the long-established sponge industry that still provides the village's main income along with fishing. This is also a traditional craft center, which is home to the talented weavers of the distinctive Andros baskets, as well as wood carvers *(see page 288)*, who use methods passed down from generation to generation.

Nicholls Town ❺, 2 miles (3 km) east of Lowe Sound, with its tall casuarina and evergreen trees, is the largest population and commercial center on the northern end of the island, with about 600

GHT: a
onge vendor
d her wares.

THE SPONGE CAPITAL

On the west side of Andros sponges can be seen drying by the roadside. Roughly 70–80 families are involved in the local sponge industry, which is Red Bay's main source of income. The locals call it "money off the mud" because the sponges are plucked from the seabed.

Red Bay has six qualities of sponge, ranging from the smoothest velvet to the more coarse wool variety, which are sold to processors and distributors in the US.

Locals free dive in the water to collect the sponges, which are strung into long lines and dragged out to sea to be cleaned. The sponges sit in corrals for six to eight days so that the worst of the mud can be washed away by the tides; this is part of the curing process. Once the sponges have dried in the Bahamian sunshine they are boxed up and sent to Florida, where most of the Greek and Cuban sponge merchants are based. In the US the sponges are washed again, softened, bleached and clipped.

Despite the success of today's sponge industry, the velvet variety and many other types were virtually wiped out in the 1960s by a hurricane that exposed them to a virulent virus. Slowly the sponges have returned to the flats and they are predicted to once again become a multimillion-dollar business for the islanders.

Androsia

The vibrant colors of Androsia textile designs are an enduring image from the Bahamas. Used in everything from clothing to table mats, straw baskets to toys and souvenirs, Bahamian batik is as popular with the local people as it is with visitors.

The Birch family of Small Hope Bay Lodge opened Androsia textiles in 1973. Its seminal inception came from a desire to assist the local community and to produce something truly unique to Andros and the Bahamas. With this in mind, Rosi Birch (the second wife of the owner of the Lodge) and her friend, Geisela Hausfield, hatched a plan. They searched Andros for just the right piece of fabric and armed themselves with wax from a couple of candles and a box of garment dye (the kind that used to be sold in the old-time dry goods stores). Next to the beach, using these raw materials, the two women created the first design on a piece of fabric, which they called Androsia after the heron.

Birch forged ahead, taking under her wing Merton Thompson, a 16-year old apprentice who remains at the company. Today, he is Androsia's General Manager. During his time at the factory Thompson has hosted visits from Queen Elizabeth II, Nelson Mandela, fashion designer Ralph Lauren, former US presidents Jimmy Carter and Bill Clinton, and leaders of African and European nations. Many dignitaries have received Androsian gifts from the Bahamian government.

Androsia textiles may have started life as a small family business at Small Hope Bay Lodge, but now it is located in an old warehouse of the defunct Lighthouse Club, 3 miles (5 km) away in Fresh Creek. In the open-air factory visitors can follow the batik printing process from start to finish, and also buy material in a variety of bright colors.

Thompson's selections of designs are inspired by the Island's plethora of shells, fish, birds, turtles, sea and sand patterns. As resident artist and manager of Androsia, he first draws his designs on paper, then copies them onto hard card to make a stencil, and finally a sponge mould is created and cut out, using specially produced foam. The walls and tables in the wax room are covered with old and new sponge images, attached to iron mesh with handles.

Androsia uses the ancient hot wax method of hand printing. The imaginative sponge designs are left in the hot molten wax for half an hour before they are hand-pressed onto either rolls of white fabric or a ready-made T-shirt. The next stage is to dye the fabric in the color-dying rooms. After the material has been washed and dried in the sunshine, the fabric is collected into six assorted layers and sent to the cutting room. Paper patterns with different garment designs are stapled to the material and a machine cutter is used to slice through the fabric. These bundles are taken to the fourth and final sewing room.

Bahamian women laugh and chat away as they sew together each piece of clothing and assorted decorative household items, living and breathing the company motto: "Caring people making quality." Nothing is wasted. Not even the scraps, which are given to the straw weavers, who use the pieces in their hats, baskets and as creative strips to add color to Bahamian straw dolls. ❑

LEFT: at the Androsia workshop.

Map on page 282

residents. The town is also home to the local government administrative offices. In September, North Andros hosts the Bahamas Free Diving Competition.

South of Nicholls Town is the tiny settlement of Conch Sound, which is notable for its blue hole lined with sponge and coral. A dive through the **Conch Sound Blue Hole**, which can be reached from the beach, drops to a depth of about 90 ft (30 meters) and should only be attempted with a qualified guide.

Central Andros

About 30 miles (50 km) south of Nicholls Town, by way of the well-paved Queen's Highway, is **Fresh Creek**, the main population center of central Andros. But don't miss stopping by the village of **Staniard Creek**, about half way to Fresh Creek. It's a lovely settlement, alongside miles of white beach framed with coconut palms.

People from Staniard Creek were considered to be the finest boat builders on the island, and to this day they are still acknowledged as the best carpenters. Most of the old houses were built on stilts and one wooden home, dating from the 1950s, is still standing today. The village occupies a sandbank and so stilts made of local cedar were built to allow hurricane flash flood waters to flow underneath the houses. The cedar hardwood is believed to be resistant to rot, as well as to destructive termites.

At Fresh Creek is the settlement of **Coakley Town**, on the creek's north bank, and **Andros Town** ❻ on the south. Andros Town is the site of the **Small Hope Bay Lodge,** the center for dive excursions to the Tongue of the Ocean reefs. Some visitors regard it as their favorite place to stay in the Bahamas.

Dolphins migrate to the creek, which runs inland, to mate. The dive center at the Lodge can organize excursions for visitors wishing to observe or swim with the marine mammals. There are also diving courses which allow anyone, from expert to novice, to dive in the waters around

:LOW: midday the Androsia ctory.

Artisans

On Andros straw weavers, woodcarvers and fabric designers *(see page 286)* incorporate the islands' marine environment, colors and traditions in their work.

Historically, Bahamian straw weavers were women who used baskets to carry their produce from the fields and to store their goods. Just about everything in a Bahamian house was made out of straw, from breadbaskets to floor mats, brooms and dolls for the children. In around the 1820s, basket-weaving was commercialized for tourism and subsequently developed into an art form.

Straw work is different in every settlement. In Red Bay, whose artists are the descendants of the Seminole Indians, the tight weave allows the baskets to carry water. A weaver known as Scrap Iron uses the Palymyra bush, which grows wild on the island, to weave. He can be found hand-stripping the reeds before tightly weaving them into a variety of baskets.

Other settlements use looser weaves for creating breadbaskets, brims of hats and straw baskets. More commercial work utilizes raffia for writing and remnants of Androsia cloth to create butterflies and flowers that are sewn on for decoration. Nothing is wasted on the island that lives very much in harmony with its environment.

Carving is another great tradition on Andros; the artists use only the old tree roots that have been naturally burnt out by forest fires, or whatever nature may leave as driftwood. Red Bay is the home of wood carver Henry Wallace, who uses primarily dead wood because he believes you should avoid cutting down living trees. Wallace has received a certificate from the Smithsonian Institute in Washington D.C., where his work has been displayed. His carvings were selected because of their unique style of folk art. Wallace's statues include bonefish, chickcharnies and portraits of local people. "We don't have cameras and so we carve people's faces to remind ourselves of loved ones or friends," he said. The artist views carving as part of Red Bay's cultural heritage. He can be found outside his house chipping away most days of the week.

In contrast to traditional crafts people, fine artists and Junkanoo costume designers are rejecting popular Western styles, which dictate having your own signature and unique individual style. Junkanoo artists are collaborating to create extraordinary costumes on Andros and the Out Islands. One artist will put up the frame, while another makes the skin, and then several people work together drawing out designs in dynamic brush strokes, always using exuberant colors.

Contemporary Bahamian art has been compared to jazz: one person starts the beat and then another answers that beat, while someone else brings in the rhythm and someone else blows the horn. Artists work together to add the colored pieces of paper, sequins, beads or little pieces of glass to produce vibrant political paintings and subversive carnival costumes. Nassau-born artist Jackson Burnside, from Doongalik Studios, explains: "One person grabs a bucket of color and throws it at it [the canvas] and then another one draws a line through the work. And then you do whatever you feel... just following your impulse." ❏

LEFT: Henry Wallace creates a carving in Red Bay.

Map
on page
282

Andros. The lodge has a long history of diving since Dick Birch, who established the lodge, broke the world record in deep sea diving in 1962.

Henry Morgan, a notorious pirate, is rumored to have buried enough gold here to buy the island several times over. However, like the name of the resort, you have small hope of finding it – although Jeff Birch, the resort manager, discovered an 18th-century cannon while swimming in the bay one afternoon.

The family-run resort, established in the 1960s, is a treasure in itself, with colorful rooms made from island stone and decorated in hand-batiked Androsia print. A short 3-mile (5-km) bike ride away in Fresh Creek is the factory where the lovely fabric is printed.

For dining, the Small Hope Bay Lodge and the Chickcharnie Hotel in Coakley Town, are reliable choices, both serving good food; and just about every settlement has a one-room bar or nightclub with dancing and music.

Androsia

A flourishing industry has been developing on Andros since 1973 – batik and the manufacture of exquisite casual clothing in Fresh Creek *(see page 286)*.

Androsia, established by Rosi Birch, began in a single room and now employs over 70 people, who use the ancient Indonesian method for handpainting and dying fabrics made from natural fibers. Visitors to the workshops, which are in a warehouse a few miles from Small Hope Bay Lodge, can watch the production process. Bright sheets of fabric hung on clothes lines flap dry in the sunshine and gentle breeze.

Androsia has a store opposite the factory site and also retail outlets in Nassau in New Providence and Grand Bahama. The stunning blue, purple, green, yellow and pink prints are known all over the Bahamas. Though not a traditional craft or product, the print has come to represent a cheerful ingenuity that is indeed traditionally Bahamian, even Androsian.

LOW: "Scrap n" weaves.

Sub exploration

Just south of Fresh Creek is **AUTEC ⑦**, the Atlantic Underwater Testing and Evaluation Center. This $160 million joint exploration venture between the United States and Great Britain is the busiest and best underwater testing facility in the world; it is being utilized increasingly by the Royal Navy to test their most advanced (possibly secret) anti-submarine weapons. Yachtsmen should be aware that this area and the harbor is off limits for casual sightseeing.

Land of water

Midway down the island is an intricate tapestry of creeks and inlets. This is a sparsely populated, little traveled region. There may be more water here than land; three long inlets (North Bight, Middle Bight and South Bight) snake between dozens of cays – Water Cay, High Ridge Cay, Linda Cay, Pine Cay, Wood Cay and others – which lie among the creeks and inlets like pieces in the world's most difficult puzzle. **Mangrove Cay ⑧** is the

largest of these cays, and its main settlement runs along the coast. The airstrip in **Moxey Town** on Mangrove Cay is served by Bahamasair. There are no rental cars here, but some local residents offer an informal taxi service.

Travel between north Andros, Mangrove Cay and south Andros is possible only by boat or plane, because no road connects the islands and cays, which are separated by the bights.

In south Andros, along the 28-mile (45-km) road from Driggs Hill to Mars Bay, you will find tiny settlements, gorgeous beaches and the beautiful resort **Emerald Palms by-the-Sea** at Driggs Hill. **Congo Town**, the main settlement, has an airstrip served by Bahamasair.

Outside the resorts, life is simple in south Andros. Most local people make their living from fishing and the sponge industry and most visitors make the journey just for the excellent bonefishing to be had here. South of Congo Town is **The Bluff** settlement, home to the area's administrative centre. Nearby is **Stargate Blue Hole**, a spectacular and dangerous inland dive site. The underground cave is believed to be around 230 ft (70 metres) at its deepest point, and has been the subject of explorations and research projects. The blue hole is for very experienced divers, and even then should be treated with caution.

Big Yard

Andros has been described in the past both as the Big Yard, because of its vast landscape, and the Sleeping Giant, because of its low level of development. But the giant has now begun to awaken from its slumber.

Direct dial digital telephone systems were established in the early 1980s, placing residents and visitors in instant communication with people in any country in the world. In 1985, Queen Elizabeth II paid a royal visit to Fresh Creek, Andros, her first visit to any of the Out Islands.

By promoting tourism, the government is attempting to spur economic growth that will arrest the steady migration of Andros' population to Nassau and Grand Bahama in search of employment. Andros is making headway in its efforts. ❑

LEFT: there i good diving the waters o Andros. **RIGHT:** an aerial vie around Andr

Map on page 296

THE EXUMAS

The dazzling array of bird, marine and wildlife on this breathtaking chain of islands and cays is of particular interest to nature lovers. The people are friendly and full of character, too

Stretching in an almost straight line for some 90 miles (160 km), the Exumas Cays, which lie in a southeasterly direction from Nassau, are perhaps the most tantalizing of the Bahamas' island groups. They are known for their beauty, the amazing colors of the sea around them and their interesting people.

The Exumas today are inhabited by approximately 3,700 people, spread between several cays but with the majority congregated on Great and Little Exuma. The largest single land mass of the Exumas is Great Exuma, which is connected to Little Exuma by a bridge across the narrow Ferry Channel.

There is one major airfield in the Exumas, in Moss Town, just north of George Town, the principal settlement. Of course one can also arrive by boat, including mailboat. However, swooping down on the Exumas from the air treats travelers to one of the most magnificent vistas in the Bahamas. Surrounding the islands, which are strung out like stepping stones, the water shimmers in huge swirls of jade, teal, turquoise, and neon blue, like whimsical abstract art.

Many Exumians are as colorful, albeit more peaceful, as pirates who once made Great Exuma's large natural harbor a favorite rendezvous. A sign in one of the bars says "Rest Awhile, Live Longer," which might seem to sum up the philosophy of these islanders, but perhaps only on the surface.

You can easily become engrossed in conversation with a number of Exumas' denizens: a midwife Minell Dames, whose brews of herbs have eased the delivery of scores of the island's babies, and who at age 90 was still going strong; a venerable farmer, Jeremiah Rolle, who at 83 was as bouncy as a young man and tending five acres of farm all by himself; taxi driver-restaurateur-farmer Kermit

Rolle, who learned herbal medicine from his great-grandmother, a feisty woman who lived to be 108 despite having been born into slavery.

Many Rolles

Visitors to these cays will soon notice that many of the residents go by the name Rolle, and that there are settlements called Rolle Town and Rolleville. During the latter part of the 18th century the British crown granted an Englishman named Denys Rolle 7,000 acres (2,800 hectares) on Great Exuma. He brought enslaved Africans and cotton seeds to the island and set to work building up five plantations. Rolle Town and Rolleville were the first; Mount Thompson, Steventon and

Ramsey followed. His son, Lord John Rolle, followed in his footsteps, and by the time of emancipation in 1834, he had some 325 enslaved men and women working on Great Exuma. Legend has it that when cotton proved to be a dismal financial failure and the prospect of emancipation loomed, Lord Rolle generously deeded all his lands to the enslaved people working his plantation. Following the custom of the day, they adopted their master's surname.

According to Bahamian historian Dr Gail Saunders, no such deed has ever been found, and Rolle's will, written three years after emancipation, asks his executors to sell all his lands in the Bahamas. In any case, the African Rolles effectively maintained their claim to the land. In consequence, both the land and the name have been passed down to their descendants.

But this very special situation of the Rolles has not gone to their heads. Today, they coexist peacefully with the rest of their fellow Exumians, continuing the island's tradition of a tranquil atmosphere. Indeed, after slavery, they were left by Rolle to eke out a living on the island as best they could, and because the land was deeded or claimed by them as a group, it has been almost impossible for many individuals to obtain clear title. The ownership status of some of the land remains in dispute even to this day.

George Town

On landing at the airport, the most noticeable landmark is a rustic bar-restaurant, a few yards off the airstrip, with a large block letter sign saying Kermit's. This establishment is owned by Kermit Rolle, one of the island's leading entrepreneurs. A self-made man who is a farmer, airport-lounge operator, taxi driver and general connoisseur of island life, he is one of the many refreshing characters of Exuma.

It is a short taxi ride to Exuma's main settlement, **George Town ❶**, where there are no traffic lights and where, under a gigantic tree at the center of town, a half

LEFT: Exuma gentleman.

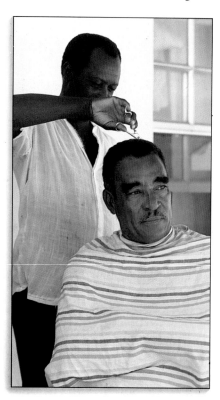

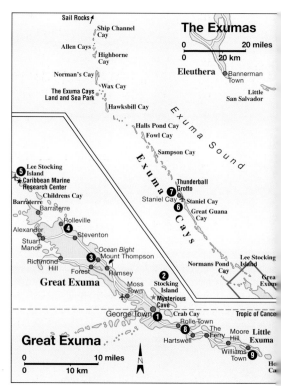

Map
on page
296

dozen ladies are likely to be found displaying their handmade straw goods and plaiting in the shade.

A few yards away is the town's largest building, the pink and white **Government Administration Building**, which was modeled on Government House in Nassau. Eschewing sidewalks and curbs, buildings hug the main road as closely as possible, and many attest to the residents' fondness for decorating their walls with pink, yellow or turquoise paint.

The main road follows the curve of the stunning **Elizabeth Harbour**, a large natural harbor protected by long, narrow **Stocking Island ❷**. Known for its beautiful beaches and the **Mysterious Cave**, which is accessible only to divers, Stocking Island is about a mile (1.5 km) offshore. A ferry links George Town to the island, which has only one hotel, solar-powered yet upscale Hotel Higgins Landing.

The fabulous harbor has prompted some Exumians to speculate that perhaps Columbus's first landfall in the New World was in the Exumas – not in San Salvador, as currently believed – because Columbus ebulliently described in his journal a harbor that could hold "all the ships in Christendom." Today, the winter months often find dozens of sleek yachts at anchor.

A few steps north of the government buildings, **St Andrew's Anglican Church** graces a low rise. The lovely, fresh white 150-year-old building is an active place of worship today.

Peace and plenty

The oldest hotel in the Exumas was a sponge market before the buildings were converted to a hotel in the late 1950s. It still has a friendly lack of pretension, though it can claim to be the center of activity in George Town. It has welcomed its share of celebrities, and its bar and dances are always enjoyed by a crowd of visitors and Exumians. Well over a century ago, the bar's two rooms, with their timbered ceilings and large fireplace, served as a kitchen for the local slave

LOW: shades colonialism the vernment ministration ilding in orge Town.

market, but today nautical memorabilia clutters the old walls.

From a wide sundeck, stone steps lead down to an azure sea. The **Hotel Peace and Plenty** richly deserves its name, except during a week in April each year when the **Family Island Regatta** takes over George Town. In this now classic race, work boats from all over the islands compete for the championship of the Bahamas. For the three days of the regatta, plus a few days before and after, visitors mob the island and liquor flows freely. As the hand-crafted work sloops compete out in Elizabeth Harbour, food stalls along the waterfront do a brisk business in fresh pineapples, grilled chicken, fried fish, and conch in all its incarnations.

Long lost friends bounce to throbbing reggae music while men play fierce games of dominoes on card tables. Thumping drums, clanking cowbells, blaring horns, and blowing shrill whistles, a Junkanoo band dances down the middle of the street. Yes, during the Out Island Regatta, there's plenty of everything in Exuma – except peace and quiet.

Farms north

Jeremiah Rolle was the first farmer in the Exumas to use a tractor on his farm and is considered the man who ushered in modern farming to the Exumas. One of his proudest accomplishments was having his produce displayed at the 1966 World's Fair. Some of his sweet potatoes weighed 10 or 11 lbs (4.5 kg), he recalled. Queen Elizabeth II was visiting around that time and saw some of his crop at an exhibition. "She talked to me for about 15 minutes and after asking me a lot of questions, she asked for a few samples, and she had them sent to the fair," he remembered.

From Mount Thompson to Rolleville, the land north of George Town has, in places, been devoted to farming since the days of the Rolle plantations. To explore this picturesque area, it is probably best to rent a car in George Town.

About 8 miles (13 km) north of George

BELOW: St Andrew's Anglican Church.

Map on page 296

Town is an area known as **Jimmy Hill**, which is not notable for a hill but for miles of empty beaches which are lovely for sun-bathing and for swimming.

Past the village of Ramsey the beach continues until you reach **Mount Thompson ❸**, where local farmers bring their produce to the packing house to be crated for the trip by mailboat to Nassau. The hill there affords a sparkling view of the sea and the **Three Sisters Rocks**, which rise unexpectedly from the water about 100 ft (30 meters) from the shore. A mile north (1.5 km) of Mount Thompson, a large bay called **Ocean Bight** laps at a treeless white-sand beach.

Hilltop life

It is well worth pressing on a few more miles, passing through **Steventon**, a quiet village named for one of the Rolle plantations. Built on a hill above a harbor, the village of **Rolleville ❹** has a curious old-world feel to it. The area has a proud history, too. The enslaved men and women of Rolleville and Steventon showed great independence and resolve in the face of cruel treatment.

With the failure of cotton as a profitable cash crop, the enslaved Rolles started cultivating plots of land, fishing and raising animals. Told at short notice of a plan to move them to a plantation on another island, they objected. A number of them fled to the woods, hiding for five weeks before stealing Lord Rolle's boat to sail for Nassau. Captured in Nassau, they were eventually returned to the plantations where they refused to work more than mornings, occupying themselves with their own projects in the afternoons. Their collective resistance continued until emancipation.

In Rolleville the **Hilltop Tavern** is the center of nightlife for visitors and locals alike. Churches play a significant part in the town's social life, too. Many years ago, Catholic sisters went out into the brush to dig and cut rock, then transported it by hand to the site of their church. It took many walks loaded down with the

heavy rocks to accumulate enough to build Rolleville's **Church of God of Prophecy**, but they persevered.

North of Rolleville the hamlet of **Barraterre** holds fish farming as its prime industry, raising tilapia in conjunction with scientists at the Caribbean Marine Research Center on nearby Lee Stocking Island. The tilapia is a freshwater fish originally from Africa. The unique aspect of the fish project here is that the fish are being sustained in saltwater cages.

Home for iguanas

Exumians claim to count 365 cays in their island chain, one for every day of the year. The string begins with **Lee Stocking Island ❺** and extends up to Sail Rocks.

To the east there is a sharp underwater drop-off to the deep Exuma Sound, but between the cays the water's depth can measure as little as 10 ft (3 meters). Some of these cays have vacation homes; on Norman's Cay, a Colombian man named Carlos Enrique Lehder ensconced himself as the head of a powerful drug smuggling ring. His activities led to him being deported from the Bahamas in 1982.

A more likable creature, the rare Bahamian iguana, also makes his home on these cays. The Exuma Cays Land and Sea Park, encompassing about 200 sq. miles (500 sq. km), is devoted to this species' preservation.

The closest major settlement to the park is **Staniel Cay ❻**, a brief charter flight or an extended charter sail from George Town. Almost everything on this tiny, friendly island is within walking distance. However, most visitors spend the majority of their time on their boats, between visits to the two rustic yacht clubs. Hand-lettered signs point travelers to the "Straw Shop on Your Right, East of Church," "the blue grocery store," and "the pink supermarket." A woman pulling a bucket of water from a roadside well is as common a sight as a satellite dish atop a suburban-style house. No matter what else you do here, be sure to go snorkeling or diving in

BELOW: the underwater cavern made famous in the Bond movies.

Map
on page
296

magnificent **Thunderball Grotto** ❼, just offshore, where two James Bond movies were filmed.

Plantations south

An excursion south of George Town leads to still another Rolle plantation – **Rolle Town** ❽, which contains a number of brightly painted buildings over 100 years old, and some old tombstones just off the main road. Many of the inhabitants of Rolle Town grow onions, mangoes, bananas and other crops.

A little bridge links Great Exuma with **Little Exuma**. Cross it to **The Ferry**, a small settlement on a hill with lovely views of the sea. A short drive farther south is **Pretty Molly Bay**, where, according to local legend, on moonlit nights a pretty mermaid may be seen sitting on a rock in the bay, combing her hair.

In the 19th century, salt held the promise of wealth and livelihood for Exumians. A few miles south of Rolle Town, a 200-ft (60-meter) white obelisk marks the site of a "mining" operation. Residents of **Williams Town** ❾ built the marker to signal potential customers on passing ships. Beyond the salt beacon is Williams Town, today an old village known for the small, fertile farms round about it.

Approximately 1 mile (1.5 km) past Williams Town, the Exumas' only standing plantation manor house can be found at the end of a driveway marked by two evergreen trees. **The Hermitage**, or **Cotton House** as it is sometimes called, is nearly 200 years old, and is home to a local "squire." Its construction is largely original. Hardly a mansion out of *Gone With the Wind,* it shows that life on these plantations for neither masters nor enslaved workers was easy. One-room cottages built for the Africans can still be seen nearby.

Although life has often been difficult for the people of Exuma, some combination of these cays' hardship, beauty and tranquillity has given many of them a resolve that has stood them in good stead for many years. ❑

iHT:
tunning
ial view of
ıma Cays.

EXUMA CAYS SEA PARK

Accessible only by water, the sprawling Exuma Cays Land and Sea Park begins just north of Staniel Cay, which is linked to George Town by plane. From here it is about an hour ride in a 24- or 36-ft powerboat.

Designated a National Park in 1958, this area was chosen because of its variety of landmasses (from limestone to mangrove) and its diversity of marine life. Fishing or removing anything else from the park is strictly prohibited. Even removing shells is taboo. A list of park rules is available at the park headquarters on Warderick Wells (open daily 9am–noon and 1–5pm), which sits on a rise above a stunning beach-rimmed bay.

Some 22 miles (35 km) long and 8 miles (13 km) wide, this preserve is full of empty beaches, pristine dive and snorkeling sites, ruins of Loyalist settlements and marked hiking trails. Animal lovers will be impressed by the tropical birds including osprey, bananaquits, terns and wildlife such as iguanas, hawksbill turtles, huge groupers, benign lemon sharks and crawfish. The park has one of the largest stands of rare pillar coral in the Bahamas.

For marked nature trails visit Hall's Pond, Hawksbill Cay, or Warderick Wells. Although the government oversees the park, it is maintained by volunteers and donations.

Map on page 305

LONG ISLAND

Visitors come here to discover scrubland where sheep farmers toiled, fertile fields of bananas and pineapple, caves and cliffs, blue holes, scenic bays and miles of sandy beaches

Stepping down the narrow stairway of the twin-engine Hawker-Siddeley airplane, you might mutter, "Here we are in sheep country." Long Island *was* sheep country for some time, and the land still has that look: vaguely inhospitable yet with just enough vegetation to allow a hearty breed to survive here. Before New Zealand and Australia made lamb their prime export, sheep was a profitable business for Long Islanders, who sent their animals live by boat to Nassau for butchering and marketing.

The island, which lies just south of Cat Island, has real variety, too. Away from the farmland, it is dotted with caves and blue holes, beautiful expansive bays and sandy beaches that stretch for miles. Here also is fabulous fishing and some of the best wall dives in the Bahamas.

Deadman's Cay

Some Long Islanders today make a meager living by farming, often using explosives or bulldozers to break through the ground's hardened limestone surface. Filling these "quarry pits" or "pot-holes" with rock, sand, vegetation trash and soil, they create plots that will support bananas, corn or pigeon peas. But none of this is immediately obvious on landing at **Deadman's Cay ❶**. At the airport a couple dozen people are normally there to meet the plane, brought by a handful of cars, seemingly from nowhere. In the worn, one-room airline terminal, a breeze filters through the open doors across the pale tile floor, past the bare counter and the man behind it, custodian of the telephone – one of the few on the island.

This is the island the Arawaks called Yuma, and that Columbus named Fernandina. Though it is now called Long Island and has a few modern flourishes, such as the bar with satellite TV down the empty airport road, once the small gathering at

the airport has dispersed, the island becomes very quiet.

The town of Deadman's Cay is home to about one-third of Long Island's population of 3,300. Deadman's Cay adjoins several smaller settlements: Lower Deadman's Cay to the north and, to the south, Buckley's, Cartwright, McKenzie and Mangrove Bush. They blend into a haphazard scattering of cinderblock houses and shops, stucco- or limestone-walled churches, schools and government administrative buildings.

Foreign enclave

Most visitors, unless they have friends on the island, fly directly to **Stella Maris ❷**, a small well-to-do town at the northern

end of the island, thus avoiding the costly and arduous drive from Deadman's Cay. Dominating the area is the **Stella Maris Resort Club**, which has spectacular views over the Atlantic coast from its hilltop location. The complex includes a world-renowned diving center, a marina, clubhouse, tennis courts, guest cottages and moderately priced vacation homes.

He had a Dream
Out of Barren Land
He Created This Haven
And Named it Stella Maris

So says the plaque on a small memorial stone dedicated to Johann Hellmuth Aufochs (1906–77), a native of Nuremberg. This small memorial to the man whose romantic appellation for this haven, which means "Star of the Sea," occupies a small lawn at the center of the Stella Maris grounds. The German connection remains, as the owner-managers of the resort are German, too – energetic people who pride themselves on running a casual, athletic, organized resort. Between 80 and 200 Long Islanders are employed here, depending on the season; as Stella Maris's fortune rises and falls, so do those of many people on the island.

From a small lookout tower on a rise near the resort's main building is a fine view of the lay of the island – mostly rocky coast and inlets, with the low, dense bushes that grow too thick even for a machete. Below are the gray ruins of **Adderley's Plantation**, a 19th-century plantation house, roofless with crumbling walls and vacant windows. Here, as on many other Out Islands, Loyalists to the British crown who fled the newly formed United States attempted to run cotton plantations in a grand style. Today, it would take a good deal of determination and a sharp machete to reach this old plantation house.

Visitors can swim at several beaches near the resort, but a drive of about 12 miles (19 km) north leads to the island's bold headland, **Cape Santa Maria ❸**, and its miles of stunning white-sand beach. Along the way is **Burnt Ground**, a

BELOW: freedom at Cape Santa Maria.

Map
below

small, quiet settlement which some say contains the oldest building on the island – a two-story stone structure laced with vines and brightened by faded blood-red paint.

Some scuba divers claim the waters off Long Island are the clearest in the world. Just south of the Stella Maris resort is the Stella Maris Marina and a dive-boat operation, which offers, as its most unusual feature, dives to **Shark Reef**, to the west. Here, intrepid divers can watch from a boat the sharks, who frequent these waters, fighting for fish poured out of a bucket.

Smooth route south

To see Long Island south of Stella Maris, rent a car at the resort. Queen's Highway, the principal road, has been paved following years of neglect, which resulted in pot holes ranging from the size of a basketball to that of a small car.

.ow:
·day dinner.

South from Stella Maris is the small settlement of Millerton. About 5 miles (8 km) farther south is **Simms**, with its

shady casuarina trees and limestone walls. One of the oldest settlements on the island, it dates from the 18th century. Just before Simms is a sign indicating the side road to the government packing house. Once a week, on mailboat days, the tin-roofed packing house bustles as farmers from all over the island bring papayas, bananas, tomatoes, pineapples and corn to be packed for the boat trip to Nassau. The farmers' sales are to the government, which buys the produce at a fixed rate.

Most Long Islanders live on the west side of the island, where the sea is shallower, quieter and where the northeast tradewinds have formed protective dunes and rocky hills. Unpaved roads and footpaths lead almost to the fishing grounds among the coral reefs on the east coast.

About 15 miles (24 km) beyond a string of villages, some of which consist of just a few houses, is Salt Pond. But linger first at **St Joseph's Church**, which stands pristine and white amid gravestones on a hill overlooking the sea.

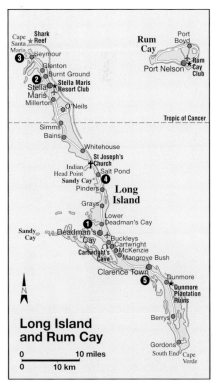

Long Island and Rum Cay

0 — 10 miles
0 — 10 km

Regatta Town

Salt Pond ❹, the next main settlement south, is best known as the site of the annual Long Island Regatta. Held each spring on Whit Monday, the race is a major commercial and patriotic event on the island. The race itself, in which only Bahamian-made boats may compete, is both a showcase for Bahamian nautical skills and a serious competition for prize money.

Unmistakable on the southwest corner of Salt Pond's single crossroad, the trim, suburban-looking Harding's Supply Center is the town's most prominent feature when the regatta is not underway. Standing on the well-stocked store's front porch, the proprietor may point out the mailboat docked a few hundred yards away and tell of the years in the 1950s when he worked on the Long Island-to-Nassau mailboat. Until the mailboats converted from sail to motor power, the trip to Nassau took eight days.

South from Salt Pond are the small settlements of Pinders, Bowers, Grays,

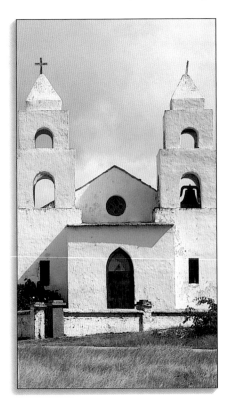

Andersons, Old Grays, Lower Deadman's Cay, Deadman's Cay, Buckley's, Cartwright, McKenzie and Mangrove Bush. This last village is the home of Laurin Knowles, one of the most respected and celebrated boatbuilders in the Bahamas.

Map on page 305

Two churches

Before the airport opened at Deadman's Cay, most people reached Long Island by boat, landing at the sheltered bay at **Clarence Town ❺**. The town still serves as the island's capital, though its business activity and population has been surpassed by those of Deadman's Cay to the north. Clarence Town's notable landmarks are two white churches on opposite hills, built in what some call Moorish and others call Mission style, one accented with red trim and the other with blue. These are the creations of John Hawes, otherwise known as Father Jerome. An Anglican minister-architect, who converted to Catholicism, he built churches throughout the Bahamas. Hawes lived as a hermit on Cat Island.

St Paul's Anglican Church perches on a hill at the western end of town, with a wide view toward the south and a glimpse of the bay. Slightly taller and more imposing, **St Peter's Catholic Church** gleams on the near eastern hill. Just as the Cat Island hermitage was built on the highest point in the Bahamas, here too the priest shows his affinity for a site with a sweeping view.

Clarence Town – quiet, more spread out than its population of 200 warrants – feels like it's the end of the earth. But there is more beyond. An hour's walk on a footpath from Clarence Town leads to a large blue hole – one of the Bahamas' seemingly bottomless pools. Just south of Clarence Town, the Public and Chancery Ponds contain old salt pans where Long Islanders have evaporated sea water to obtain salt since the early 18th century.

Few foreign visitors or tourists spend time on Long Island, its settlements enduring with few amenities and largely beyond reach of the outside world. But there are plantation ruins to see here, and lovely beaches at **South End**. ❏

LEFT: St Paul Anglican Church, Clarence To **RIGHT:** a gra fringed bea and rocky coast line in Long Island

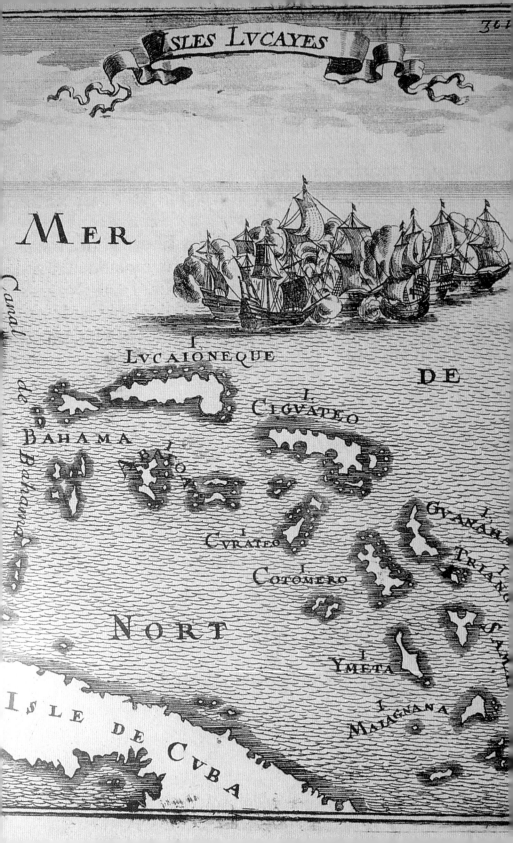

ISLES LVCAYES

MER

Canal de Bahama

DE

I. LVCAIONEQUE

I. CIGVATEO

BAHAMA

I. CVRATEO

COTOMERO

I. GVANAHA

TRIANG

NORT

I. YMETA

ISLE DE CVBA

I. MAIAGNANA

Map
on page
316

THE SOUTHERN ISLANDS

*Shallow reefs protect this scattered chain of remote, mostly
uninhabited islands and cays that lie north of Cuba and Haiti.
As a result, endangered species are flourishing*

On a good day, the hazy bulk of Cuba, to the southwest, is just visible from the observation platform of the Matthew Town lighthouse in Inagua. A few degrees to the left is only the unbroken horizon over the ocean. Yet only some 75 miles (120 km) away lies Tortuga Island, off the north coast of Haiti.

Through these waters have passed the treasure-laden ships of Imperial Spain, as well as countless freighters and merchant ships plying their trade between the Caribbean and North America.

The route is hazardous. Low-lying cays and shallow reefs await the unwary and those hopelessly driven on by storms and hurricanes. A few miles north of Great Inagua, the rusting hulk of a freighter sits perched atop the treacherous Hogsty Reef, while the remains of many more vessels are scattered along the reefs and ocean depths to the north and west.

Big island

Great Inagua ❶, is the third largest island in The Bahamas, and also the most southerly in the Bahamian archipelago. Sandwiched between Cuba in the west and the Turks and Caicos Islands to the northeast, its salt flats and low hills spread across the peak of an isolated undersea mountain rising almost 10,000 ft (3,000 meters) from the ocean floor.

The terrain of Inagua is harsh. With little freshwater, low rainfall and constant trade winds, only the most hardy vegetation can survive. Yet it is these very factors that have brought comparative prosperity to the island. Salt has been concentrating in Inagua's shallow lakes for thousands of years. Today, the Morton Salt Company speeds up the process by controlling the flow of water and produces some 1 million tons of sea salt annually. The salt that is piled high after extraction is exported to a variety of com-

panies, such as fisheries and water softening facilities, after first being processed in the US.

It was salt that first brought settlers to this largest of the southern Bahamian islands. The name of the island was most likely derived from two Spanish words *lleno* (full) and *agua* (water). An English corruption of these words, Henagea, apparently persisted for some time, and was the name of the island when settlers first came here to harvest salt. In 1803, it was recorded that there was only one inhabitant on Inagua, and by 1848, a mere 172. However, the harvest of salt and its sale to passing ships was so successful that, by 1871, the population had risen to over 1,000, a number that is close to the present population.

These good times were not to last, for the mining of salt in the USA, and protective tariffs imposed by that country, reduced the market, and the Inagua salt industry went into decline.

The author G.C. Klingel, who was shipwrecked upon Great Inagua in the 1930s, and who later described his experiences in his book, *Inagua,* wrote: "The place was a ruin. Vacant and broken windows stared at us from tumbled and deserted houses. Roofs careened at crazy angles, and through great gaping holes in their surfaces we could see golden splashes of sunlight that filtered into the darkened interiors. Flattened fragments of long-deserted garden walls lay in piles where they had fallen, dislodged by the elements and the flowers of these gardens had long since run riot and were strewn in hopeless profusion in a tangle of weeds and broadly padded Prickly Pear."

In the 1930s, the Erickson brothers revived the salt industry into a successful operation that was later taken over by the Morton Salt Company. Today, **Matthew Town**, the main settlement, reflects its former prosperity and its relatively affluent residents enjoy a lifestyle unequalled in the southern Bahamas.

A good number of the town's population make a living from the salt and this is without doubt a company town. Visitors interested in salt production can call in advance to ask for a short tour of Morton's salt plant (tel: 339-1847), north of town.

Inagua's low rainfall and persistent trade winds are ideal for salt production, a natural process that is guided and assisted by humans at every step. Some 12,000 acres (4,800 hectares) are now set aside for salt production. Sea water is pumped into the island by powerful diesel engines, and carried to the interior through natural creeks lined with mangroves. Man-made dikes separate this sea water from the increasingly saline brine in the evaporating lakes.

From the air, the ponds are a quilt of many colors. Different species of algae, minute floating forms of plant life, thrive

BELOW: flamingos in Inagua National Park

Map on page 316

in the changing concentrations of brine. Indeed their presence is welcomed, for by coloring the water, they increase the absorption of heat, and thus speed up evaporation and salt production.

At the end of the line, the brine flows into crystalizing ponds to a depth of some 18 inches (46 cm). When the salt has crystalized, the remaining liquor containing other mineral salts is pumped out into an adjacent area, a moonscape punctuated by the skeletal remains of dead trees. The salt left behind is harvested with heavy machinery, and carried away by trucks.

The salt ponds may not produce only salt. Experiments are currently being carried out to grow various forms of marine life in the salty water. Brine shrimps, stonecrabs, and prawns are all potential harvests. The old salt ponds to the north on Long Island have already been converted to this purpose.

Although there is little worth seeing in Matthew Town itself, south of town is a well-preserved historic landmark, the

Great Inagua Lighthouse. Built in 1870, the lighthouse is fuelled by kerosene, and the lighthouse keeper continues to use traditional methods of winding to keep it going. However, the white beacon's days as we know it may be numbered because there is talk of automation. From the top of the lighthouse tower, on a clear day, you can see the entire island and, to the southwest, Cuba.

Natural aviary

Long before the lakes of Inagua were utilized for salt production, water birds gathered here to enjoy nature's bounty. In 1771, English naturalist Mark Catesby wrote about the flamingo: "...the flesh is delicate and nearest resembles that of a partridge in taste. The tongue, above any other part, was in the highest esteem with the luxurious Romans for its exquisite flavour... A man, by concealing himself from their sight, may kill great numbers of them, for they will not rise at the report of a gun, nor is the sight of those killed

LOW: a
shorebird's
signature.

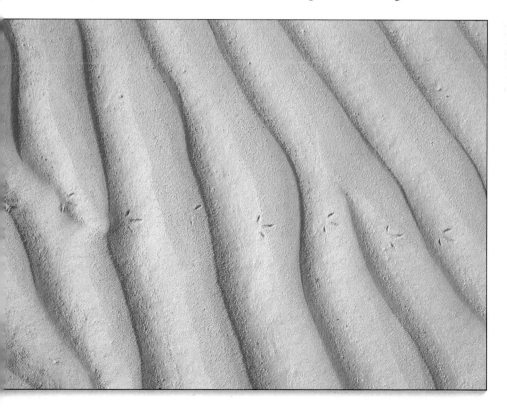

close by them sufficient to terrorise the rest, and warn them of the danger, but they stand gazing, as if it were astonished, til most or all of them are killed."

By the 1950s, Inagua's **Lake Rosa** was the last stronghold of the flamingo in the Bahamas. Fortunately for the species, an organization was formed to protect the birds in a declared protected area. Later, this organization became the Bahamas National Trust, and the flamingo reserve is now called the **Inagua National Park ❷**, a 300 sq-mile (750 sq-km) area comprising almost 50 percent of Great Inagua.

The West Indian flamingo, which is the national bird of the Bahamas, appears in the national coat of arms, and has made a spectacular comeback. Hunting of the colorful creatures is prohibited and carries a punitive fine and possibly imprisonment. Today, as many as 60,000 of these birds may congregate at Inagua between November and July to engage in complex courtship rituals and to raise their young. Wardens have established a camp at the western edge of the park, some 23 miles (37 km) from Matthew Town, upon a low sand dune optimistically known as **Long Cay**. While the constant breeze keeps away the bugs, the flamingos, spoonbills, and other waterbirds parade past in their search for food, probing the heavily organic mud for their supper. (Arrangements for visitors to stay at the camp, and tours of adjacent areas, may be made through the Bahamas National Trust, Nassau; tel: 393-1317.)

At the eastern end of the lake are remote creeks, ponds, and luxuriant mangroves where myriad waterbirds build their nests. Here are cormorants, pelicans, spoonbills, herons, and the rare reddish egret, the local version is easily distinguished from its North American cousins by its pure white plumage.

Rocks and wind

Not all of Inagua is swamp or lake; the southern and eastern portions of the island are mostly raised a few feet above sea

BELOW: the roseate spoonbill dips its food from Inagua's saline lakes.

Map on page 316

level, and covered with either low coppice or thorny scrub. There are more cactus here than in any other part of the Bahamas, from the tall elongated dildo cactus to the woolly-nipple cactus, a 6-inch (15-cm) ball of ferocious spines.

The rocky landscape, thin soil, and low rainfall make Inagua a harsh environment for plants to survive in. Trees of possibly great age rise no more than a few feet above the rocky terrain. Such a growth is even more of a struggle along the southern coast, where the unrelenting trade winds, and the almost continuous salt spray from the jagged rocks below, have flattened the vegetation against the rocky soil. Short, but mature trees, molded to the contour of the land, rise above the rock and blanket the ground with their trailing stems and branches.

From these rocky, windblown slopes there is a fine view of one of the most graceful of seabirds, the white-tailed tropic bird. After spending months out in the Atlantic Ocean, this species comes ashore along the rocky cliffs of the eastern Bahamas to mate and lay its single, mahogany-colored egg. Wheeling and swooping, the birds utilize the air currents coming off the ocean as they search for a suitable nesting hole. Evidence from tagged birds suggests that they always return to the same nesting hole each year.

Farther inland and better protected from the influence of the sea, the taller broadleaf coppice is home to the Bahamas parrot, a species that today survives only on the northern island of Abaco, and here on the southern island of Inagua some 350 miles (560 km) away. The Bahamas parrot is closely related to parrots of Cuba and the Cayman Islands, and in its Abaco habitat is the most northerly species of parrot anywhere in the world.

Little Inagua

Just to the north of Great Inagua, and surrounded by water thousands of feet deep, is **Little Inagua ❸**, an uninhabited wilderness of some 30 sq. miles (78 sq. km).

LOW:
anas
abit cays
the Bight
Acklins.

Local mythology has it that Henri Christophe (1767–1820), one-time flamboyant ruler of Haiti, buried his treasure either on Little or Great Inagua.

Fishermen sometimes visit the island, and turtles come here to nest. Inland, in an inhospitable pothole terrain is found the only natural stand of royal palms in the Bahamas. The seeds may have been brought from the island of Hispaniola in the digestive tracts of birds.

Short on human inhabitants, the islands of Great and Little Inagua are home to herds of brown, black and gray wild donkeys, goats and herons.

Another world

Some 60 miles (96 km) north of Inagua, across the Caicos passage, is the island of **Mayaguana ❹** one of the few Bahamian islands to retain its Amerindian name. Although a medium-sized Bahamian island of about 285 sq. miles (735 sq. km), its population has always been small. Today, a little under 300 people live in the

"capital" of **Abraham Bay**, on the island's south coast, and in the two even smaller settlements of Betsy Bay and Pirates Well. Out in the western coastal settlement of **Betsy Bay**, many of the homes have a rural innocence from another era.

Fishing, farming, and a few government positions are the only source of work on the island. Such being the case, many of the younger residents have left to seek alternative careers in Nassau. However, plans are afoot to increase the numbers of tourists visiting Mayaguana.

Continuing to the north and west along the island chain are a small cluster of uninhabited cays. These are **Samana Cay ❺**, sometimes known as **Attwood's Cay**, and the east and west **Plana Cays**. Two of these small islands are of particular interest for their unusual plant and animal species.

Samana Cay has been inhabited seasonally by farmers from nearby Acklins, and by collectors of cascarilla bark. This small tree, also known in the islands as sweet

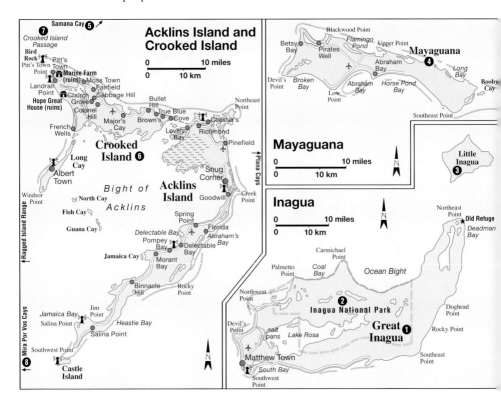

Map on page 316

wood or Eleuthera bark, has a rich spicy aroma. The pieces of bark are an important ingredient in the production of the popular liqueur Campari. Today, Samana Cay ranks third in importance in the production of cascarilla bark behind the Acklins and Crooked islands, where many of these trees have been planted around homes for the later harvesting of the bark.

Rediscovery

A somewhat barren and nondescript little island, **East Plana Cay** has an area of less than 1,000 acres (400 hectares). It was here on this cay, in the mid-1960s, that the unique Bahamas hutia, an animal which was long thought to have been extinct, was rediscovered.

Hutias are plant-eating rodents about the size of a small rabbit *(see page 311)*. They have living relatives in Cuba, Hispaniola and Jamaica, but for a long time were known in the Bahamas only by their skeletons. In 1747, Catesby wrote about the hutia: "The Bahamas Coney…

is a little less than the common wild rabbit, and of a brown colour without a mixture of grey hairs. Its ears, feet and tail resemble those of a rat, in the other parts it is somewhat like a rabbit, they feed wholly on wild fruits and vegetables, when surprised by hunters they retreat to holes in the rock. Their flesh is esteemed very good, it has more the taste of a pig than that of a rabbit."

In early colonial times, the edibility of local wildlife was of critical importance, for supplies from elsewhere were sporadic and unreliable. Even today, with American-style supermarkets on several of the islands, the first question many Bahamians will ask about animals is "Can it eat?" – local dialect for "is it edible?"

The protected population of between 5,000 and 10,000 hutias on East Plana Cay is still thriving. Smaller populations are also growing on two cays within the Exuma Cays Land and Sea Park *(see page 301)*. A small number of hutias were placed here a few years ago by scientists.

LOW: nesting brown booby.

Sheltered lagoon

About 223 miles (360 km) southeast of Nassau the islands of Crooked and Acklins encircle a shallow lagoon known as the **Bight of Acklins**. Geologically this is actually the smallest of the true Bahamian Banks. Banks are shallow sandy platforms often bordered by narrow islands, and isolated from other shallow water regions by water of great depth.

Crooked Island ❻ was not settled by Loyalists until after 1783, but by the beginning of the 19th century there were more than 40 cotton plantations worked by more than 1,000 enslaved men and women. The plantations were short lived, for the soil was thin and could not support crops for more than a few years. Soon the homes of the plantation owners began to fall into disrepair. Today, fewer than 500 people live on Crooked Island. Most of them make a living from the land and the sea. At best, the plantation houses are now scattered ruins. Two, however, are worthy of note: the ruins of **Hope Great**

Map on page 316

House, built in the 19th century, and **Marine Farm** in the north of the island; both are preserved by the Bahamas National Trust.

On the extreme northwestern tip of Crooked Island, near Bird Rock, is where it is believed that Columbus anchored during his passage through the islands on his first voyage.

In 1492, he spent several days in the area searching for "Samaot," a place where it was rumored that gold was to be found. He found only an Amerindian village near his anchorage.

Recent evidence shows that there was a major Amerindian community occupying 4 miles (6 km) of coastal **Acklins Island** between Jamaica Cay and Delectable Bay. This was quite possibly the largest Amerindian community in the entire Bahamas at that time. To this day there is still no hard evidence to suggest that gold existed on or had been brought to the island.

Before the advent of steamships, the monthly packet from Jamaica to England would pass through the **Crooked Island Passage** ❼ en route to Britain. Here it would drop off and pick up not only the mail, but passengers and freight for shipment to Nassau and elsewhere.

The first general post office of the Bahamas was located at **Pitt's Town**, close to both Marine Farm plantation and to Bird Rock. On a cay west of Crooked Island's north coast, 1½ miles (2 km) from Pitt's Town, is the **Bird Rock Lighthouse**. Erected in 1876, the lighthouse and its out-buildings are being restored following years of neglect.

Just to the south of **Acklins** is a small group of cays that still retains its original Spanish name. The **Mira Por Vos Cays** ❽ have never been inhabited, but are one of the most important seabird nesting sites in the entire Bahamas. On the cays is probably the most northerly colony of brown booby, a tropical gannet with a 4½-ft (1.4-meter) wing span.

For those requiring structured vacations, the southern Bahamas is out, but for those seeking a new experience, the southern islands offer a great deal. ❑

LEFT: *lignum vitae*, the national tree of the Bahamas and common throughout the Southern Islands. **RIGHT:** salt crystals of Inagua's lak

INSIGHT GUIDES
TRAVEL TIPS

New Insight Maps

Maps in Insight Guides are tailored to complement the text. But when you're on the road you sometimes need the big picture that only a large-scale map can provide. This new range of durable Insight Fleximaps has been designed to meet just that need.

Detailed, clear cartography
makes the comprehensive route and city maps easy to follow, highlights all the major tourist sites and provides valuable motoring information plus a full index.

Informative and easy to use
with additional text and photographs covering a destination's top 10 essential sites, plus useful addresses, facts about the destination and handy tips on getting around.

Laminated finish
allows you to mark your route on the map using a non-permanent marker pen, and wipe it off. It makes the maps more durable and easier to fold than traditional maps.

The first titles
cover many popular destinations. They include Algarve, Amsterdam, Bangkok, California, Cyprus, Dominican Republic, Florence, Hong Kong, Ireland, London, Mallorca, Paris, Prague, Rome, San Francisco, Sydney, Thailand, Tuscany, USA Southwest, Venice, and Vienna.

� INSIGHT GUIDES
The world's largest collection of visual travel guides

CONTENTS

Getting Acquainted

The Place

Area: Over 700 islands make up the Bahamas. The archipelago begins 60 miles (97 km) off the eastern coast of Florida and stretches southeast for 500 miles (900km) to the edge of the Caribbean Sea. Just over 30 of the islands are inhabited and 20 are well developed for tourism.
Capital: Nassau.
Population: 305,000.
Language: English.
Religion: mainly Anglican.
Time zone: Eastern Standard Time. Eastern Daylight Savings Time from April to October.
Currency: the Bahamian dollar (B$). US dollars (US$) are accepted.
International Dialing Code: 242.
Weights and measures: imperial.
Electricity: 110 volts/60 cycle alternating current – the Northern American standard.

Climate

Bahamian weather is mild year round, with only a 12 degree average difference between the warmest and coolest months. Winter (mid-December through mid-April) has average temperatures of 70–80°F (21–26°C). The sun shines nearly every day and there is very little rain. Summer stretches from mid-April to mid-December, and temperatures rise to about 80–90°F (26–32°C). Humidity also increases (yearly average 75–80 percent), and short tropical showers fall occasionally. Mid-summer visitors from the US may well find Bahamian temperatures and refreshing breezes a relief from the heat at home.

Hurricanes

Like its neighbors in the Caribbean and Southern US, the Bahamas lies in the hurricane zone. These powerful tropical storms can strike anytime from June to November: August, September and October being high-risk months. But history shows that the storms strike land only once every nine years.

If a hurricane strikes

• During the storm stay indoors once the storm begins.
• Tune in to local radio stations and follow instructions if ordered to evacuate.
• Wait for the all clear from the authorities before venturing out.

Economy

Bahamians enjoy one of the highest standards of living in the Americas. Tourism is the leading industry, providing close to two thirds of the nation's revenue, and employing roughly three-quarters of the population. International banking is the second biggest industry. The country's economic and political stability, as well as its many tax breaks, attract foreign investment.

Maps

In addition to high quality atlas and fold-up maps, small maps are included in most tourist literature. Not all brochure maps are entirely accurate.

Government

A British imperial outpost for over 300 years, the Bahamas became a sovereign state in 1973. The nation retains the British monarch as its official head of state, represented by the Governor General and is also part of the Commonwealth. A bicameral parliament and a prime minister govern the country with a 16-member government and a 40-member house of assembly, elected for a five-year term.

Planning the Trip

What to Bring

Lightweight casual clothes are the most popular dress in the Bahamas. During the day, you will probably wear a swim suit, shorts or lightweight trousers. Bathing suits are appropriate only on the beach or around the pool. Avoid wearing skimpy clothing in town. In the evening there are more occasions to dress up.

In the winter peak season, dress is generally more formal. Long skirts, cocktail dresses, and dressy pantsuits are acceptable for women. A wrap or sweater may come in handy too, when winter ocean breezes push temperatures to 50°F (10°C).

In the summer, temperatures are higher, prices are lower, and dress is more casual. Fewer restaurants require men to wear jackets at that time of year, but it is still advisable to bring one. An umbrella comes in handy in summer for the brief showers that sometimes fall in the afternoon.

Entry Regulations

United States citizens do not need a visa to enter the country if their stay is limited to eight months or less. However, carrying a passport and a return ticket is essential (although not legally required) if one intends to re-enter the United States. US Immigration requires proof of US citizenship such as an original or certified birth certificate (no photocopies). Voter cards and driver's licences are supporting documents, but not proof in themselves.

Citizens of Canada and the

United Kingdom do not need passports for visits of up to three weeks. But passports and return tickets are required for entry to, and departure from, the UK.

Visas are not required from citizens of British Commonwealth countries (except Pakistan), Cameroon and Mozambique, for a stay not exceeding eight months. Permanent residents of the US (green card holders) must have with them their green card and a passport from their place of birth.

Citizens of the following countries must have passports and visas to enter the Bahamas for any purpose: Dominican Republic (except in transit), Haiti, Columbia, Thailand, China and several other Asian and Eastern European countries. To check entry requirements for visitors from your home country, or to extend your stay for longer than eight months, write to the Director of Immigration, Immigration Department, P.O. Box N-831, Nassau, tel: 322-7531; fax: 326-0977.

Admission of Animals

No animals may be taken into the Bahamas without an Import Permit from the Ministry of Agriculture, Trade and Industry, Box N-3028, Nassau, tel: 325-7502/9. To obtain a permit, you must apply in writing to the Ministry and pay a $10 processing fee. Dogs and cats require a Rabies Vaccination Certificate. A Veterinary Health Certificate must also be issued by a licensed vet within 24 hours of the time you leave for the Bahamas. A licensed Bahamian vet must examine the dog or cat within 24 hours of its arrival.

Customs

In the Bahamas, customs officials have made it easy. Only an oral declaration is required. All bags are subject to inspection and cleared luggage receives a sticker.

Bahamian law allows visitors to bring in personal belongings, one quart of liquor, 50 cigars or 200 cigarettes, one quart of wine and small gifts worth $100 or less.

There are no restrictions on the amount of foreign currency you can bring in.

Prohibited items include firearms, unless you have a Bahamian gun license, animals, unless you have a permit from the Ministry of Agriculture, Trade and Industry; and of course, marijuana or narcotics of any kind.

US Customs regulations allow each returning resident to take home purchases totaling $600 without paying duty, provided the resident has been out of the country at least 48 hours and has not claimed the exemption within the past 30 days. Family members living in the same household can pool their exemptions. Only one customs declaration form per couple or family traveling together is required.

If you think you might exceed the limit, consider mailing home some gifts. You can send an unlimited number of gifts worth up to $50 each, as long as one person doesn't receive more than $50 worth in one day. However, these gifts may not include cigars, cigarettes, liquor or perfume.

For more information, call US Customs at Nassau International Airport, tel: 327-7126, or write for the booklet, *Know Before You Go*, from the US Customs Service, Washington D.C. 20229.

Returning residents of Canada who have been out of the country over 48 hours may bring back CAD$300 worth of merchandise without paying duty. The merchandise must accompany the resident, and the exemption, claimed in writing, may be taken no more than once per quarter. Canadians who have been abroad for seven days or more can claim goods valued at not more than CAD$750, once per calendar year. These goods may be shipped separately, but must be declared when the traveler reaches Canada. The $300 duty-free total may include up to 200 cigarettes, 50 cigars, 2 pounds (0.9 kg) of tobacco for residents over 16, 40 ounces of wine or liquor, or 24 cans

of beer, if you meet the legal age requirement of the province you are traveling to.

The total exemption for residents returning to the United Kingdom from outside the EC is £34. This may include nine fluid ounces (225 grams) of toilet water, two fluid ounces of perfume (50 grams), and for persons over 17, half pound (250 grams) of tobacco, or 200 cigarettes, or 100 cigarillos or 50 cigars. If you live outside Europe, double the tobacco limits. Duty-free alcohol is a liter of spirits or two liters of sparkling wine, plus two liters of still table wine.

Health

A yellow fever vaccination certificate is required from travelers over one year old who arrive in the Bahamas from an infected area, or within seven days of leaving one of the following:
Africa: Burkina Faso, Gambia, Ghana, Nigeria, Sudan, Zaire.
Latin America: Bolivia, Brazil, Colombia, Peru.

Few precautions are necessary for a trip to the Bahamas. Tap water in Nassau and Freeport is pure and tropical diseases were wiped out long ago. The biggest hazard may be the sun. At the beach, be sure to apply a strong sunscreen, avoid direct noonday rays, and build up exposure gradually – no matter what your skin color.

Money

If you plan to visit the Out Islands, consider changing your money before you arrive. On some islands, banks are open only a few days a week and then only for a few hours. The B$, or Bahamian dollar, is held equivalent to the US dollar, and both currencies are accepted throughout the country. Coins come in 1, 5, 10, 15, 25, and 50-cent pieces. Special $1, $2, and $5 coins are less common.

Credit cards are accepted at most large stores, restaurants and resorts in Nassau and Freeport, but somewhat less often in the Out

Islands. There you should come prepared to pay with cash or traveler's checks. The better known international brands of traveler's checks are usually accepted throughout the islands.

Getting There

BY AIR

Several major airlines make stops in Nassau or Freeport and several charter services fly from Florida direct to the Out Islands. With over a million visitors flying into Nassau and Freeport every year, the Bahamas air travel market is competitive and so it pays to shop around.

Bahamasair, the national carrier, serves Nassau and Freeport from Miami; Nassau from Orlando; Marsh Harbour and Abaco from West Palm Beach; and Nassau and Exuma from Fort Lauderdale, and is the major air link to the Out Islands. **Delta** flies from Atlanta, Fort Lauderdale, Dallas, Denver and New York to Nassau; Delta's affiliate, **Comair**, has a popular route between Fort Lauderdale and Freeport and connections to cities in the Midwest. **USAir** flies direct to Nassau from Fort Lauderdale, West Palm Beach, Philadelphia, Baltimore or Charlotte. **USAir Express** flies from Miami to Abaco and Eleuthera. **American Airlines** serves Nassau and several Out Islands (American Eagle) from Chicago, Dallas, Nashville, New York, Raleigh and Miami (American Eagle). **AirTran Airways** flies daily to Grand Bahama from Atlanta.

Air Canada flights originating in Montreal and Toronto serve Nassau.

British Airways connects Nassau and Freeport with London.

Chalk's International is a commuter airline with scheduled service from downtown Miami or Fort Lauderdale to Paradise Island and Bimini, and a charter service to Cat Cay. **Continental** flies from Newark to Nassau; **Continental Connection** flies from Fort Lauderdale, Miami and West Palm

Beach to Nassau. **TWA** connects JFK in New York to Nassau; La Guardia in New York to Freeport. For more information contact your local travel agent or the individual airline. (800 numbers are toll-free only when dialed from within the country of origin):

Air Canada, tel: 800-776-3000; 327-8411 (Nassau); 352-7266 (Freeport)
AirTran Airways, tel: 1-800-AIR-TRAN
American Airlines, tel: 800-433-7300; 327-5124 (Nassau)
Bahamasair, tel: 800-222-4262; 327-8511/9 (Nassau); 352-8341 (Freeport)
American Eagle, tel: 800-222-7466; 800-8-AIRFUN
British Airways, tel: 800-247-9297; 322-8600 (Nassau)
Chalk's International, tel: 363-2845 (Paradise Island)
Comair (Delta), tel: 800-354-9822; 800-241-1212
Delta, tel: 377-7774 (Nassau); 800-241-4141
USAir, tel: 800-423-7714; 327-3791 (Nassau); 377-8222 (domestic); 377-8518 (international)

BY SEA

Cruises

Travelers who prefer the leisurely life aboard ship and the shorter stay ashore can choose among the many cruise lines serving the Bahamas. Most ships dock in Nassau, but quite a few also stop at Freeport, Grand Bahama.

Some cruise lines, such as the **Star Princess** and **Nordic Prince**, make a circuit of several Caribbean ports. **Holland America Lines** and **Norwegian Caribbean Lines** also visit Great Stirrup Cay in the Out Islands. Cruises on **Premier** ships can include visits to four Out Islands. Phone numbers for cruise lines are:

Carnival Cruise Lines (*Carnivale, Mardi Gras, Jubilee, Fantasy*), tel: 800-327-9501
Crown Cruise Lines (*Viking Princess*), tel: 800-841-7447

Public Holidays

- **New Year's Day:** January 1
- **Good Friday:** variable
- **Easter Monday:** variable
- **Whit Monday:** eighth Monday after Easter
- **Labour Day:** first Friday in June
- **Independence Day:** July 10
- **Emancipation Day:** first Monday in August
- **National Heroes Day:** October 12 (replaces Discovery Day)
- **Christmas Day:** December 25
- **Boxing Day:** December 26

Disney Cruise Lines (*Disney Magic, Disney Wonder*), tel: 407-566-7000
Holland America (*Westerdam*), tel: 800-426-0327; 206-281-0351
Norwegian Cruise Lines (*Sunward, Seaward, Norway*), tel: 800-327-7030
Premier Cruise Lines (*Oceanic, Royale, Atlantik, Majestic*), tel: 800-327-7113
Princess Cruises (*Star Princess*), tel: 800-421-0522
Seascape (*Scandinavian Sky, Scandinavian Sun*), tel: 800-432-0900
Royal Caribbean Cruise Lines (*Nordic Prince*), tel: 800-327-6700

In the Bahamas, two steamship agencies that handle cruise bookings are: **R. H. Curry**, tel: 322-8681/7 (Nassau), Telex: 20-155 and **United Shipping**, tel: 322-1330/3 (Nassau), tel: 352-9315 (Freeport), Telex: NS. 16.

The Bahamas are a popular destination for yachts from the US. All sailors entering the Bahamas must pay a single entry fee of $100 (for four persons or less). This covers a cruising permit, customs and immigration charges, and departure tax. Each additional person must pay a $15 departure tax. Sailors who don't have their own vessels can rent one from the numerous bareboat yacht charter companies on the Florida coast.

EUROPE

United Kingdom: 3 The Billings, Walnut Tree Close, Guildford, Surrey GU1 4UL, tel: 01483 448900; fax: 01483 571846; email: btogfd@bahamas.com
France: 60 Rue St Lazare, 75009 Paris, tel: 1 45 26 62 62; fax: 1 48 74 06 05; email: btoparis@bahamas.com
Germany: Leipziger Strasse 67d, Frankfurt-Main D-608487, tel: 69 970 8340; fax: 69 970 83434; email: btofrank@bahamas.com

UNITED STATES AND CANADA

Chicago: 8600 West Bryn Mawr Avenue, Suite 820, Chicago, Illinois, tel: 773-693-1500; fax: 773-693-1114; email: astuart@bahamas.com.
Los Angeles: 3450 Wilshire Blvd., Suite 208, Los Angeles, California 90010, tel: 213-385-0033; fax: 213-383-3966; email: jjohnson@bahamas.com.
New York: 150 East 52nd Street, 28th Floor North, New York, NY 10022, tel: 212-758-2777; fax: 212-753-6531; email: vbrown@bahamas.com.
Toronto: 121 Bloor Street East, Suite 1101, Toronto, Ontario M4W3M5, tel: 416-968-2999; fax: 416-968-6711; email: aadderle@bahamas.com.

Out Island Promotion Board
Florida:
1 Turnberry Place, 19495 Biscayne Blvd., Suite 809, Aventura, Florida, 33180, USA, tel: 305-931-6612; fax: 305-931-6867; email: boipb@ix.netcom.com

Website
You can also get information on the official tourism website at: www.bahamas.com

Practical Tips

Business Hours

Most businesses operate from 9am to 5pm, Monday through Friday, though some open and close up to an hour later. Banking hours are 9.30am to 3pm, Monday through Thursday, 9.30am to 5pm on Friday. Banks in the Out Islands are open fewer hours. Check with your hotel for further information.

All banks can provide currency exchange but even branches located at airports and cruise ship terminals operate only during regular banking hours.

Some hotels will change limited amounts of foreign currency at more convenient hours, but be warned they also charge a high commission and may not give as good a rate as the bank.

Foreign Investment

The Bahamas' stable government, strict bank secrecy laws, tax breaks and special incentives make it attractive to investors. Foreign investment is a leading industry, second only to tourism in revenues. There are no income, sales, withholding, corporation, capital gains, estate or inheritance taxes. The Industries Encouragement Act offers exemption from duties and taxes on equipment, raw material, and earnings. The Hotel Encouragement Act and the Agricultural Manufacturers Act also give generous packages of exemptions.

The Bahamas Agricultural and Industrial Corporation provides information about investment opportunities and acts as a link between investors and the government.

Tipping

A 15 percent tip is standard for most services, but make sure you don't pay twice: many resorts and restaurants automatically add a service charge to the bill.

Religious Services

Christian churches predominate in the Bahamas, but there are also Ba'hai, Jewish, and Muslim congregations. Visitors are welcome at most religious services, but do dress appropriately. For a more personal introduction to religious services, join the Bahamas' **People-to-People** program which introduces visitors to Bahamians with similar interests. For more information contact the tourist office.

Media

NEWSPAPERS AND MAGAZINES

There are three national daily newspapers, appearing Monday through Saturday: the **Nassau Guardian** and **The Tribune** in the morning, and the **Bahama Journal** in the afternoon. Readily available in Nassau and Freeport, their arrival in the Out Islands usually keeps pace with the slow moving mail boats. The **Freeport News** is a Grand Bahama newspaper published Monday through Friday. Foreign papers including the New York Times, Wall Street Journal, The Times, and Daily Telegraph, are available at hotels and newsstands on Nassau and Freeport one day after publication.

The **Island shop**, on Nassau's Bay Street, has the biggest selection of books by and about Bahamians. Newsstands in the larger cities and towns carry a large array of foreign magazines.

RADIO AND TELEVISION

The country's four major radio stations, **ZNS 1**, **2**, **3** and **ZNSFM** and its only television station, **ZNS**

Channel 13, are owned and operated by the government. They are financed, however, by advertising. **100 jamz** was the first privately owned radio station to win a license in the early 1990s. Other non-government controlled radio stations which have since hit the airwaves include: **Island 102.9 FM**, **MORE FM** and **LOVE 97** in Nassau, **COOL 96** in Freeport, **Radio Abaco**, and **Splash 89.9** on Eleuthera.

Satellite TV is popular in the islands because it allows the Bahamians access to the full range of US television programs via a backyard dish, even on the remotest of Out Islands.

Embassies

Canada
Honorary Consul Robert Nihon, Out Island Traders Building, Nassau
Tel: 393-2123 (office hours)
Tel: 393-2124 (after hours.)
United Kingdom
British High Commission, Bitco Building, East Street, Nassau
Tel: 325-7471 (emergencies only)
Tel: 323-4286 (after hours.)
United States of America
Queen Street, P.O. Box N-8197
Tel: 322-1181 (office hours.)

Postal Services

Only Bahamian stamps are valid for items mailed in the Bahamas. In Nassau and Freeport, post office hours are 8.30am to 5.30pm, Monday through Friday, and 8.30am to 12.30pm on Saturday. Out Island post offices are open fewer hours. Check at your hotel.

Beautiful Bahamian stamps deserve more attention than a passing lick. The General Post office on East Hill Street at the top of Parliament Hill in Nassau has a Philatelic Bureau (323-7814/5) that is worth visiting.

Mail from the Out Islands moves slowly. Speed mail services for delivery to postal boxes and International High Speed mail services are available. For more information, call the main Post office (322-3344).

Telecommunications

In the Bahamas, the telecommunications system **BaTelCo** (323-4911) is a government enterprise, except on Grand Bahama, where the private Grand Bahama Telephone Company operates. Direct dialing is available to many of the islands from North America, the United Kingdom and the rest of Europe and Japan. It is also possible access to cellular phone networks and paging services. However, long distance calls from some Out Islands still require operator assistance.

Making a call from a public pay phone costs 25 cents.

A fully automated telex service is available at the **Centralised Telephone Office** on East Street, at Nassau International Airport, and in Freeport at BaTelCo's office on Pioneer Way, and the Freeport International Airport.

US Access Codes

When dialing the US from the Bahamas use the following access codes: 1 800-888-8000 (MCI); 1 800-389-2111 (Sprint); 1 800-872-2881 (AT&T).

Tourist Information in the Bahamas

Over three million people visit the Bahamas annually, making it one of the most popular island vacation spots in the world. To help these travelers, the Bahamas Ministry of Tourism and its many branch offices provide an endless amount of information on accommodation, restaurants, sightseeing and other pastimes. For travelers interested in specialized sightseeing, the ministry issues the **Bahamahost Roster**, a list of official well-trained tour guides.

Through its highly successful

The Out Islands

For information about the Bahamas Out Islands check out the Bahama Out Islands Promotion Board website: www.bahama-out-islands.com.

cultural exchange program, **People-to-People**, the ministry can also arrange for you to meet socially with Bahamians who share your interests or occupation. Ideally, to participate, you should return a simple form to the Ministry of Tourism (P.O. Box N-3701, Nassau) at least three weeks prior to your visit. Forms are available from the ministry and its branches.

Guided walking tours of historic sites and major points of interest in Nassau can be booked by appointment, and are well worth the $5 per person. There is also a monthly tea party coordinated by the Bahamas Ministry of Tourism and hosted at Government House in Nassau, the residence of the Governor General.

There are information booths at the airport, Rawson Square, Nassau, or the International Bazaar, Freeport.

TOURIST OFFICES

Bahamas Ministry of Tourism
Headquarters
Market Plaza, Bay Street
Nassau
Tel: 322-7500/1/2/3/4); 356-4231/5216.
Email: tourism@bahamas.com
Grand Bahama
International Bazaar
Freeport
Tel: 352-8044/5.
Eleuthera
Queen's Highway
Governor's Harbour
Tel: 332-2142.
Bay Street
Harbour Island
Tel: 333-2621.
Abaco
Queen Elizabeth Drive
Marsh Harbour
Tel: 367-3067

Information Booths

Nassau International Airport
Tel: 327-6806/6782.
Rawson Square
Bay Street, Nassau
Tel: 326-9772/9781.
Nassau/Paradise Island
Promotion Board Hotel House
Bay Street
Tel: 322-8383/2/3/4.
Grand Bahama Island Tourism Board
International Bazaar
West Sunrise Highway
Tel: 352-8044.
There are also tourist information booths at **Freeport International Airport** and at **Freeport Harbour** cruiseship port.

Family Travel

Most hotels offer substantial discounts for children, and often children under 12 receive free accommodation in their parents' room. If you are traveling with children, you may find that an apartment or villa complex with cooking facilities is more convenient than a hotel.

Some complexes offer lessons in watersports and other activities that children will enjoy. Most hotels and resorts will find a baby-sitter for you if you request one in advance.

Emergencies

SECURITY & CRIME

Don't be fooled by the laid-back atmosphere and seemingly crime-free streets of the Bahamas. Visitors to new Providence, Grand Bahama and Paradise Island should take the same precautions they would in any other cosmopolitan metropolitan area.

Watch out for your wallet and don't leave valuables unattended in your room, rental car, or at the beach. Avoid deserted streets after dark and keep car doors locked. A late evening stroll might be pleasant, but don't do it alone. The Out Islands are generally

very safe. Still, it's always wise to look after your valuables wherever you go.

In New Providence and Freeport, you can get help by calling the Fire and Police emergency number, **919**.

MEDICAL SERVICES

A large number of physicians practise in Nassau and Freeport, where the major hospitals are located:
Princess Margaret Hospital
Shirley Street
Tel: 322 2861
Doctor's Hospital
Centreville and Shirley Street, Nassau,
Tel: 322 8411
Rand Memorial Hospital
East Atlantic Drive, Freeport
Tel: 352 6735

Ambulance

Ambulance Service, tel: 322 2221 (New Providence) or, tel: 352 2689 (Freeport).

If accident or illness strikes in the Out Islands, you'll probably be flown to Princess Margaret Hospital, or possibly to Miami, Florida.
Air Ambulance Associates
Tel: 305-776 6800
National Air Ambulance
Tel: 305-525 5538/ 800-327 3710
Based in Fort Lauderdale, Florida, offer emergency transportation in medically equipped aircraft to hospitals in the United States or the Bahamas.

Less urgent problems can be taken care of at one of the 50 clinics which serve the Out Islands. In addition to nurses, many have doctors on staff and visiting dentists.

At Sea

If an emergency occurs at sea contact:
BASRA (Bahamas Air Sea Rescue Association)
Tel: 322-3877.
Emergency frequencies: VHF 16, single sideband 2182 kHz and AM2738 kHz or,
the **Coast Guard** (2182 SB).

Getting Around

On Arrival

If you fly to the Bahamas, you'll be asked to fill out an immigration form on the plane. Save the duplicate. You will need it for departure. All travelers must have a return or continuing ticket upon entry.

If you sail to the Bahamas on a yacht or arrive in a private plane, you must clear customs and immigration at an official port of entry. Boats must fly a yellow quarantine flag and only the captain is permitted ashore until the vessel has been cleared. The excellent **Yachtsman's Guide to the Bahamas**, published annually, lists ports of entry and procedures for boaters.

From the Airport

Unless your tour package includes airport transfers, you will probably need to take a taxi from the airport. On New Providence, fares run approximately $14 to Cable Beach, $19 to Nassau and $23 to Paradise Island. It costs around $15 to hotels in downtown Freeport. In the Out Islands, taxi fares can be quite expensive. It's wise to check the cost of transportation to and from the airport when making hotel reservations.

Water Transportation

Bahamas Fast Ferries

The 177-seat, air-conditioned **Bo Hengy** sails to Eleuthera, Spanish Wells, and Harbour Island twice daily; and between Nassau and Governor's Harbour twice weekly. The high-speed catamaran has expanded its inter-island routes to

Andros and Abaco, after becoming an instant hit with both locals and visitors when it first sailed in summer 1999.

The 90-minute trip on the catamaran from Nassau to Eleuthera is far more reliable than a flight on Bahamasair, which is often subject to delay. For more information: PO Box N-3709, Nassau, N.P., tel: 323-2166 Email: www.bahamasferries.com.

Airline Reservations

Bahamasair
United States
Tel: 800-222-4262
Nassau
Tel: 322-4727
Freeport
Tel: 352-8346
Eleuthera
Tel: 332-2196
Email: www.bahamasair.com

Chalk's Ocean Airways
Miami
Tel: 305-871-1192/84; or
800-432-8807
Broward County
Tel: 305-947-1308
United States (except Florida)
Tel: 800-327-2521
Nassau
Tel: 363-1687
Bimini
Tel: 347-2024
Email:
www.chalksoceanairways.com

Nassau Charters
Bahamasair Charter Service
Tel: 327-8223
Condorair
Tel: 327-6625
Trans Island Airways
Tel: 327-8329
Pinder's Charter Service
Tel: 327-7320
Reliable Air Service
Tel: 327-7335/6

Freeport Charters
Helda Charters
Tel: 352-8832
Lucaya Air Service
Tel: 352-8885

Mailboat

For spectacular scenery and some local color, try traveling between Nassau and the Out Islands by mailboat. In addition to the mail, cargo on these battered diesel powered boats often include cases of rum, mattresses, oil drums and provisions. All the boats are a far cry from any luxury liner – you share the same food and shelter as the crew – but some do have comfortable, basic accommodation and good Bahamian cooking. They also give visitors a chance to get to know Out Islanders who are on their way home from the city.

When boarding, note the location of the **life rafts**. More than one of these boats has run into trouble in a storm.

A number of boats leave Nassau on Tuesday, returning later in the week; the days for weekly departure and return depend on the destination. Trips can take anywhere from four hours to all day, sometimes even overnight, also depending on destination. One-way fares average about $30. First class passengers get a bunk bed and (usually) clean sheets; second class passengers sit on the deck.

The Ministry of Tourism provides information about rates and travel times, but for the most current information, inquire personally at the **harbormaster's office** at Potter's Cay Dock, next to the bridge to Paradise Island.

Domestic Air Travel

Bahamasair, the national airline, flies to 19 destinations around the country, and offers package rates for stays of three nights or more in the Out Islands. Daily service runs from Nassau to Great Abaco, Andros, Eleuthera and Exuma.

There are flights two or three times a week to the less populated islands. British Hawker-Siddeley twin engine planes are used for domestic trips. Almost all flights to the Out Islands originate in Nassau, so would-be island hoppers must fly back to the capital before soaring on to the next destination.

Although these prop planes have been criticised for delays and suddenly-changed schedules, Bahamasair is the most economical way to travel between Nassau and the Out Islands.

Another option is **Chalk's International Airline**'s seaplanes, flying between Miami, Paradise Island and Bimini and (by charter only) to Cat Cay. An excellent safety record and meticulous adherence to schedules make Chalk's the first choice of many. Chalk's also flies to Fort Lauderdale.

A bit more costly, but more convenient for island hopping, are the charter services operating from Nassau and Freeport. Round trip fees fall in the $500 to $700 range for a plane seating four to six persons.

Some hotels in the Out Islands fly guests to and from Nassau. Check with your hotel for prices and details on this service.

Public Transport

Taxis

In the Bahamas, taxi rates are set by the government. The first quarter mile costs $3 and each additional quarter mile, 40 cents.

Beyond two passengers, there is an additional $2 charge for each extra rider. Most taxis have meters – although the meter may not be visible from the passenger seat. Unfortunately, a few drivers take advantage of this, so agree on the fare before setting out, and look at the meter before paying.

Taxis can also be hired on an hourly basis for sight-seeing. There is a maximum rate of $20 per hour for a five passenger cab; each additional half hour is $10.

On the Out Islands, taxi tours are a good way to sightsee, and can be arranged by your inn or resort. Usually several drivers are on hand at the airport when flights arrive.

Bus

Also known as the jitney. In New Providence privately owned buses serve tourist and residential areas. The fare is $1 ($1.25 on Grand

Live it up!

Ride through the past in a trishaw and be welcomed into the future by lions.

or the time of your life, live it up in Singapore! xplore historic back lanes and shop in malls of e future. Take part in a traditional tea ceremony t a quaint Peranakan house, then tee off for birdie at one of our challenging golf courses.

Spice things up with some hot Pepper Crab and unwind in a world-class spa. Join a Feng Shui Tour to harness positive energy and later channel it into a night on the town. Come to Singapore and catch the buzz and excitement of Asia's most vibrant city.

Singapore NEW ASIA

www.newasia-singapore.com

or more information, mail to: Singapore Tourism Board, Tourism Court, 1 Orchard Spring Lane, Singapore 247729 or Fax to (65) 736 9423.

ame: _____ Address: _____

_____ Email: _____

Holiday villas beyond indulgence.

BALEARICS ~ CARIBBEAN ~ FRANCE ~ GREECE ~ ITALY ~ MAURITIUS
MOROCCO ~ PORTUGAL ~ SCOTLAND ~ SPAIN

If you enjoy the really good things in life, we offer the highest quality holiday villas with the utmost privacy, style and true luxury. You'll find each with maid service and most have swimming pools.

For 18 years, we've gone to great lengths to select the very best villas at all of our locations around the world.

Contact us for a brochure on the destination of your choice and experience what most only dream of.

INTERNATIONAL
CHAPTERS

Toll Free: 1 866 493 8340
International Chapters, 47-51 St. John's Wood High Street, London NW8 7NJ. Telephone: +44(0)20 7722 0722
email: info@villa-rentals.com www.villa-rentals.com

Bahama). In Freeport, a regular bus service is available, and a special red double decker bus makes stops at all hotels and sightseeing attractions. On Paradise Island, buses (50 cents) circle the island every 20 to 30 minutes.
• Be aware that all buses cease service after sundown.

Private Transport

Car rentals
Nassau, Freeport and Paradise Island are served by the major car rental companies such as Hertz, Avis, National and others. Typical rates run from about $60 to $70 per day, depending on the model, and $350 to $415 weekly. On the Out Islands, smaller concerns – sometimes the local filling station or an individual with an extra car – offer rentals. Some Out Island hotels also rent cars to guests.
Motor Scooters rent for about $35 for a full day, $20 for half day, plus $5 insurance and a deposit. Bicycles rent for $10 per day.
Caution: Whatever you drive, remember to drive on the left.

Specialist Tours

In Nassau and Freeport, there are dozens of bus tours of historic sites, tropical gardens and nature areas, shopping districts and the nightclub circuit. Most large hotels have a tour desk, or you can call one of the agencies below. Fares range from about $12 to $45 for a tour including nightspots. If you'd rather walk, take advantage of the free Goombay Guided Walking Tours offered all year round. Walks begin at the Rawson Square Information Booth in Nassau. Tour companies include:

Nassau
Happy Tours
Tel: 323-5818
Playtours
Tel: 322-2931
Majestic Tours
Tel: 322-2606
Bahamas Taxi Unions
Tel: 323-4555

Freeport
Executive Tours
Tel: 352-8858
Fantasy Island Tours
Tel: 352-6223
Reef Tours Ltd
Tel: 373-5880
Sun Island Tours
Tel: 352-4811

On Departure

If you are flying from Nassau, arrive at the airport at least two hours before your flight is scheduled to leave. In contrast to the usually relaxed and efficient arrival process, long lines and cramped quarters for departure check-in can add a sour note to an otherwise perfect visit, if you are not prepared.

On leaving the Bahamas, you'll be required to pay a $15 departure tax in Nassau and $18 in Freeport. Children under three years old are exempt. You will also be asked to surrender the copy of the Immigration Card you filled out on arrival. Visitors leaving Nassau and Freeport for most destinations in the United States clear US Customs prior to departure. No further customs formalities are required on arrival in the US. Canadian and European passengers clear customs at their final destinations.

Where to Stay

Hotels

Accommodation in the Bahamas ranges in size from intimate inns and seaside cottages to huge resort and casino complexes; and in location from Nassau's cosmopolitan atmosphere to the most secluded corners of the Out Islands. Accommodations orient to particular kinds of activities. Relaxation on the beach is the mainstay of most hotels. But if you favor scuba diving, golf or game fishing, you may prefer one of the specialty hostelries scattered through the islands.

On the whole, the Bahamas is not an inexpensive destination. But prices are lower during the summer and the autumn Discovery Season from September through November. Price categories relate to the cost per person per night and are intended as a guide only. The upper price limit for many of the luxury hotels is off the scale entirely for the average traveler.

A word of warning, a tax of around 8 percent will be added to all nightly room rates and Cable Beach and Paradise Island have an additional 2 percent surcharge.

NASSAU & CABLE BEACH

British Colonial Hilton
Cnr Bay and Marlborough streets
Tel: 322-3301 or 322-3311 (room reservations only)
Fax: 302-9010
Website: www.nassau.hilton.com
Impressive building constructed in 1922 on the original site of Fort Nassau. More than 300 rooms on 8 acres (3 hectares) of land. A popular choice with business

travelers. Comfortable, spacious rooms and a choice of restaurants. Secret agents should check out the James Bond Suite *(see page 149)*. The only hotel in downtown Nassau with its own stretch of beach. **$$$**

Clarion South Ocean Beach Hotel & Golf Club
South Ocean Village
P.O. Box N-8191
Tel: 326-4391/2/3/4
Large hotel with golf course, private beach and other facilities. **$$$**

Compass Point Resort
West Bay Street
Cable Beach
Tel: 327-4500; 1-305-531 8800 (US)
Fax: 327-3299
Website:
compasspoint@islandoutpost.com
21 rooms in studio. One and two bedroom huts and cottages and a three-bedroom penthouse, minutes from the airport. Nassau's most colorful property. **$$$**

Days Inn Casuarinas
P.O. Box N-4016
Cable Beach
Tel: 327 7921/2.
An alternative to grand hotel style with nearly 80 rooms. **$$**

Dillet's Guest House
PO Box N-204, Nassau
Tel: 325 1133
Fax: 325 7183
Website: www.islandeaze.com
Bahamian culture exudes in this transformed homestead. Internet café on the property. **$$**

Grand Central Hotel
P.O. Box N-4084
Charlotte Street
Nassau
Tel: 322-8356/7/8
Small hotel in the heart of downtown Nassau. **$$**

Graycliff Hotel
West Hill Street
P.O. Box N-10246
Nassau
Tel: 322-2796
Fax: 326-6110
Website: www.graycliff.com
Georgian style hotel in a 260-year old mansion with 14 suites furnished with antiques, and the only 5-star restaurant in The Bahamas. The **Graycliff Cigar Company** is next door. **$$$$**

Nassau Beach Hotel
P.O. Box N-7756
Cable Beach
Tel: 327-7711
Fax: 327-8829
Website:
www.nassaubeachhotel.com
Large, well-furnished hotel in Cable Beach. **$$$**

Nassau Marriott Resort & Crystal Palace Casino
P.O. Box N-8306
West Bay Street
Cable Beach
Tel: 327-6200; or 800-222-7466 (US and Canada)
Fax: 327-6818
Website: www.marriotthotels.com
Massive upscale place with cabaret shows, restaurants and bars. **$$$**

Price Categories

Prices quoted are for a standard room per night:

$$$$	$200 or more
$$$	$125–$200
$$	$65–$125
$	$65 or less

Ocean Spray Hotel
West Bay Street
P.O. Box N-3035
Nassau
Tel: 322-8032
Fax: 325-5731
Budget establishment near Long Walk Beach. **$–$$**

Radisson Cable Beach Casino & Golf Resort
P.O. Box 4914
West Bay Street
Cable Beach
Tel: 327-6000
Fax: 337-6987
Website: www.radisson.com
Grand, Las Vegas-style hotel complex, lots of facilities. **$$$**

Sandals Royal Bahamian Resort & Spa
P.O. Box 39
Cable Beach
Tel: 327-6400
Fax: 327-6961
Website: www.sandals.com
Large, luxurious all-inclusive for couples. Part of a popular Caribbean resort chain. **$$$**

SuperClubs Breezes Bahamas
P.O. Box N-3026
Cable Beach
Tel: 327-8231
Fax: 327-5155
Website: www.superclubs.com
All-inclusive SuperClubs luxury resort and a neighbor of the Forte. No children under 16 years. **$$$**

PARADISE ISLAND

Atlantis
P.O. Box SS-6333
Paradise Island
Tel: 363-2000/3000
Website: www.atlantis.com
Massive mega-resort with restaurants, bars, its own cinema, casino and cabaret shows, golf, tennis and ocean theme park. **$$$**

Club Med
P.O. Box N-7137
Paradise Island
Tel: 800-258-2633
Modern block. No children under 12 years. **$$$**

Ocean Club
P.O. Box N-4777
Paradise Island
Tel: 363-2501
Fax: 363-2424
Website: www.oceanclub.com
Upscale small hotel with golf course bordered by pretty gardens. Celebrity guests enjoy the clubs exclusivity. **$$$$**

Radisson Grand Hotel
P.O. Box SS-6307
Tel: 363-2998
Fax: 363-3900
Website: www.radisson.com
Excellent facilities. Some rooms with Atlantic views.**$$$**

GRAND BAHAMA

Castaways Resort and Suites
The East Mall
P.O. Box F-2629
Freeport
Tel: 352-6682
Fax: 352-5087
Busy hotel near the International Bazaar, with transport to the beach. **$$**

Our Lucaya

P.O. Box F-42500
Royal Palm Way
Lucaya
Tel: 373-1333/7777; or
800-772 1227 (US and Canada)
Fax: 373-2396
Website: www.ourlucaya.com
A Luxurious family resort on the
beach across the road from
shopping and entertainment at the
colorful Port Lucaya marketplace.
An emphasis on watersports and
golf. **$$$–$$$$**

Port Lucaya Resort and Yacht Club
Bell Channel Bay Road
P.O. F-42452
Freeport
Tel: 373-6618
Fax: 373-6652
Website: www.portlucaya.com
Adjacent to the Port Lucaya
Marketplace and UNEXSO. **$$$**

Paradise Cove
P.O. Box F-42771
Freeport
Tel: 349-2677
Fax: 352-5471
Email: pcove@batelnet.bs
Simple, apartments, cottages and a
villa near a with a secluded beach
off Deadman's Reef. **$$**

Resort and Casino at Bahamia
The Mall at Sunrise, Freeport
Tel: 350-7000/352-6721; or
800-223 1818 (US and Canada)
Website: www.bahamia.com
Largest resort on the island
comprising golf courses, a man-
made beach, the Country Club at
Bahamia and the Towers at
Bahamia. **$$–$$$**

Xanadu Beach and Marina Resort
Sunken Treasure Drive
Freeport
Tel: 352-6782/3; or
800-333 3333 (US and Canada)
Fax: 352-5799
Website:
www.xanadubeachhotel.com
Hotel with a pink theme hence its
nickname, the "Pink Palace". The
reclusive multimillionaire, Howard
Hughes, lived on the top floor for
many years. **$$$$**

BIMINI

All My Children Hotel
Alice Town
Tel: 347-3334
Fax: 347-3333
Basic accommodation near great
snorkeling waters. **$$**

Bimini Big Game Fishing Club
P.O. Box 699
King's Highway
Alice Town
Tel: 347-3391/3
Fax: 347-3392
Good angling location, comfortable
rooms. **$$$**

Bimini Blue Water Resort
P.O. Box 627
Alice Town
Tel: 347-3166
Fax: 347-3293
Email: bluewaterresort@boipb.com
Small hotel with rooms, suites,
cottages and Hemingway's former
hideaway. Private beach. **$$**

Compleat Angler Hotel
P.O. Box 601
Alice Town
Tel: 347-3177/3122
Fax: 347-3293
Hemingway stayed here. Faded but
it has a popular bar. **$$**

Sea Crest Hotel
P.O. Box 654
Alice Town
Tel: 347-3071
Small place in town. **$$**

THE BERRY ISLANDS

Chub Cay Club
Chub Cay
Tel: 325-1490
Fax: 322-5199
Website: www.chubcay.com
Two-, three- or four-bedroom
accommodation. Great deep-sea
fishing. **$$$**

THE ABACOS

Abaco Beach Resort
PO Box AB-29511
Marsh Harbour
Tel: 367-2158
Fax: 367-4154
Email: info@abacobeachresort.net
Small, comfortable resort with
watersports, a lively bar and its own
marina. **$$$$**.

Abaco Inn
Hope Town
Tel: 366-0133
Fax 366-0113
Email: info@abacoinn.com
Friendly place with spacious
secluded accommodation. **$$$**.

Ambassador Hotel
PO Box AB-20484
Abaco
Tel: 367-2022
Simple decor. Coffee-maker in
room. **$$**

Banyan Beach Club
PO Box AB-22158
Treasure Cay
Tel: 365-8111
Fax: 365-8112
Website: www.banyanbeach.com
Luxury beachfront condos.
$$$–$$$$

Bluff House Beach Hotel
Green Turtle Cay
Tel: 365-4247
Fax: 365-4248
Email: BluffHouse@oii.net
Spacious, elegant rooms with lovely
views. **$$$**

Conch Inn Hotel & Marina
PO Box AB-20469
Marsh Harbour
Tel: 367-4000
Fax: 367-4004
A no-frills, small, casual hotel and
marina designed for those who want
to spend a little time on land but
still be near their vessel. **$$**

Different of Abaco
PO Box AB-20092
Marsh Harbour
Tel: 366-2150
Fax: 327-8125
Website: www.differentofabaco.com
Bird watching, hiking trails and a
great restaurant in Nettie
Symonette's eco-lodge. No
telephone or TV. **$$$**

Green Turtle Club
PO Box AB-270
Green Turtle Cay
Tel: 365-4271
Fax: 365-4272
Website: www.greenturtleclub.com
Relaxed elegance with rooms and
cottages.**$$$**

Hope Town Harbour Lodge
Elbow Cay, Hope Town
Tel: 366-0095; or
800-316 7844 (US and Canada)
Fax: 366-0286
Website: www.hopetownlodge.com
Located just 30 feet (9 meters)
from a coral reef and an excellent
snorkeling site. **$$–$$$**

Hope Town Hideaways
Elbow Cay, Hope Town
Tel: 366-0224
Fax: 366-0434
Website: www.hopetown.com
Luxury home rentals near the much-
photographed candy-striped
lighthouse. **$$$–$$$$**

Treasure Cay Hotel Resort & Marina
Treasure Cay
Tel: 954-525-7711; 800-327-1584
(US)
Fax: 954-525-1699 (US)
Website: www.treasurecay.com
Rooms and villas near a large
marina. **$$$–$$$$**

Walker's Cay Hotel & Marina
Walker's Cay
Tel: 352-5252
Tennis, watersports and white
sandy beach. **$$**

Inns and villas on Abaco

D's Guest House
PO Box AB-20655
Marsh Harbour
Tel: 367-3980. **$$**

Island Breezes Motel
Marsh Harbour
Tel: 367-3776. **$$**

Lofty Fig Villas
PO Box AB-20437
Marsh Harbour
Tel/fax: 367-2681. **$$**

Marsh Harbour Airport Hotel
Tel: 367-3658
Fax: 367-4401. **$$**

Pelican Beach Villas
Marsh Harbour
Tel:367-3600
Fax: 367-3603
E-mail:pelican@g-net.net. **$$**

ELEUTHERA/HARBOUR ISLAND

Buccaneer Club
PO Box EL-86
Governor's Harbour
Tel: 332-2000
Family-operated guest house. Five
rooms. **$$**

Cigatoo Resort
P.O. Box 86
Governor's Harbour
Tel: 332-3060
Fax: 332-3061
Website: www.cigatooresort.com
Simple rooms in a quiet, friendly
resort overlooking Governor's
Harbour. No children under 16. **$$$**

Price Categories

Prices quoted are for a standard
room per night:
$$$$ $200 or more
$$$ $125–$200
$$ $65–$125
$ $65 or less

Cocodimama
Governor's Harbour
Tel: 332-3150
Fax: 332-3155
Website: cocodimama.com
Rooms in brightly-painted beachfront
cottages. **$$$–$$$$**

Coral Sands Hotel
Harbour Island
Tel: 333-2350/5
Fax: 333-2368
Website: www.coralsands.com
This luxury resort is situated on 3
miles (5 km) of pink sand and good
facilities. **$$$**

The Cove Eleuthera
Gregory Town
Tel: 335-5142
Fax: 335-5338
Website: TheCoveResort.com
Rooms and cottages nestled in a
small cove. Relaxed, friendly beach
atmosphere. **$$$**

Edwina's Place
Rock Sound
Tel: 334-2094
Fax: 334-2280
Simple rooms in an establishment
with a good reputation. **$$**

Ethel's Cottages
Tarpum Bay
Tel: 334-4233
A family place. **$**

The Landing
PO Box EL-190
Harbour Island
Tel: 333-2707
Fax: 333-2650
Website:
www.harbourislandlanding.com
Old world charm meets the elegant
Bahamian Bed and Breakfast. **$$$**

Pink Sands
PO Box EL-87
Harbour Island
Tel: 333-2030/305-531-8800 (US)
Fax: 333-2060
Website: www.islandoutpost.com
Twenty-four luxury cottages on 16
lush acres of landscaped grounds
leading to a pink sand beach. **$$$$**

Romora Bay Club
Harbour Island
Tel: 333-2325
Fax: 333-2500
Website: www.romorabay.com
Comfortable rooms near the ocean.
$$–$$$

Unique Village
Governor's Harbour
Tel: 332-1830
Fax: 332-1838
Small resort. Simple rooms and
villas with ocean views. **$**

CAT ISLAND

Bridge Inn
New Bight
Tel: 342-3013
Fax: 342-3041
Has a bar with live rake and scrape
music Friday and Saturday nights. **$**

Fernandez Bay Village
New Bight
Tel: 305-474-4821 (US)
Fax: 305-474-4864 (US)
Thirteen beach villas; relaxed and
friendly with good watersports and
a great beach nearby. **$$**

Greenwood Beach Resort
Port Howe
Tel/fax: 342-3053
Website:
www.greenwoodbeachresort.net
Small resort with 20 comfortable
rooms and a pink sand beach. **$$**

Orange Creek Inn
Orange Creek
Tel: 354-4110
Cozy establishment with roadside
inn ambience near Arthur's Town. **$**
Sea Spray Hotel
Orange Creek
Tel: 354-4116
Fax: 354-4161
Inexpensive family hotel facing the
beach. **$**
Twin Palm Beach Resort
New Bight
Tel: 342-3108
Quiet, clean and unpretentious. **$$**

SAN SALVADOR

Riding Rock Inn
San Salvador
Tel: 331-2631
Fax: 331-2020
Website: www.ridingrock.com
Luxury rooms some with ocean
views. Ideal for watersports
enthusiasts. **$$–$$$**

ANDROS

Chickcharnie Hotel
Fresh Creek
Tel: 368-2025
Simple hotel with ocean views. **$**
Emerald Palms By-the-Sea
Driggs Hill
Tel: 369-2661
Fax: 369-2667
Relaxed elegance. **$$**
Lighthouse Yacht Club & Marina
Andros Town
Tel: 368-2305
Fax: 368-2300
Website:
www.androslighthouse.com
All-inclusive accommodation. On the
property is a lighthouse that was
built in 1836. **$$$**
Small Hope Bay Lodge
Fresh Creek
Tel: 368-2013/4
Fax: 368-2015
Website: www.smallhope.com
Family-run all-inclusive resort with a
popular diving center and beach
huts. **$$$$**

THE EXUMAS

Club Peace and Plenty
George Town
Tel: 336-2551/2
Fax: 336-2093
Website: www.peaceandplenty.com
Large resort complex which includes
the **Beach Inn** and the **Bonefish
Lodge**. A ferry to Stocking Island
beach is available to guests. **$$$**
Coconut Cove Hotel
George Town
Tel: 336-2659
Small hotel with 12 rooms and a
lovely beach. **$$**
Flamingo Bay Club & Villas
George Town
Tel: 336-2661
Small hotel and villas. **$$$**
Hotel Higgins Landing
Stocking Island, Exuma
Tel: 336-2460
Website: www.higginslanding.com
An eco-lover's delight. Solar energy.
Five comfortable cottages. **$$$**
Staniel Cay Yacht Club
Staniel Cay
Tel: 355-2024
Fax: 355-2044
Website: www.stanielcay.com
Cottages on edge of a national park.
Popular with sailors and divers. **$$**
Two Turtles Inn
George Town
Tel: 336-2545
Fax: 336-2528
Small, quaint inn near the straw
market and the shops. **$**

LONG ISLAND

Cape Santa Maria Beach Resort,
Beach Road
Tel/fax: 338-5273
Website: www.capesantamaria.com
Small resort with oceanfront cot-
tages in the north of the island. **$$**
Stella Maris Resort Club
P.O. Box SM-105
Tel: 338-2051; or
800-426 0466/954-359 8236 (US)
Fax: 338-2052
Website: www.stellamarisresort.com
Top island resort built in plantation
style, with its own marina. Good
facilities. **$$–$$$**

CROOKED ISLAND

Crooked Island Beach Inn
Cabbage Hill
Tel: 344-2321/336-2096
Small guest house-style. **$**
Pittstown Point Landings
Landrail Point
Tel: 344-2507/704-878 8724 (US)
www.pittstownpointlandings.com
Simply furnished, with "downhome"
atmosphere. Homemade food. **$$**

INAGUA

Morton Main House
Matthew Town
Tel: 339-1267
Fax: 339-1265
Modest guesthouse run by the
Morton Salt Company. **$**

Renting

The Bahamas has a good
selection of rental villas and
apartments, an alternative for
groups, families, business
travelers and visitors planning
longer stays. A few sources are:
Bahamas Home Rentals
230 Lawrence Avenue
Pittsburgh, Pennsylvania
USA 15238
Tel: 412-828 1048.
Bay View Village
P.O. Box SS-6308
Paradise Island
Tel: 363-2555.
Cable Beach Manor
P.O. Box N-8333, Cable Beach
Tel: 327-7785.
**Dillet's Guest House and
Apartments**
P.O. Box N-204, Nassau
Tel: 327-7743/325-1133.
**Henrea Carlette Apartment
Hotel**
P.O. Box N-4227, Cable Beach
Tel: 327-7801/3.
The Orchard Apartment Hotel
Village Road, P.O. Box N-1514
Nassau
Tel: 393-1297/393-1306.
Note: Camping is not permitted
in the Bahamas.

Where to Eat

If you are staying in Nassau or Freeport, the cuisine of the Bahamas may at first seem largely American spiced with a touch of the tropics. Most hotels and resorts serve a variety of continental food, including Italian, Chinese and French. But the real delight is Bahamian home-cooking.

Throughout the islands there are restaurants and take-out stands serving Bahamian specialties. Usually these are family run businesses with ingredients bought fresh at local markets. For the most part, the fewer the frills of the dining setting, the truer the island flavors. While beef, pork, and chicken are widely available, the home-style cooking here revolves around the sea.

Fish turns up for dinner, lunch, and even breakfast, with snapper and grouper being the most common. "boil fish" (cooked with salt pork, onions, and green peppers) is a popular morning eye-opener that comes with grits. Also eaten as the day's first meal, stewed fish comes in a delicious brown gravy. Steamed fish is not eaten before noon and is cooked with a savory tomato base.

Traditional Bahamian fare is tasty, sometimes spicy and filling. Seafood favorites include turtle steaks, crawfish, the delicious clawless Bahamian lobster, grouper, and conch (pronounced conk).

Among the top incarnations are cracked conch, for which the conch is pounded until tender, battered, and deep fried; steamed conch (cooked with sauteed onions, peppers, thyme, tomatoes, and maybe okra or carrots). Conch chowder is a rich, spicy soup with vegetables and conch salad contains minced raw conch, marinated in lime juice, and mixed with chopped onions and peppers.

Star of the Show

The star of the culinary show is conch (pronounced "conk"). In testament to the popularity of this tasty mollusk, huge mounds of discarded conch shells stand at the edge of the water near boat docks everywhere. These are the shells with the shiny pink spiral interior, the kind that children put to their ears to hear the waves. Bahamians claim that conch gives men "strong back," meaning that it can pump up the volume between the sheets. No wonder the meat is transformed into so many local favorites.

Minced lobster, usually served in the shell, is made by shredding the meat and cooking it with tomatoes, green peppers, and onions. Among other favorites, but harder to find outside of Bahamian homes are crab and rice, okra soup, chicken and dough (dumplings), and wild boar. Accompanying lunch and dinner are heaped portions of peas and rice (usually made with pigeon peas), potato salad, coleslaw, or macaroni and cheese – sometimes all of the above.

Bahamian chefs also have a flair with curried chicken and mutton. Souse, slow boiled and spiced pig's head, feet, or sheep's tongue, traditionally served with hot johnny cake, which is like sweet cornbread.

Kalik, the locally-brewed beer, is great for washing it all down. And for dessert, few visitors in the know pass up warm slices of guava duff topped with creamy white sauce.

Price categories are based on the average cost of dinner per person excluding wine. Breakfast prices for the same categories range from under $10 ($) to over $15 ($$$); and lunch from under $10 ($) to over $20 ($$$).

Bahamian Kitchen
Trinity Place, off Market Street
Tel: 325-0702
Mena's in her kitchen and at your table, offering her restaurant's impressive array of everything from salads to turtle steak cooked to order. Excellent value. Open Mon–Sat 11.30am–10pm. **$**
Buena Vista
Delancy Street
Tel: 322-2811
A Nassau establishment in an old 19th century residence. Serves Continental food. Dinner from 7pm Reservations advised. **$$$**
Chippie's Wall Street Cafe
Colony Place
Bay Street
Tel: 356-2087/356-2092
One of the few places in downtown Nassau offering internet cafe service, it also has selection of fine wines and cigars to consume after dining on a balcony overlooking Nassau's main street. **$$**

$$$	$50 and over
$$	$30–$50
$	$30 and under

Conch Fritters
Marlborough Street
Tel: 323-8778
Specializing in its namesake with both American and Bahamian dishes. Open 7am to midnight. **$$**
Graycliff
West Hill Street
Tel: 322-2796
Upscale, excellent continental cuisine. Dinner 7pm to 10.30pm. Reservations requested. **$$$**
Green Shutters
Parliament Street
Tel: 322-3701
Promising the best of Britain in the Bahamas, this restaurant and pub serves draft beer on tap, steak and kidney pie and the like. Open for lunch and dinner. **$**

Montague Gardens

East Bay Street
Tel: 394-6347
A converted mansion that overlooks a gazebo, pool and Grecian statues in the garden, which has changed little since its original ownership. Bahamian dishes prepared simply but effectively, including grouper and conch. **$$**

Pink Pearl Cafe
East Bay Street
Tel: 394-6413
A residence from the 1940s has been restored and now serves up jazz with its elegant dinners. The Bahamian-Caribbean cuisine is enhanced by original works by Bahamian artist, John Cox. Open for lunch and dinner. Reservations recommended. **$$$**

Portofino Italian Cafe
British Colonial Hilton
Tel: 322-3301
Casual dining, Bahamian and European buffet or a la carte, in a sedate atmosphere with a great beachfront view of the cruise ships in Nassau Harbour. **$$**

CABLE BEACH

Androsia Steak & Seafood Restaurant
West Bay Street
Cable Beach, Shoppers Paradise
Tel: 327-7805
Specialties include dishes from Andros and a Parisian peppered steak. Reservations advised. **$$$**

Cafe Johnny Canoe Restaurant & Bar
next to Nassau Beach Hotel
Tel: 327-3373
Not to be missed, this restaurant's walls are filled with original photos of the early city and unusual straw and Junkanoo art. Bahamian and American cuisine is served promptly and service is excellent. Open daily, 7.30am until midnight. **$$**

Capriccio Ristorante
West Bay Street
Tel: 327-8547
A true taste of Italy, from the herb garden and ornaments on the outdoor patio to the tiramisu and opera music indoors. Open

Mon–Sat 11am–10pm; Sundays and holidays 5–10pm. **$$$**

Compass Point Restaurant
West Bay Street
Tel: 327-4500
A hands-down winner for dinner, offering breathtaking sunsets by the sea. The restaurant is decorated with vibrant Junkanoo colors; the menu is New Age Caribbean-American. Unpretentious but classy, patronized by the rich and famous, but still affordable. Open daily for breakfast, lunch and dinner. Reservations recommended. **$$**

Traveler's Rest
West Bay Street
Tel: 327-7633
Casual indoor and outdoor dining at an establishment known for "killer" banana and strawberry daiquiris, minced crawfish and – the house specialty – guava cake. Open daily 11am–11pm. **$$**

PARADISE ISLAND

Blue Lagoon Seafood Restaurant and Grill Terrace
Club Land'Or, Paradise Beach Drive
Tel: 363-2400
Romantic dining by candlelight on the third floor of Club Land'Or, overlooking the Atlantis marina. Music wafts up from the piano bar on the second floor. Specialties are seafood crepes and peach flambé. **$$**

The Blue Marlin Restaurant
Hurricane Hole Shopping Plaza
Tel: 363-2660
While it offers vegetarian specialties and chicken and seafood dishes, the soups and burgers are hard to beat for subtle flavorings. Fire dancing and steel pan entertainment on weekends. Open daily 11am–10pm, weekdays and midnight on weekends. **$$**

Atlantis
Paradise Island
Tel: 363-3000
Restaurants include **Bahamian Club**, Continental and American; **The Boathouse**, steaks and prime rib; **Seagrapes**, Bahamian and American buffet; **Villa d'Este**, Italian. **$$$**

Lunchtime and dinner cruises
Calypso Cruises
Paradise Island Terminal
Tel: 363-3577.
Daytime and evening cruises with live music. Reservations advised.

GRAND BAHAMA

Buccaneer Club
Deadman's Reef, Eight Mile Rock
Tel: 349-3794
Bahamian and Continental. Closed on Monday. **$$**

Cafe Michel
International Bazaar, Freeport
Tel: 352-2191
Expensive, but worth every penny. Its white-gloved service and the romantic decor place it among the top restaurants on the island. **$$$**

Ferry House Restaurant
Opposite Port Lucaya Marketplace
Tel: 373-1595
Simple, but elegant decor. Gourmet seafood and steak dining. A glass enclosed patio overlooks the picturesque ferry dock and marina. Open for breakfast, lunch, and dinner. **$$$**

Freddie's
Hunter's, just outside Freeport
Tel: 352-3250
Bahamian specialties. **$$**

Lucaya Lobster and Steak House
Midshipman Road, Lucaya
Tel: 373 5101. **$$**

Luciano's
Port Lucaya Marketplace
Tel: 393-9100
Gourmet European fare, white glove service and romantic ambiance Open for dinner only. **$$**

Pier One Seafood Restaurant
Freeport Harbour
Tel: 352-6674
Steak and seafood. Sunset shark feedings below the verandah. **$$$**

Ruby Swiss European Restaurant
West Sunrise Highway, Freeport
Tel: 352-8507
Gourmet breakfast, lunch and dinner; Swiss specialties and flambés. **$$$**

The Stoned Crab
Taino Beach, Lucaya
Tel: 373-1442
Fresh seafood and steaks. **$$**

Our Lucaya
Royal Palm Way, Lucaya
Tel: 373-1333
Restaurants at the mega-resort include **Willie Broadleaf,** international buffet; **Iries** with a Caribbean menu; the **Arawak,** Continental and Bahamian cuisine and **Churchill's Chop House. $$$**

BIMINI

The Anchorage
Bimini Blue Water Resort
Alice Town
Tel: 347-3166
Seafood. **$$**
Bimini Big Game Fishing Club
King's Highway
Tel: 347-2391/3394
Fish specialties in an elegant dining room. Popular with yachties. **$$–$$$**

Price categories

$$$	$50 and over
$$	$30–$50
$	$30 and under

Red Lion Pub
King's Highway, North Bimini
Tel: 347-2259
Local, Continental and American. **$$**

THE ABACOS

Abaco Beach Resort
Marsh Harbour
Tel: 367-2158
Seafood and Continental served in restaurant overlooking fabulous yachts docked in the resort's marina. **$$**
Abaco Inn
Elbow Cay
Tel: 366-0133
Elegant restaurant, which serves excellent seafood. **$$**
Conch Inn Restaurant
Marsh Harbour
Tel: 367-4000/2319
Friendly waterfront bar and bistro. Seafood. **$$**

Green Turtle Yacht Club
Green Turtle Cay
Tel: 365-4237
Dine al fresco or in the classy dining room. American and Bahamian. **$$**
Sea View Restaurant and Bar,
Green Turtle Cay
Tel: 365-4111
Seafood. **$$**

ELEUTHERA

Angela's Starfish Restaurant
Nesbit Street, Harbour Island
Tel: 333-2253
Good Bahamian home-cooking; serves some of the best cracked conch and peas and rice. Popular for breakfast so reservations advised. Closes around 8.30pm. **$**
Club Eleuthera
Rock Sound
Tel: 334-2020
Seafood and American fare. **$$**
Edwina's Place
Rock Sound
Tel: 334-2094
Seafood. **$$**
Romora Bay Club
Dunmore Street, Harbour Island
Tel: 333-2325
Bahamian food with a French touch. Reservations recommended. **$$**

ANDROS

Chickcharnie Hotel,
Fresh Creek
Tel: 368-2025
Fish restaurant in the hotel. Located just a short walk away from the Androsia factory, home of the national batiked cotton designs. **$$**
Small Hope Bay Lodge,
Andros Town
Tel: 368-2014
Seafood and American beef. **$$**

EXUMA

Kermit's Lounge
Opposite Exuma Airport
Tel: 345-0002
Breakfast, lunch and dinner. Takeaway. **$**

Peace and Plenty,
George Town
Tel: 336-2551
Fish dishes. Dancing on Saturday night. **$$**

LONG ISLAND

Stella Maris Resort Club,
Tel: 336-2106.
Bahamian, Continental and American cuisine. **$$$**

Drinking Notes

The Bahamas have contributed their share to the world's exotic cocktails with specialties like the *Bahama Mama*: rum, orange juice and creme de cacao; and the *Goombay Smash*: coconut rum, Galliano, pineapple juice, sugar and a dash of lemon. You'll also find plenty of tropical classics like *Banana Daiquiris, Piña Coladas* and *Planter's Punch*.

Drink prices in restaurants and bars run high because of the duty on imported liquor (which is a bargain in liquor stores). The best buy is rum distilled locally, including all Bacardi products, coconut rum from Grand Bahama and Eleuthera's pineapple rum.

There are also soft drinks in abundance. *Goombay Punch* is a super-sweet soda with a hint of pineapple; *Malta* and *Mauby*, made from tree bark, have a bittersweet treacle taste. Finally, there's tap water. It is faintly salty tasting, which is due to the high sodium content. Therefore bottled water is recommended. Sold in most restaurants, it can also be purchased at half the cost of hotel shops, at grocery stores and supermarkets.

The legal drinking age in the Bahamas is 18 years.

Nightlife

Casinos, bars and nightclubs line the shores of Nassau, Paradise Island and Freeport, and some stay open all night. In Nassau, popular attractions include Las Vegas style revues at the **Rain Forest Theatre** in

Marriott Crystal Palace Resort and Casino. It presents singers, comedians, magicians, acrobats and animal acts. Another hit is the so-called "native show" featuring local Bahamian talent and some very unBahamian acts such as fire-eating.

For dancing in Nassau try **Club 601**, at 601 Bay Street, with in house band and recording artists, Visage; the mega disco complex **The Zoo** on Bay Street opposite Saunders Beach, and **Waterloo**. On Cable Beach try the **Out Island Bar** at the Nassau Beach Hotel and the **Junkanoo Lounge** at Marriott Crystal Palace Resort. Then there are the casinos on Cable Beach and Paradise Island: vast, sparkling and seductive.

In Freeport, the main attraction is the **Casino at Bahamia**, a huge Moorish palace, with an extravagant French cancan revue at the **Casino Royale Theatre**. Freeport/Lucaya also have native shows including **The Yellow Bird Show Club** at the Castaways Resort. Also worth a look is **Captain Kenny's** at Taino Beach.

Nightlife on the Out Islands is tamer: a quiet drink at the hotel bar or perhaps some after-dinner dancing on the terrace. If you want more action, ask where the locals go.

Culture

Art

Art Exhibitions are hosted by various galleries on the islands – including the Temple, Marlborough Antiques, Kennedy Gallery, The Art Gallery, Nassau Glass, Lyford Gallery – and are displayed in the foyer of the Main Post Office. The Archive Department holds an annual exhibit at the Post Office during February.

Many local artists continue to take their inspiration from the islands and its people, notably Amos Ferguson, R. Brent Malone, Mal Flanders, Macmillan Hughes and the playwright Winston Saunders. Foreign writers and artists have been drawn to the island ever since novelist Ernest Hemingway made the Bimini Islands his home during the 1930s.

Theater, Dance and Music

The lively arts scene is thriving in the Bahamas with its fertile mixture of international and regional culture. Check newspaper entertainment sections, especially during the winter, when the benefit and concert season is in full swing.

A **National Centre for the Performing Arts** opened on Shirley Street in Nassau, in summer 2001. The $4 million renovated movie theatre house's some interesting cultural Bahamian memorabilia in the lobby, and is the venue for theatre, dance, and other live performances.

The **Dundas Centre for the Performing Arts** on Mackey Street also hosts performances in Nassau; call 322-2728 for more information. In Freeport, the

Regency Theatre (Tel: 352-5535) is a hub of artistic activity and the group, **Friends of the Arts**, sponsors guest performers from abroad. The Nassau Players, Bahamas School of Theatre, Grand Bahama Players, the Dundas Repertory Company and Freeport Players Guild are a few of the better known theatrical groups. James Catalyn & Friends is an excellent professional company which regularly performs productions in Bahamian dialect, a revived art form linked to a resurgence of interest in Bahamian culture and heritage.

Amateur dance groups include the New Breed Dancers, Nassau Civic Ballet and National School of Dance. Popular local choral ensembles include the Diocesan Chorale, Lucayan Chorale, Chamber Singers and Nassau Operatic Society.

Cinema

Bahamian cinemas show mostly American movies. RND Cinema has two multiscreen theatres in Nassau, and one each in Freeport and Abaco.

The Bahamas has been the set for many feature films, including the James Bond thrillers *Never Say Never Again* and *Thunderball*. Also, *Jaws: The Revenge, Cocoon II, Shoot to Kill, The Abyss, Blood Relations* and *Deadly Spy Games* have all had their share of Bahamian scenery. The Bahamas was home to a man who made his name as both an actor and an accomplished director in Hollywood. Sidney Poitier grew up on one of the Out islands – Cat Island.

Attractions

With sun and sea as common denominators, each island in the Bahamas has its own set of possibilities. Away from the cities in the Out Islands sightseeing is more or less built into the landscape, both natural and manmade. In town touristic activities tend to be more structured.

Wildlife Parks

The Bahamas are home to a number of exotic birds, plants and rare animal species. Often these require a good bit of persistence and luck to view first hand. Once found throughout the islands, iguanas still inhabit secluded islands and cays. Living separately on their islands, they have evolved dozens of forms, including iguanas on Andros that grow to be over 5 ft (1½ meters) long. The hutia may be Bahamas' only unique mammal. Once widespread, it can now be seen only on East Plana Cay. The most spectacular of the Bahamas' birds is the flamingo, whose nesting ground is protected in Inagua National Park.

Funded entirely by private donations and memberships, **The Bahamas National Trust** administers many sites designed for the protection of wildlife. These include **Black Sound Cay Park, Exuma Cays Land and Sea Park, Inagua National Park, Pelican Cays Land and Sea Park, Peterson Cay Park, Conception Island Park** and **Lucayan National Park.** Park wardens protect land and sea life in the parks, and provide information. For more details on visiting the parks, write to the Trust at P.O. Box N-4105, Nassau, The Bahamas or call 393-1317.

City Gardens

Attractions in Nassau and Freeport:

NASSAU

Ardastra Gardens, Zoo and Conservation Centre
Chippingham Road, off West Bay Street. Tel: 323-5806
Tours through 5 acres (2 hectares) of exotic gardens. Tropical plants, animals and flamingos, which perform three times daily in a marching flamingo show.
Botanic Gardens
Chippingham Road, off West Bay Street. Tel: 323-5975
18 acres (7 hectares) of tropical flora, near Ardastra Gardens.
Calypso Getaway Cruise
Paradise Island Terminal.
Tel: 363-3577
Sail to an island lagoon with water sports and dining. Reservations.
Hartley's Undersea Walk
Nassau Yacht Haven, East Bay Street. Tel: 393-8234/393-7569
Boat cruise culminates in a walk on the sea floor. Reservations.
The Retreat
Village Road. Tel: 393-1317
Headquarters of the Bahamas National Trust with an 11 acre tropical garden, including one of the largest collections of rare palms.

FREEPORT

Garden of the Groves
Corner of Midshipman Road and Magellan Drive. Tel: 352-4045
Botanical garden with many rare species, plus a small museum of Bahamian history. Closed Wednesday.
Rand Memorial Nature Centre
Settler's Way East
Tel: 352-5438.
Trails and guided tours through a 100-acre (40-hectare) park. Closed Saturday.
Water World
Tel: 373-2197
Two 18-hole upscale miniature golf courses, with licensed restaurant and ice cream parlour.

Festivals

Events

Junkanoo is an African derived celebration creolized into the most spirited and lighthearted holiday in the Bahamas. In Nassau on Boxing Day and New Year's Day, Bahamians take to the streets in colorful crepe paper costumes and masks. Thousands parade along Bay Street in a dancelike motion called "rushin'" to the beat of cowbells, goatskin drums and clackers. The Boxing Day parade begins in the wee hours (usually at dawn), and is the culmination of months of preparation.

Many Bahamians belong to Junkanoo groups sponsored by local businesses, pooling their talents to create the costumes. Amid secrecy and keen competition, groups choose the themes that their costumes will illustrate – for example, the Valley Boys' "Just Say No to Drugs", the Fox Hill Congos' "Bahamian History" or the Saxons' "Let the World Know the Bahamas is Our Pride and Joy". Lively scrap gangs join the parade with impromptu costumes, horns, bells and whistles. Some of the Bahamas' most prominent citizens are seen ringing in the New Year in a scrap gang. There are also parades on Grand Bahama and several other islands.

JUNKANOO IN JUNE

In 1999, the Bahamas Ministry of Tourism, along with vendors at the very popular Arawak Cay, launched **Junkanoo in June.** Every weekend during that month there is live entertainment by Bahamian recording artists at an outdoor bandstand at Arawak Cay. Festivities also include storytelling sessions and poetry readings on a porch patio, demonstrations of Junkanoo costume-making, and cowbell creations. An instant hit with locals and visitors alike, it has rejuvenated this otherwise quiet summer month.

LOCAL CULTURE

There are also several neighborhood festivals including the **Fox Hill Day Festival**, and **Seafood Festival** (October). During these special weeks of celebration there are concerts, storytelling, indigenous (rake and scrape) music, art and photographic exhibitions and demonstrations in handicrafts such as cooking local specialties, sewing and plaiting.

October was designated **International Culture Month** by the Bahamas Ministry of Foreign Affairs. Mid-month, the Botanical Gardens at Fort Charlotte in Nassau is the venue for scores of food stalls, dance troupes, and oral presentations by international residents of the Bahamas, who gather to celebrate their heritage at the event.

In a somewhat different vein, the **National Arts Festival**, sponsored by the Ministry of Education, in the early spring, showcases talent in music, drama, and poetry. It is open to all school-aged children, with a section for adult entrants.

Shopping

What to Buy

With no sales tax and low tariffs, the Bahamas can be a bargain-hunter's delight. Some merchants sell imported goods at prices 30 to 50 percent lower than in the US, but compare the prices of goods at home before you go.

Bay Street in Nassau offers the biggest and best selection of shops. For fine china, crystal and figurines, visit **Treasure Traders, Little Switzerland,** and **John Bull**. The largest selection of French perfumes are at **LIghtbourne's,** the **Perfume Shop** and the **Perfume Bar**. Several stores, like **Colombian Emeralds,** feature fine gems. Look for handcrafted conch and coral jewelry. For Bahamian batik fashions, visit **Mademoiselle,** especially the **Androsia Boutique**. For guaranteed Bahamian-made goods, try **Bahamian T'ings** (cards, art work and pottery) and **The Plait Lady** (straw work).

Finally, there is the open-air straw market selling handwoven goods. Bargain here, but not at other Bay Street establishments.

At Cable Beach you'll find **Sea Grapes Too** for unusual local gifts, and **Androsia** for batiks and other items made on Andros.

On Grand Bahama, the **International Bazaar** in Freeport and **Port Lucaya Marketplace** dominate the shopping scene.

The Bazaar is a huge arcade containing over 70 shops, while Port Lucaya Marketplace is a more interesting mixture of small thematic shops, boutiques, bars and live entertainment.

In the Out Islands you can find gifts at roadside stands throughout the islands selling straw goods.

Sport

Outdoor Activities

The key fact to remember about sports in the Bahamas is the toll free phone number of the **Bahamas Sports Information Center** Tel: 800-32-SPORT. They offer guidance and a useful calendar of events.

Spectator Sport

Baseball may be the most popular team sport among Bahamians, but cricket and rugby also have loyal followings. On New Providence, the **Queen Elizabeth Sports Center**, tel: 323-5163 is the major complex, with a stadium and track and field arena. April and May is the season for fly-ins, air shows and aviation races. Sailing regattas checker the calendar from January through October in the waters off Exuma, New Providence, Long Island, Cat Island, the Abacos and Eleuthera.

Throughout the year, runners take to the streets in numerous road races and triathalons. At this point the lines between spectator and participant sports begin to blur; a visitor can be running in the track for one event and the next minute cheering from the sidelines for another.

Participant Sport

Not surprisingly, watersports opportunities abound. The larger hotels offer windsurfing and snorkeling. Many islands have a fleet of charter boats for deep sea fishing, and bareboat yacht rental facilities. Dive operations are everywhere. Despite the pre-eminence of watersports, golf and tennis buffs and even equestrians will find plenty to do here.

Sailors can consult the current edition of the *Yachtman's Guide to the Bahamas* for an up-to-date review of marinas and suppliers.

GOLF

Ocean Club Golf Course
Paradise Island
Tel: 363-6682
Cotton Bay Golf Club
Eleuthera
Tel: 334-6161
Fortune Hills Golf and Country Club
Grand Bahama
Tel: 373-1066
The Lucayan and **The Reef** courses
At Our Lucaya
Grand Bahama
Tel: 373-1333/373-1066
Features the Butch Harmon School of Golf.
South Ocean Beach Hotel & Golf Club
New Providence
Tel: 362-4391
Treasure Cay Hotel Resort and Marina
Abaco
Tel: 367-2570

Swim with Dolphins

Swimming with dolphins is a popular way to enjoy the water and have a close encounter with the fascinating mammals. The Dolphin Experience organises excursions to Sanctuary Bay, off Grand Bahama.
Tel: 373-1250; Fax: 373-3948.
Website:
www.dolphinexperience.com
There is also an information booth at UNEXSO in Port Lucaya.

DIVING

New Providence
Bahama Divers Ltd.
Tel: 393-5644
Coral Harbour Divers Ltd.
Tel: 362-4171/241-6573
Dive Dive Dive
Tel: 362-1401

New Providence Divers Ltd.
Tel: 362-4391/ 414-251 8283 (US)
Sun Divers Ltd.
Tel: 325-8927

Grand Bahama
Underwater Explorers Society (UNEXSO)
Tel: 373-1244/800-992 3484

Abaco
Brendal's Dive Shop
Tel: 365-4411
Dive Abaco Ltd.
Tel: 367-2787
Island Marine Dive Shop
Tel: 366-0282
Treasure Cay Divers
Tel: 305-763 5665
Walker's Cay Dive Shop
Tel: 432-2092/800-223 6961/305-522 1469

Andros
Small Hope Bay Lodge
Tel: 368-2014/800-223 6961/305-463 9130

Bimini
Bimini Undersea Adventures
Tel: 800-327 8150/305-763 2188

Cat Island
Hawk's Nest Club
Tel: 800-426 4222/904-368 2500
Eleuthera
Romora Bay Club BDA
Tel: 333-2325
The Valentine's Dive Center
Tel: 333-2142

Exuma
Exuma Aquatics
Tel: 336-2600
Exuma Divers
Tel: 336-2030

Long Island
Stella Maris Resort
Tel: 336-2106

Rum Cay
Rum Cay Club
Tel: 305-467 8355

San Salvador
Guanahani Dive Ltd.
Tel: 800-272 1492

Further Reading

History, Politics & People

Hazel I. Albury, *Man-O-War, My Island Home*. Holly Press, 1977.
Paul Albury, *Paradise Island Story*. London: Macmillan Caribbean, 1984.
Paul Albury, *The Story of the Bahamas*. London: Macmillan Caribbean, 1975.
P.J.H. Barratt, *Grand Bahama*. London: Macmillan Caribbean, 1972.
E. Clement Bethel, *Junkanoo - Festival of The Bahamas*
Michael Bloch, *The Duke of Windsor's War*. New York: Coward McCann, 1983.
Donald Cartwright and Gail Saunders, *Historic Nassau*. London: Macmillan Caribbean, 1979.
Philip Cash et al, *The Making of the Bahamas: A History for Schools*. London: Collins, 1978.
Michael Craton, *A History of the Bahamas*. London: Collins, 1962.
Steve Dodge, *Abaco: The History of an Out Island and its Cays*. Decatur, Illinois: White Sound Press, 1983.
Sir Etienne Dupuch, *A Salute to Friend and Foe*. Nassau: The Tribune, 1982.
Sir Etienne Dupuch, *The Tribune Story*. London: Ernest Benn, Ltd.
Cleveland W. Eneas, Bain Town. Nassau, 1976.
Collin A. Hughes, *Race and Politics in the Bahamas*. New York: St Martin's Press, 1981.
Randolf W. Johnston, *Artist on His Island, A Story of Self Reliance*. Park Ridge, New Jersey: Noyes Press.
H. Malcom, *Historical Documents Relating to the Bahamas Islands*. Gordon Press, 1976.
Timothy O. McCartney, *Neurosis in the Sun*. Nassau: Executive Ideas of the Bahamas, 1971.
Michael Pye, *The King Over the Water*. London: Hutchinson, 1981.

Sandra Riley, *Homeward Bound: A History of the Islands to 1850*. Miami: Island Research, 1983.

S. Russell, *Nassau Historic Buildings*. Bahamas National Trust.

Gail Saunders, *Bahamian Loyalists and Their Slaves*. London: Macmillan Caribbean, 1983.

Gail Saunders, *Slavery in the Bahamas, 1648-1838*. Nassau 1985.

Michael A. Symonette, *Discovery of a Nation*. Nassau: Bahamas International Publishing Co.

Anthony Thompson, *An Economic History of the Bahamas*. Nassau: Commonwealth Publishers, Ltd.

Mackay Williams, *A History, A Memoir*. Nassau: Williams Publishing Co., 1984.

Everild Young, *Eleuthera: The Island Called Freedom*. London: Regency Press, 1966.

David Zink, *The Stones of Atlantis*. Engelwood Cliffs, New Jersey: Prentice Hall, 1978.

Natural History

P.G.C. Brundenell-Bruce, *The Birds of New Providence and the Bahama Islands*. London: Collins, 1975.

David G. Campbell, *The Ephemeral Islands: A Natural History of the Bahamas*. London: Macmillan Education, 1978.

Dee Carstarphen, *The Conch Book, All You Ever Wanted to Know About the Queen Conch from Gestation to Gastromony*. Pen & Ink Press, 1982.

Mark Catesby, *Natural History of Carolina, Florida and the Bahama Islands*. Johnson Reproductions.

Drs. Donovan and Helen Correll, *Flora of the Bahama Archipelago, including the Turks and Caicos Islands*. Monticello, New York: Lubrecht & Cramer, 1983.

Idaz Greenberg, *Guide to Corals and Fishes*. Miami: Seahawk Press.

Hannau, Hans, *Tropical Flowers of the Bahamas*. Miami.

Lawrence A. Hardie, *A Sedimentation of the Modern Carbonate Tidal Flats of Northwest Andros Island, Bahamas*. Baltimore: John Hopkins University Studies in Geology, 1977.

G.W. Lennox and S.A. Seddon, *Flowers of the Caribbean: The Bahamas and Bermuda*. London: Macmillan Caribbean, 1980.

Lennox G.W. and Seddon, S.A., *Trees of the Caribbean: The Bahamas and Bermuda*. London: Macmillan Caribbean, 1980.

Jack Patterson and George Stevenson, *Native Trees of the Bahamas*. Hope Town, Abaco, Bahamas.

Food

Marie Mendelson and Marguerite Sawyer, *Gourmet Bahamian Cooking*. Green Turtle Cay, Abaco, Bahamas, 1985.

St Andrew's School Committee, *It's Cookin' in the Bahamas*. Nassau, 1983.

Cindy Williams, *Bahamian Cookery*. Boynton Beach, Florida: Star Publishing Co., 1976.

Deby Nash, *Nassau Memories*, Memories Press, 2000.

Religion & Folklore

Daniel J. Crawley, *I Could Talk Old-Story Good: Creativity in Bahamian Folklore*. Berkeley: University of California Press, 1966.

W. Eneas, *Let the Church Roll On: A Collection of Speech and Writings*. Nassau.

Leslie Higgs, *Bush Medicine in the Bahamas*. Nassau: Bahamas Nassau Guardian, 1969.

Timothy O. McCartney, *Ten Ten the Bible Ten*. Nassau.

Language

John A. Holm and Alison W. Shilling, *The Dictionary of Bahamian English*. New York: Lexik House, 1982.

Fiction & Poetry

Desmond Bagley, *Bahama Crisis*. London: Collins, 1980.

College of the Bahamas, *Bahamian Anthology*. London: Macmillan Caribbean, 1983.

Jack Culmer ed., *A Book of Bahamian Verse*. Gordon Press, 1977.

Ernest Hemingway, *Islands in the Stream*. New York: Charles Scribner & Sons.

Wilhelmina Kemp Johnstone, *Bahamian Jottings: Poems and Prose*. Nassau: Bruce Publishing Co., 1973.

Andre Norton, *The Opal Eyed Fan*. New York, 1977.

Dennis Ryan, *Bahamas: In a White Coming On*. Ardmore, Pennsylvania: Dorrance & Co., 1981.

General

Bahamas Handbook and Businessman's Annual. Nassau: Etienne Dupuch, Jr. Publications. Updated Annually.

F.C. Evans and N. Young, *The Bahamas*. New York: Cambridge University Press, 1977.

Patricia Glinton-Meicholas, *Talkin' Bahamian* and *More Talkin' Bahamian*, Guanima Press

George Hunte, *The Bahamas*. London, 1975.

Charles Ives, *The Isles of Summer: Or Nassau and the Bahamas*. Elliots Books, Reprint of 1880 edition.

H. Kline, *Bahama Islands*. New York: Charles Scribner & Sons.

G.J. Northcroft, *Sketches of Summerland: Nassau and the Bahama Islands*. Gorden Press, 1976.

Bill Robinson, *South to the Caribbean*. New York: W.W. Norton & Co., 1982.

Gail Saunders, *The Bahamas: A Family of Islands*. London: Macmillan Caribbean.

Gail Saunders and D. Cartwright, *Historic Nassau*. London: Macmillan Caribbean.

Johann D. Schoepf, *Travels in the Confederation, 1783–1784*. Ben Franklin, 1968. Reprint of 1911 edition.

Secondary School Atlas for the Commonwealth of the Bahamas. Ministry of Education, Bahamas Kingston, Jamaica: Kingston Publishers.

Yachtman's Guide to the Bahamas. Miami: Tropic Isle Publishers, Inc. Updated annually.

Other Insight Guides

In Apa Publications' flagship series of more than 200 Insight Guides, destinations in this region include *Caribbean, Barbados, Bermuda, Cuba, Dominican Republic and Haiti, Florida, Jamaica* and *Puerto Rico*.

The vivid text and spectacular photography in **Insight Guide: Caribbean** brings to life the serenity, the allure, the diversity of this part of the world – from the beauty of a Caribbean sunset to the charm of the Caribees.

POCKET GUIDES

Also available are companion volumes in the Pocket Guides series: *Bahamas, Barbados, Bermuda, Cayman Islands, Jamaica* and *Puerto Rico*. These books feature the author's personal recommendations and are especially suitable for visitors with limited time to spare. A practical and easy-to-use pullout map smooths the way through the islands and sights.

Insight Pocket Guide: Barbados comes complete with a pullout map. Written by a knowledgeable local host, the guide comprises a series of full- and half-day itineraries designed to help visitors get the most out of Barbados during a short stay.

COMPACT GUIDES

Insight Compact Guides are handy mini encyclopedias which are both fact-packed and intensely practical, with text, pictures and maps all cross-referenced. Titles in this series include *Bahamas, Barbados, Dominican Republic* and *Jamaica*.

INSIGHT FLEXIMAP

Insight FlexiMaps combine clear cartography with photography of top destinations and practical information. The laminated finish is weather-resistant.

ART & PHOTO CREDITS

Cartographic Editor **Zoë Goodwin**
Production **Linton Donaldson**
Design Consultants
Klaus Geisler, Tanvir Virdee
Picture Research
Hilary Genin, Britta Jaschinski

Index

Numbers in italics refer to photographs

"I was first drawn to the Insight Guides by the excellent "Nepal" volume. I can think of no book which so effectively captures the essence of a country. Out of these pages leaped the Nepal I know – the captivating charm of a people and their culture. I've since discovered and enjoyed the entire Insight Guide series. Each volume deals with a country in the same sensitive depth, which is nowhere more evident than in the superb photography."

Sir Edmund Hillary

INSIGHT GUIDES

The world's largest collection of visual travel guides

Insight Guides – the Classic Series that puts you in the picture

Alaska	China	Hungary	Munich	South Africa
Alsace	Cologne			South America
Amazon Wildlife	Continental Europe	Iceland	Namibia	South Tyrol
American Southwest	Corsica	India	Native America	Southeast Asia
Amsterdam	Costa Rica	India's Western	Nepal	Wildlife
Argentina	Crete	Himalaya	Netherlands	Spain
Asia, East	Cuba	India, South	New England	Spain, Northern
Asia, South	Cyprus	Indian Wildlife	New Orleans	Spain, Southern
Asia, Southeast	Czech & Slovak	Indonesia	New York City	Sri Lanka
Athens	Republics	Ireland	New York State	Sweden
Atlanta		Israel	New Zealand	Switzerland
Australia	Delhi, Jaipur & Agra	Istanbul	Nile	Sydney
Austria	Denmark	Italy	Normandy	Syria & Lebanon
	Dominican Republic	Italy, Northern	Norway	
Bahamas	Dresden	Italy, Southern		Taiwan
Bali	Dublin		Old South	Tenerife
Baltic States	Düsseldorf	Jamaica	Oman & The UAE	Texas
Bangkok		Japan	Oxford	Thailand
Barbados	East African Wildlife	Java		Tokyo
Barcelona	Eastern Europe	Jerusalem	Pacific Northwest	Trinidad & Tobago
Bay of Naples	Ecuador	Jordan	Pakistan	Tunisia
Beijing	Edinburgh		Paris	Turkey
Belgium	Egypt	Kathmandu	Peru	Turkish Coast
Belize	England	Kenya	Philadelphia	Tuscany
Berlin		Korea	Philippines	
Bermuda	Finland		Poland	Umbria
Boston	Florence	Laos & Cambodia	Portugal	USA: On The Road
Brazil	Florida	Lisbon	Prague	USA: Western States
Brittany	France	Loire Valley	Provence	US National Parks: East
Brussels	France, Southwest	London	Puerto Rico	US National Parks: West
Budapest	Frankfurt	Los Angeles		
Buenos Aires	French Riviera		Rajasthan	Vancouver
Burgundy		Madeira	Rhine	Venezuela
Burma (Myanmar)	Gambia & Senegal	Madrid	Rio de Janeiro	Venice
	Germany	Malaysia	Rockies	Vienna
Cairo	Glasgow	Mallorca & Ibiza	Rome	Vietnam
Calcutta	Gran Canaria	Malta	Russia	
California	Great Britain	Mauritius, Réunion		Wales
California, Northern	Greece	& Seychelles	St Petersburg	Washington DC
California, Southern	Greek Islands	Melbourne	San Francisco	Waterways of Europe
Canada	Guatemala, Belize &	Mexico City	Sardinia	Wild West
Caribbean	Yucatán	Mexico	Scandinavia	
Catalonia		Miami	Scotland	Yemen
Channel Islands	Hamburg	Montreal	Seattle	
Chicago	Hawaii	Morocco	Sicily	
Chile	Hong Kong	Moscow	Singapore	

Complementing the above titles are 120 easy-to-carry Insight Compact Guides, 120 Insight Pocket Guides with full-size pull-out maps and more than 100 laminated easy-fold Insight Maps